D0844840

WITHDRAWN

The Autobiography of Du Pont de Nemours

PIERRE SAMUEL DUPONT
Conseiller d'État, Ch.er de l'Ordre de Vasa
PROPRIETAIRE ET CULTIVATEUR

Député du Bailliage de Nemours
à l'Assemblée Nationale de 1789.

Gros del.

Courbe sc

From the engraving published in 1790

The Autobiography of Du Pont de Nemours

Translated and with an
Introduction by
Elizabeth Fox-Genovese

SR Scholarly Resources Inc.
Wilmington, Delaware

Scholarly Resources Inc.
104 Greenhill Avenue
Wilmington, Delaware 19805

Library of Congress Cataloging in Publication Data

Du Pont de Nemours, Pierre Samuel, 1739–1817.
The autobiography of Du Pont de Nemours.

Translation of: L'enfance et la jeunesse de Du Pont
de Nemours, racontées par lui-même.
Includes bibliographical references and index.
1. Du Pont de Nemours, Pierre Samuel, 1739–1817.
2. Du Pont family. 3. France—History—18th century.
4. Intellectuals—France—Biography. I. Title.
DC131.9.D85A3413 1984   944.04′092′4 [B]   84–10645
ISBN 0–8420–2132–9

For Ted,

en souvenir de nos enfances entrelacées

Contents

Preface

In 1800, Du Pont, upon arrival in the United States, sent Thomas Jefferson a copy of his work on education with the suggestion that Jefferson have it translated immediately so that it could contribute to the preservation and prosperity of the new republic. Jefferson replied: "You say you propose to get it translated; but I believe that it is impossible to translate your writings. It would be easier to translate Homer which yet has never been done. Several of us tried our hands on the memoire you gave me for the Philosophical society; but after trial, gave it up as desperate and determined to print it in French."[1] Jefferson's words afforded me a kind of grim solace during the translation of this text, although, having ignored his warning, I am prepared to take my medicine from irate reviewers.

In translating, I have tried to remain as close as possible to Du Pont's original rendition. Intelligibility in English has dictated some modification of his punctuation and occasional liberties with literal translation. On the whole, it seemed preferable to retain as much of his tone and emphasis as possible. Since he apparently used capitalization for emphasis, his practice has been followed precisely, although the effect in English is sometimes strange. Similarly his underlinings have been retained and set as italics. The translation follows in all respects, including Du Pont's idiosyncratic spellings of proper names, the manuscript version at the Eleutherian Mills Historical Library.

Translating Du Pont, as Jefferson delicately implied, presents problems beyond the inevitable problems of any translation. Jefferson was much too polite to risk hurting Du Pont's feelings by criticizing his style in French. But with Du Pont now beyond the stings of putative slights, it can—with no disrespect intended—be confessed that he did not write French especially well, even by the standards of physiocratic prose, which itself fell short of the proverbial brilliance and wit of the French Enlightenment. Yet for all its infelicities, Du Pont's style has a distinctive flavor.

Since the point of translating an autobiography is, at least in part, to capture such flavor—to capture an individual in his or her own idiom—I decided to remain as close to Du Pont's original as respect for correct English would allow. This decision has had many consequences that will hardly escape the attentive reader. For example, I have made every attempt to avoid breaking up his interminably long sentences, even in cases in which the English rendition would have gained. In the interests of clarity, I have occasionally altered his punctuation, especially (but not only) in those cases in which it simply would have been incorrect in English. These changes consist primarily in substituting semicolons or dashes, or more rarely colons, for his ubiquitous commas. To the objection that many sentences are simply incorrect as English, I can only reply that they faithfully reproduce his incorrect French.

Conversely, I have retained as much of his own vocabulary as possible, even in cases in which it might seem odd to the modern reader. In Chapter 13, for example, when he writes of various fetters upon the free market, I retained his "inquisitions" in the sequence "all regulations, all inquisitions, all prohibitions on labor or commerce" even though "interventions" might have seemed more natural. There is every reason to believe that the inquisition represented a threat of censorship or intervention to Du Pont, and that he chose the word because of its political resonance.

In his autobiography, Du Pont strove, albeit intermittently, for literary effect. Sometimes he succeeded; sometimes he did not. His style and diction contribute to the charm of such passages as his description of his plans to take Corsica. But he did not have good control of his literary effects, and he was doubtless either rushed, or lazy, or both. Thus in the marvelous passage in which he describes his response to his little sister's return from her wet nurse, he apparently intended to use the present tense to record his own thoughts at the time and the past tense to describe the scene as a whole. The intent was good: he did capture the quality of the child's mind. But the execution was sloppy: he did not stick faithfully to his distinction. Here and elsewhere he mixed tenses erratically. I have followed him.

No translator, not even the best, such as the late Ronald Meek, has ever succeeded in rendering physiocratic prose as graceful English. It was awkward in the original and earned its progenitors mockery for its turgidity and obscurity. It is worse in translation. Du Pont's account of the principles of this science, notably in Chapter 13, provides no exception. But it is perfectly faithful to Du Pont's other writings on the subject and faithfully conveys the allure of physiocracy in its own day. I have tried, accordingly, to remain faithful to it myself.

For forms of civil address and their abbreviations, I have retained the French: Monsieur for Mr., with its abbreviation, M., and the plural form thereof, MM; Madame and Mme for Mrs.; Mademoiselle and Mlle for Miss. I have normally translated such noble titles as Duc and Comte. All translations from the French, including poetry, are my own unless otherwise indicated. To the extent possible, potentially unfamiliar persons, places, and references are identified in the footnotes to the text of the autobiography, which also include relevant references to scholarly sources. Additional information on Du Pont's ancestors may be found in Henry A. du Pont, *The Early Generations of the Du Pont and Allied Families.*[2]

When my husband Gene, my best comrade and critic, read the draft of the introduction, he protested against its fifth section: "I hate introductions that interpret the text I am about to read!" Happily, he had no quarrel with what I had written, but then he had already read the autobiography. Those who share his feelings about interpretive introductions would be well advised to read the fifth section after reading the text itself.

When my parents, my staunchest supporters but also my advisers on the probable response of the outside world, read the draft, they protested the inclusion of the first and fourth sections, which they claimed to find perfectly fine for their proper place—discrete articles—but not for the introduction. At this point, I began to think that it would be advisable to add a prefatory word about the introduction. Perhaps, in the spirit of the subject matter, I can get away with a brief confession.

Where I had intended initially to offer a few brief remarks, I have written a very long introduction, long enough to try the patience of readers. As I worked on the translation of Du Pont's remarkable text, it increasingly seemed to me that it touched upon many topics and many intellectual interests and, accordingly, that its value for modern readers might be enhanced by explicit identification of its multiple contexts. In this introduction, I have attempted to review some of the contexts that seemed most compelling: that character-istically bourgeois or modern form of individualism which emerged sharply from the shift in *mentalités* of the second half of the eighteenth century and was consolidated by the French Revolution; Du Pont's own life, especially as it reflected the culture and politics of his era; the history of his manuscript; and the problems of reading an auto-biographical text. Every reader will find one or another reason to quarrel with my specific choice of topics, or my treatment of them. For some, the discussions of bourgeois individualism and auto-biography—the more theoretical sections, not to put too fine a point on it—will offer a good deal more than they may ever have wanted to know or are prepared to swallow. For others, they will offer a good deal too little on complex questions on which they may have strong ideas of their own. Ideally, both sections should help readers to situate the text and to understand its many tiers, but they are no more than sketches. I have no wish to offer a disclaimer and no illusions about disarming criticism. In truth, I have taken the liberty of writing the introduction that I wanted to write, that I hoped would contribute to the text rather than in some way reduce it, and that I thought would do proper homage to Du Pont.

To translate a man's work is to live with him for an extended period of time; to translate his autobiography is to come to know him very well. And with all due respect to those who would sever texts from their authors, I do believe that I have come to know the man as well as the text. In my judgment, Du Pont's autobiography is a charming, impressive, and revealing document. Not least, it reveals with amazing, if conflicted, honesty the spirit of a man who is taking stock of his life in the face of imminent death.

There are those who will find some contradiction between my protestations of admiration for Du Pont and my unabashed use of Freudian theory to explicate his text. I can only say that no such contradiction exists. Du Pont wrote a text that could pass as a classic case study of the oedipal conflict in action. He, not I, graph-ically detailed his love for his mother, his quest for her likeness in all other women, his sibling rivalry, and, above all, his relentless struggle with his father, first over her and then over his own destiny. The challenge is not to unearth the traces of oedipal conflict in Du Pont's text, but to understand what also lies behind their explicit enunciation. And yes, I have tried, gently, to probe those secrets, those hidden meanings—but never, I trust, in an attempt to reduce the man or his text to raw material for abstract theories. I have tried, rather, to use theories that seem especially useful and appropriate as an aid to understanding the man. The exploration contributes to my conviction that he was a man of integrity and courage: in every way, a man of respect.

One final word on terms is in order. Du Pont entitled his text *Mémoires*; I usually refer to it as the autobiography. The recent interest in autobiography as a genre has generated some discussion of the appropriate use of the terms "memoirs" and "autobiography," and I concur with those who differentiate between the two according to whether the author and narrator of the text constitutes his or her own main subject. Autobiography presents the narrative of a self, memoirs that of others. Both rely on a nonfictional, first-person narrator, but assign him or her a different status in the text. According to this distinction, Du Pont's text constitutes an autobiography, although the word was not yet in use and he labeled his text a memoir.[3]

I first read Du Pont's autobiography in 1972 while pursuing research on physiocracy at, and thanks to the generous support of, the Eleutherian Mills Historical Library. At the time it seemed absurd to me that such an extraordinary text had never been published except as a private edition for the Du Pont family,[4] and never in English at all. Several years later, Philip G. Johnson, now my editor, encouraged me to translate and edit it. He is, on his own authority, a patient man, which is all to the good since the time that elapsed before I delivered the manuscript would have exhausted the patience of one who was not. I am indebted to him for much more than encouragement and simple endurance. His interest in and support for the project have eased its way to completion. I would also like to thank Ann M. Aydelotte, formerly of the Eleutherian Mills Historical Library, now of Scholarly Resources, who offered me the invaluable support and assistance that only an editor who knows the content of the work as well as the craft of editing can.

My own enthusiasm for Du Pont, from the start, has been nourished by Mrs. Betty-Bright Low, research and reference librarian at the Eleutherian Mills Historical Library, and peerless authority on all matters concerning Du Pont and his papers. Throughout, I have tested my intuitions about the manuscript against her expertise, traded perceptions of Du Pont and his family with her, and above all learned from her many things I needed to know but had no way of knowing. Although I am loathe to hold Mrs. Low responsible for my own errors, I would hardly have committed the manuscript to publication over her objections. And, in thanking her, I am also thanking all those who made the library such an extraordinary place in which to work. Without the gracious permission of the director of the library, Dr. Richmond D. Williams, to publish a translation of the text of the autobiography, this project would not have been possible at all. I fully appreciate the opportunity so generously extended.

An early version of part of the introduction was written for a Colloque at Aix-en-Provence and benefited from the penetrating and friendly, if skeptical and bemused, criticism of Traian Stoianovitch, Françoise Brunel, Michelle Fogel, François Hincker, and Claude Mazauric. A somewhat later version was presented at the Seminar on Commerce and Culture at the National Institute for the Humanities, Research Triangle Park, North Carolina, thanks to the interest of Werner Dannhauser. I hope the present version has benefited as much from the encouragement of that stimulating seminar as the participants have a right to expect. My colleague, Mary Lynn Broe, read the section on autobiography, offered valuable suggestions, and promised that I would be neither totally disgraced nor lynched. My colleague, Thomas W. Africa, read the entire introduction with the acumen, learning, and skepticism for which I cherish him. Dominick LaCapra gave meaning to that overworked phrase, "intellectual community," by his generous reading and penetrating comments. Tracy Mitrano read, challenged, and encouraged throughout; her interest, like that of so many of my students, proved a marvelous incentive. Antoinette Emch shared perceptions of late eighteenth-century professionals and men of letters, as well as valuable insights from her own work on Samuel Tissot. Katherine Combellick entered on word processor the entire text of the autobiography, and then all the endless corrections. Throughout, she retained her interest in the project and contributed insights from her own work on women's forms of closure. Jennifer "Jendy" Murphy tirelessly endured my strange requests for odd books and bits of information. Without her energy and interest, I might never have made it halfway through the footnotes to the autobiography.

Without the uncommon expertise, research skills, and sheer deductive brilliance of my mother, Elizabeth Simon Fox, the final intractable problems of identification would never have been solved at all. No one without her professional training could have understood the material, and almost no one with it would have so generously given of her time to help another. Who else would have thought to bring me the pictures of the polar bear that accompanied the original edition of Gerrit de Veer's account of Barents's voyages to the Arctic? I especially thank her and Jendy for learning with me to think as Du Pont thought, to become sufficiently acquainted with his mental universe to pick up his references, especially when unidentified and misspelled.

If I think I have some empathy for Du Pont's investment in his family, I can only hold my own responsible. My father, Edward Whiting Fox, read the draft of the introduction and gave freely not merely of his general wisdom as a historian; not merely of his books, which I have been borrowing for years; but even more of those wonderful conversations about this point of telling detail and that—in this instance especially the lure of military careers in the eighteenth century—with which he has blessed me since my own earliest memories. His longstanding empathy for and attempt to understand me contributed in no small way to my sense of Du Pont's attitudes toward his sons.

My sister, Rebecca MacMillan Fox, and my brother-in-law, William Scott Green, both read when they could hardly spare the time and contributed variously and richly, as they always do. My sister-in-law, Helen Fox, and my nieces, Nondini, Maria, and Cybelle Fox, put up with my obsessive interest in Du Pont and even entered into the spirit of the game. Gene proved once again that the family of choice is as strong as that of nature, that my adopted career as Sicilian has not been a mistake. He read everything, reread, edited, encouraged, forgave the time taken from our work together, and, best of all, came to share my enthusiasm for Du Pont.

My brother Ted, to whom this book is dedicated, contributed nothing directly. Indirectly, he contributed everything, mostly by being the kind of brother to me that Du Pont wanted his sons to be to each other and by having shared those castles in Spain of our own childhood.

Notes

[1]Gilbert Chinard, ed., *The Correspondence of Jefferson and Du Pont de Nemours* (Baltimore: Johns Hopkins University Press, 1931), p. 28.

[2]2 vols. (Newark: University of Delaware Press, 1923).

[3]See Yves Coirault, "Autobiographie et mémoires (XVIIe-XVIIIe siècles) ou existence et naissance de l'autobiographie," *Revue d'histoire littéraire de la France* 75, no. 6 (1975): 931–56.

[4]Henry A. du Pont, *L'Enfance et la jeunesse de Du Pont de Nemours racontées par lui-même* (Paris, 1906).

Introduction

Pierre Samuel du Pont de Nemours's *Mémoires de Pierre Samuel Du Pont adressés à ses enfans* offers a rare and captivating autobiographical account of childhood and adolescence in the middle years of the eighteenth century. Drafted in 1792 in the shadow of the French Revolution, it deserves a place with that first generation of modern autobiographies, notably those of Benjamin Franklin and Jean-Jacques Rousseau, which apparently influenced Du Pont's attempt to construct his own. Rousseau's *Confessions,* which appeared in 1782, immediately captured the attention of the literate world to which Du Pont belonged. He always harbored mixed feelings about Rousseau, whose work he carefully read, generally admired, and frequently criticized sharply. Jealousy, too, may have played its part in his reaction, and perhaps a touch of uneasy identification. At any event, in his own autobiography Du Pont has the Abbé de Voisenon, in conversation with the Duc de Choiseul, point to the striking similarities between the circumstances and backgrounds of Rousseau's life and Du Pont's. For Franklin, Du Pont nourished much less ambiguous feelings of affection and respect. When Franklin's autobiography first appeared in an unauthorized French translation in 1791, Du Pont must have read it immediately. He certainly seems to have taken his lead from Franklin, who cast the first part of his autobiography in the form of a letter to his son.[1]

If the autobiographies of Franklin and Rousseau help to account for Du Pont's undertaking his own, they cannot be credited with direct influence on its tone or content. Du Pont's narrative manifests not merely a distinct voice, but distinct concerns. Less the self-portraitist of the social man than Franklin, he is also less the brooding introspectionist than Rousseau. He blends his concerns with the social and the personal in a special fashion.

Du Pont proves an engaging autobiographer with a special sensitivity to the feelings, concerns, dreams, and illusions of childhood and adolescence. His text brings to life the wonder of children's stories; the quality of life at school; the importance, especially for a young prodigy, of boxing; the defiance of parental discipline; and adolescent fantasies of glory. He simultaneously pokes fun at and forgives the peccadilloes of the earlier self he is invoking. He conjures up the imaginative universe of a young Parisian Protestant of the artisanal class whose mother nurtures him on dreams of military grandeur and quotations from the plays of Corneille. In short, his autobiography is a delight, as well as a very special view of a young man's coming of age.

Although Rousseau and Franklin retain their status as outstanding autobiographers by any standards and for any generation, their efforts, like that of Du Pont, were embedded in a culture in which autobiography suddenly flowered as a genre. To cite only French examples, Marmontel and Morellet were merely the better known of the many who, after the Revolution, would publish accounts of their lives under the *ancien régime*.[2] Recently, the autobiography of a young peasant turned professional intellectual, Valentin Jamerey-Duval, and a young artisan who remained an artisan, Jacques-Louis Ménétra, have come to light.[3] Others may yet follow. Our own age, in which bourgeois individualism may be approaching its demise, shares the fascination with the history of the self that characterized bourgeois individualism a-borning. Among this company of early autobiographers, Du Pont deserves a respected place.

It is hard not to like the Pierre Samuel du Pont de Nemours who lives in this autobiography. His account of himself restores the personality that breaks through the public writings only occasionally and then often deceptively. The autobiography goes far toward explaining the devotion of his descendants to their *Bon Papa*, the efforts they expended in collecting and editing his papers, the attention they gave to writing the story of his life—sometimes only for private publication—and the veritable cult they constructed around his memory.[4]

Friend, disciple, and lieutenant of the great and the near-great, Du Pont forged a commendable career as public servant, author, and editor during the final decades of the *ancien régime,* and as deputy, committee member, and even president of the Constituent Assembly during the early years of the Revolution. But his abiding reputation results primarily from his passionate defense of the doctrines of physiocracy, of which he became one of the premier publicists, and his loyal service to the person and causes of Anne-Robert-Jacques Turgot, whose secretary, associate, and first important chronicler he became.[5]

Du Pont had talent and set his sights high. He worked indefatigably. His separately published writings on a wide variety of topics well exceed fifty in number. His contributions to the various journals he edited or published further swell his total output. He was never shy concerning the merits of the causes to which he devoted himself, or concerning his own role in the projects in which he participated. Believing himself in the service of an absolute truth, he highly valued his personal contributions to the progress of humanity through enlightened legislation. He also attributed the failure of others, notably Jacques Necker, to recognize and reward his services to their willful opposition to the principles for which he stood. A quick and enthusiastic learner, he would, as the occasion demanded, immerse himself in a fresh body of knowledge and emerge a self-appointed expert. He cultivated the great and powerful, but never indiscriminantly: he chose his masters, and they seem to have rewarded his loyalty with their own. Among his friends he could count not merely Quesnay and Turgot, but the great chemist Lavoisier, Franklin, Jefferson, and the Mirabeaus, father and son. Among his acquaintances or correspondents he could number Rousseau, Voltaire, Diderot, Madame de Staël, Lafayette, and Talleyrand.[6]

In 1787, writing to Madame Blondel, the custodian of Turgot's papers, about his intention to bring out an edition of Turgot's works, he bemoaned the injustice and slander that plagued him because of his association with the so-called sect of the *économistes* and concluded: "For the rest, so much the better if there are three hundred citizens that are worth more than I."[7] Du Pont's concern with numerical precision reflects his own uncertainty about his precise standing among the great with whom he worked, as well as a preoccupation, shared by many of his most illustrious peers, with how history would judge him. Merit normally resists such exact classification, but Du Pont's figure at least demonstrates how small was that republic of enlightened citizens who were making some public mark during the last years of the *ancien régime*.

Du Pont never ranked among those who stand alone, whose views, actions, and lives command attention for the compelling brilliance of their minds, the originality of their formulation of problems, their political genius, or their pathbreaking contributions. He was not Prince Hamlet, "nor was meant to be," but he also was no lackey and could correctly see himself in attendance on history and progress, rather than on men. Most of us nonetheless require some external reason to be interested in him, and he has especially attracted the attention of students of physiocracy, but also that of students of the Constituent Assembly, the Institute, the making of the conservative bourgeoisie, and social policy. His protean interests and activities touched upon innumerable aspects of French government, society, and intellectual life in those decisive years before, during, and after the Revolution. But among the numbers of the second rank—a rank, after all, that few attain—he made his mark. He can be distinguished among the throng of the prerevolutionary elite and their postrevolutionary successors.

This autobiography and the massive documentation of Du Pont's career testify to a private success that probably exceeded his public accomplishments. Du Pont found his vocation as a father, the head of a family. As a son of the artisanal, petty bourgeoisie of the *ancien régime*, he became the father of postrevolutionary bourgeois capitalists. In his own life, he lived that transition; he adjusted to meet the demands of his times; he winnowed values and attitudes that he had inherited and bound them to those he acquired; and he forged a personality that could command the allegiance and win the love of his sons, and their sons and daughters after them.

Du Pont's personal and public life constitutes an exemplary view of the making of a bourgeois individual. One of the more important changes of the mid-eighteenth century consisted in the growth in the numbers of professional intellectuals and administrators, and the prominence of lawyers among the Jacobins especially has long been recognized. Also recognized has been the beginning of the bureaucratization of public service, the growth in governmental functions—for example, the compilation of statistics—the increase in the numbers of books published on a variety of topics, and, in general, the decisive increase in the size of a salaried professional class. This was the world in which Du Pont, like so many others of his and adjacent generations, forged his career. For when Du Pont began to work for Blaise Méliand, the intendant of Soissons, he was not embarking on a clearly defined career. He could not expect regular advancement to reward adequate performance of clearly specified responsibilities. He maneuvered in a world permeated with vestiges of patronage and clienteleship, albeit one that was moving in the direction of formal professional careers. He exemplified the self-made man who lifted himself from one social rank and level of income to another, and in so doing he helped to identify the employments that would justify social and economic promotion.

His sense of himself thus derives from a multitude of sources, not some ready-made mold. His career resulted from a series of ad hoc responses to disparate opportunities. Its unity, if it ever really had one, resulted from his having done specific things in sequence, from the unity afforded by his sense of his life as a coherent story. His advance foreshadows the career open to talent of the postrevolutionary generations, but only imperfectly. If Stendhal shows the persistence of patronage and family connection in his unfinished novel *Lucien Leuwen,* he also depicts the corridors of power as the hallways that connect defined offices. The world in which Du Pont came of age lacked that bureaucratic regularity.

Du Pont's autobiography provides the personal history and background for the development of his public career. It offers his readers a privileged access to his private feelings and memories, which permit us better to understand the quality of an individual life under the *ancien régime.* But his recollections are shaped by his commitment not merely to the claims of subjective experience, but to the claims of individualism as the governing principle of a just society. In his own life, he experienced the bloody transition from a society based on hierarchical principles to one based on those of bourgeois individualism. Whatever his reservations about the violence and excesses of the transition, he committed himself heart and soul to what he took to be its essence. An understanding of the reinterpretation of his life that he presents in the autobiography requires consideration of the nature of the epoch-making social and political revolution through which he lived and under whose shadow he wrote.

I

An emergent individualism—the sense of the self—did not appear as something new in the eighteenth century. Classical, Christian, and Renaissance individualism, to name but the most obvious forms, had all testified to awareness of the excellence or responsibilities of the self. There is something rash, even condescending, in assuming that peoples in all times and places have not taken account of the perceptions and stimuli experienced in the individual body and mind. The recent and widespread tendency among scholars to point to the modern personality as qualitatively different in some way from its predecessors easily leads into such related and offensive propositions as that until the fairly recent past parents did not love their children. At its mindless worst, it suggests that premodern personalities did not attain the autonomy and maturity of modern personalities. Such attitudes easily explain the reactions of other scholars who insist upon the individualism of, say, the Middle Ages.

The debate, as it has been cast, frequently misses the point, in ways analogous to debates over the economic acquisitiveness or the sense of property. Only blind condescension or romanticization can explain the view that medieval and early modern peoples displayed no sense of acquisitiveness or no sense of possession. The turbulent history of the violent quest for personal advantage clearly stamps such an idea as silly. But the reverse position that, upon recognizing a struggle for plunder and possession, one discovers the spirit of capitalism and of absolute property throughout history serves us no better. Acquisitiveness, the desire to increase one's own even at the expense of others, like the desire for domination over others, appears a ubiquitous dimension of human history. The interesting question concerns how those feelings changed over time, how social relations and the dominant language shaped and endowed them with different kinds of historical and personal implications.

Bourgeois individualism did not introduce the self into human experience, but it did register a changing perception of the self, its legitimacy, and its relation to the fundamental values of society. With the triumph of bourgeois individualism, the self—individual right—became the basic unit of social organization, the source of political legitimacy, and the self-conscious locus of first knowledge and, ultimately, of truth. This transformation of the accepted view of the nature and role of the individual occurred in tandem with momentous changes in the social organization of economic production that were themselves consolidated by the development of staggering advances in the material forces of production: the transformation we call capitalism, which preceded but was made irreversible by the industrial revolution.

The novelty of the modern world that was visibly coming into being by the second half of the eighteenth century has impressed most of its celebrants and detractors ever since. The growing numbers of political economists and sociological historians in England, Scotland, and France, especially those now known collectively as the Scottish Historical School, were among the first to chart the emergence of the distinctive new social forms they associated with succeeding stages in social organization.[8] Almost as soon as intellectuals began to reflect on these changes, they engaged in drawing lines of transformation and emphasizing distinctions between societies, understood to include values, theories, and personal and political relations as well as social and productive relations.

Early in the first half of the nineteenth century, John Stuart Mill and his contemporaries were pointing to the demise of feudalism, which they took to have occurred in the recent past; by the second half of the century, Ferdinand Tönnies was distinguishing between *gemeinschaft* and *gesellschaft*, or societies based on community and those based on economic contract.[9] Before the century reached its close, Max Weber had sketched a bold outline of the new personality of the capitalist, which he linked to Protestantism and to the triumph and internalization of an ethic of work, thrift, and accumulation.[10] Weber dissociated the spirit of capitalism as manifest in the discrete personality from the rigid categories of class he attributed to Marxism, but in any case his own analysis reflected a more subtle appreciation of values and ideology than had been current among Marxists of his day.

In our own time, theorists of "modernization" have insisted upon the emergence and significance of a modern personality type, which they take to be more autonomous, goal-oriented, and rational—among other stellar attributes—than its ancestors.[11] The central debates have more directly concerned the character of this new personality and the date and causes of its emergence than they have disputed its existence. But in large measure, the discussion has unfolded as a function of the spread of what we might call the objective conditions of modernization or, better, the emergence of capitalism. Modernization theories have primarily considered the spread of modern social, political, and economic institutions and have projected, on the strength of such aggregate evidence as voting behavior, the existence of a Modern Personality. The tools of social science upon which these students of the modern world rely lend themselves poorly to the close investigation of changes in specific personalities, the transmission of new, or subtly altered, values between generations in specific families, or the language and culture through which people represent new values to themselves.

Freudian theory has much more to offer, but has not normally provided a compelling alternative to the implicit or explicit behaviorism of the modernization theorists and their sympathizers. For in historical practice, Freudian theory has reflected the two principal tendencies in this historical study of individualism in general. Freudian theorists have tended either to adhere to the most rigid strain in Freud's thought and to postulate identity of psychodynamics across time and space, or to adhere to a largely American neo-Freudianism that discerns progress in personality formation across time and space.[12] In this respect, the modern individual of neo-Freudianism differs only in having the semblance of an unconscious life from the modern personality type of the modernization theorists.

There can be no dispute about the massive social changes attendant upon the rise of capitalism, however ferocious the disputes about terminology and timing may remain. Nor can there be serious dispute about the emergence of what I call bourgeois individualism, and what others call modernity. But important disputes persist about the relation between aggregate social and economic change; the relation of these changes to political change, especially revolutionary change; the distinctiveness of modern subjectivity and its form of expression; and the relation between social and personal change. The issues assume specific form in the debates about the nature and significance of the French Revolution in relation to the development of capitalism and individualism in France.

Although these debates are much too complex and extensive for exhaustive review here, a few principal issues are worth recalling. Marxists, conservatives, and liberals long concurred in identifying the Revolution as a watershed in French history.[13] They also tended to converge in portraying the Revolution as the product of enlightened thought, fiscal and social irresponsibility on the part of the monarchy, and administrative inefficiency. They even concurred in a general social analysis: the Revolution heralded the triumph of the bourgeoisie, the France of the politicians, the place seekers, and the notables. They diverged in their assessment of the result. For the conservatives, especially the more reactionary ones, the Revolution destroyed the nobility, the king, and the Church; destroyed organic social relations; and ushered in the world of competition, greed, and illegitimate exploitation. For the liberals, the Revolution opened the door to responsible political institutions, career based on talent, and the triumph of a socially responsible class of propertied citizens. The Marxists also saw the Revolution as the triumph of the bourgeoisie, but they muted their enthusiasm for this outcome, which they recognized as of world-historical significance for the triumph of capitalism and thus its ultimate overthrow, but which they also recognized as having been accomplished over the bodies of the popular classes that had made it possible in the first place.

Recent scholarship has challenged the older consensus about the nature of the Revolution on every front. The principal onslaughts have been directed against certain central notions. Against the notion that the Revolution accurately reflected the concerns of identifiable social classes, it has argued that no prerevolutionary bourgeoisie existed to make the Revolution. Against the notion that postrevolutionary France departed in any significant particulars from prerevolutionary France, it has argued that the monarchy—shades of Alexis de Tocqueville—had been effecting administrative reform and that the nobility remained as powerful after the Revolution as before. And against the notion that enlightened thought, whatever it might be, reflected the concerns of a specific class, much less a bourgeoisie that did not exist as a class, it has been argued that the nobles were as, if not more, likely than non-nobles to figure among the propagators of the Enlightenment.

Each point of contention suffers from a lack of clarity. Discussions of class in the Revolution generally confuse the subjective intentions and self-perceptions of a clearly defined group of individuals with objective changes in social, political, and legal institutions that would favor the interests of a specific social class—of a group of individuals prepared to identify with new values, new forms of acquisition, and new ways of ordering society. To take the example of property, which emerges as central in Du Pont's political economy and autobiography: the emotional force of the individual's devotion to the distinction between thine and mine can be equally intense under a system of decomposing feudal property relations, in which possession or disposition of the surplus is determined by customary reciprocal obligations and joint rights in a piece of land, and a system of bourgeois property relations in which possession is theoretically absolute and control of the surplus is determined by the free exchange of all goods, including property and human labor power. But the different forms of property have vastly different implications not merely for social and economic relations, but for the individual's sense of self in relation to society.

The violence of the French Revolution crystallized in political struggle the general tendency that dominated the entire Western world in the eighteenth century to transform archaic, collective, albeit rigidly hierarchical relations into modern individualistic relations. The most portentous aspect of this transformation lay in the triumph of absolute bourgeois property and its principal corollary, the absolute right to dispose of one's own labor power, itself frequently viewed as just another form of property. This transformation ensured the triumph of bourgeois individualism as a dominant ideology, or better, the dominant ideological tendency, since it long jostled with persistent collective and hierarchical views. But in establishing the foundations for institutions that would promote the generalization of individualism as a practice and in providing the dominant justification for social, political, and economic relations, it inaugurated a social system that differed fundamentally from its predecessors.

Bourgeois individualism in this sense does not refer to personal feelings, but to the forms of property; to sovereignty's deriving from the sovereignty of individuals in contradistinction to individuals' having rights as members of the collectivity; to the abolition of guilds and the attendant coercion of labor via the market, rather than via custom; to the existence of civil legitimation and registration of marriages and births, which effectively allowed some degree of freedom in choice of religious affiliation; to the election of representatives on the basis of individual if not yet universal suffrage; and more. Changes of such magnitude entail comparable changes in the response of individuals to their circumstances, which is to say an adaptation of personalities to meet new conditions. It is hard to believe that a revolution in objective conditions does not engender—if it does not result from—a revolution in the perception and representation of the self, not merely in isolation, but in relation to others. Recent work on changes in the nature of family relations belongs to this current of thought. But we are still far from a clear picture of the relation between objective change and subjective life. The hegemony of bourgeois individualism not merely as a theory of social and political relations, but as a world view that helped to explain the individual to himself or herself in relation to others, can hardly be understood without some knowledge of its subjective dimension.

Unilinear theories of the bourgeoisie's rise and triumph in the Revolution have proved easy marks for their critics. The events, ideas, and struggles that led to the Revolution bore the marks of their origin under the *ancien régime.* Those who would become revolutionaries once the Revolution broke out pursued a variety of occupations, held a variety of opinions, and had belonged to different social groups. The calling and initial meeting of the Estates General in 1789 mobilized the enthusiasm of vast numbers of people, who would begin to differ among themselves as events began to give political substance to ubiquitous wishes for reform. Language itself would be honed in the revolutionary struggles. The fate of the monarchy, the status of the Church, the abolition of feudal dues and services, the disposition of the estates of the *émigrés,* the floating of the *assignats,* and the many other issues that culminated in the ultimate test posed by the execution of the king presented choices that would gradually give shape to political groups. If initially individuals decided on discrete issues according to their conscience, increasingly issues were recognized as interrelated. If it is deceptive to speak of political parties in a modern sense during the Revolution, it is no less deceptive to ignore the emergence of political tendencies and groups.

For many, notably Du Pont, the Revolution provided the test, the winnowing, and the distillation of their prerevolutionary views. Only after the fact could they recognize themselves as members of a new bourgeois elite. Before the Revolution, their opinions lacked the social and institutional foundations that would permit them to identify with any specific class consciousness or even any putative will to revolution. They invariably sought reform within the existing social, political, and institutional system. And when, as frequently occurred, their goals implied something more than minor tinkering, they hid the implications from themselves.

Physiocracy, the political economy to which Du Pont so passionately adhered, offers a nice example. Physiocracy, as formulated by Quesnay and Victor de Riqueti, Marquis de Mirabeau, and as described in the autobiography by Du Pont himself, combined contradictory strands.[14] As the first modern analysis of the circular flow of economic life, it presented a comprehensive view of production that, in retrospect, can only be called capitalist. Yet the physiocrats staunchly refused to recognize the productive force of industry. Drawing on time-honored pastoral tradition, they asserted the unique productivity of agriculture and the special value of the rural, as against the urban, sector. In addition, although they developed a theory of the individual's presocial right to absolute ownership and of property as the sacred foundation of any legitimate social order, they insisted with equal force on the absolute power of the monarch, a theory of sovereignty they dubbed "legal despotism." In short, having cogently outlined the economic and social structure of bourgeois individualism, they repudiated its possible political consequences: political representation, they held, could only lead to the disorder that would inevitably result from the irresponsible pursuit of individual self-interest. They had their eyes on the nobility's disquieting tendency to defend archaic, antieconomic forms of property—and on the mob of landless laborers.

The physiocrats argued that the realization of the potential wealth of agriculture depended upon complete freedom of trade for the products of agriculture, notably grain.[15] This superficially innocuous policy recommendation contravened the received wisdom that had governed the growth of cities and the monarchy itself throughout the early modern period. All municipal and royal officials, like the urban residents with whom they were concerned, had argued that urban peace depended upon the regular availability of grain at a regular and manageable price. To achieve this end, they had hedged in the growing urban markets with a wall of restrictions to govern the buying and selling of grain from farmer to final consumer, and the export of grain from the kingdom. The physiocrats' modest proposal to restore natural freedom to this trade appeared to many as the most wanton possible disregard not merely for the well-being of numerous individuals, but for the social peace of the kingdom as a whole. They retorted that these policies of provisioning violated the justice due to property as well as the natural order of free exchange and actually decreased the aggregate supply and optimal distribution of grain within the kingdom, not to mention that they deprived the monarchy of the revenues it could expect from a free and healthy economy.

Physiocracy, at the time that Du Pont became committed to it, contained important elements of what subsequently would be called liberal thought. But its liberalism blended with a denial of the potential of industry and a disquieting political authoritarianism. Members of what would be called the "sect" yielded nothing to the sensibilities of their potential converts: they cast their views in a rigid, formulistic language such as that which Du Pont echoes in his defense of the doctrine. For them, the truth was an all-or-nothing proposition. They had scant patience with those who wanted to trim on the margin, to compromise with popular sensibilities, or to appeal to the more sophisticated and less dogmatic Paris fashions.

In the 1760s and 1770s, the physiocrats were taken to constitute a group, or a sect. They did not constitute a political party, for none existed in the modern sense; they did not even normally admit that they had political goals. They sought administrative reform to free the economy of the chains that precluded its natural growth. Georges Weulersse, in his classic history of the physiocrats, refers to them as a party.[16] He means those writers, editors, and royal administrators who systematically propounded physiocratic views and sought its implementation through existing institutions: the originators of the doctrine, Quesnay and Mirabeau; and their associates, Louis-Paul Abeille, Nicolas Baudeau, Guillaume-François Letrosne, Pierre Le Mercier de la Rivière, and Du Pont. Many others associated themselves with and defended physiocratic views during the final decades of the *ancien régime*. But most of those who were moving toward more liberal positions on a variety of matters rejected complete identification with the sect, primarily because of its political authoritarianism. Turgot, Du Pont's patron and a great reforming minister, and Marie Jean Antoine Nicolas Caritat, Marquis de Condorcet, both transcended and opposed many specific physiocratic formulations, but nonetheless passionately defended many of physiocracy's liberal economic policies and its theory of absolute property and free labor.

For reasons explored below, the allure of an absolute truth helps to account for Du Pont's initial attraction to physiocracy, especially to Quesnay. But although Du Pont remained a physiocrat throughout his life, continued to preach its virtues to Thomas Jefferson, and wrote to Jean-Baptiste Say that political economy could not be reduced to narrow economic analysis but must be understood as the entire science of man in society, he adapted his own views to changing historical conditions. Technical problems of administration, like changing political possibilities, led him to modify specific policy prescriptions and, ultimately, to accept first the principles of constitutional monarchy and then those of a conservative republic with a franchise limited to property owners. The continuity in his thought remains clear. For one who had lived through such a tumultuous period, he proved remarkably consistent.[17] But the Revolution opened opportunities of which he had not dreamed in his youth, offered him a political language that permitted him to express his conservative individualism, and ultimately helped him to forge a coherent interpretation of his rightful place—and that of those like him—in society.

Although the changes in his economic views have received some attention, the changes in his political views have received little. He did not himself write of his political evolution explicitly. He espoused some positions at one moment in his life, others at another. The consistency in his devotion to the ideals of individualism and of property saves his thought from radical disjunctures or from any imputation of concealment. Probably, he did not perceive the differences that might interest modern commentators as of special significance or even as disjunctures. Changing circumstances simply permitted fuller expression of views that, once he held them, he may have thought that he had always held. In this respect, as in many others, he offers a window on how individuals registered and assimilated the changes of the Revolution. For Du Pont the Revolution fully exposed the dangers he had always expected from what he would have considered a rabble dominated by irresponsible leaders. It also opened the way to desirable change. He quickly dropped his infatuation with the nobility, although by the time hereditary nobility had been abolished, he himself enjoyed noble status. As the autobiography records, he had some slight claim to noble blood, but he clearly never felt himself a noble in the full sense. And the disappearance of that superior social status and its extraordinary pretensions appears to have occasioned in him relief and even a bit of satisfaction.

For Du Pont, the king, not the nobility, or even the mob, constituted the decisive issue of the Revolution. His personal attraction to authority, his physiocratic attitudes in general, and his complex attitudes toward paternal authority in particular all led him to defend Louis XVI. He did not, or did not want to, see that the constitutional monarchy of 1789–92 remained deeply permeated with the absolutism of the *ancien régime*. Believing in monarchy and abhorring the mob, he failed to recognize that the constitutional in constitutional monarchy risked being subsumed under a resurgence of pure monarchy. Many others—for example, Pierre-Louis Roederer—shared his views. But the crisis of 1792 left scant place for civilized debate.[18] From the perspective of the more radical revolutionaries, Louis XVI himself posed an unacceptable threat to everything that had been won thus far. Du Pont's loyalty to the person of the king, which was interpreted as royalism rather than as a responsible defense of the Revolution, placed his life in jeopardy. Only after the dangerous years of 1792–94 would he subordinate his commitment to monarchy, which he assumed to be compatible with decisive institutional and political change, to his commitment to republican institutions.

Du Pont nonetheless accepted the institutional aspect of bourgeois individualism with something like a sign of recognition. It was what he had meant all along: he had only lacked the language in which to articulate it, the institutions in which to realize it.

Before the Revolution, Du Pont had been an ennobled bourgeois within the *ancien régime*'s system of estates. He had been grappling with the need to forge a career and an identity for himself and, simultaneously, with the desire to elaborate a program and language of reform. During the Revolution, he had been at first an enthusiastic, if moderate, participant and subsequently a horrified potential victim of popular rage. After the Revolution, he became a liberal notable, a propertied if far from wealthy member of the intellectual and administrative elite. Although he remained loyal to the initial formulation of physiocracy, which marked his views on political economy as tangential to the swelling mainstream of bourgeois classical economics, his general view of the proper relations of men in society fit easily into the dominant ideology of the newly born bourgeois France.

In recent years social history, and especially the history of "*mentalités*," has increasingly explored the changes in culture and attitudes that characterized the eighteenth century. This work, which attempts to reveal the changes in the ways in which people lived in and perceived the world and their specific societies, shows how the impersonal forces of the economy and ideology were perceived by ordinary people in everyday life. Social history and the history of *mentalités* almost inevitably consider the external traces of collective habits and perceptions; they constitute, as it were, a kind of history of collective behavior, of social patterns and group culture. Collective behavior and values appear to change very slowly, especially before the modern period, but they do change. In some periods, evidence for a constellation of apparently disparate incremental changes permits historians to speak of a recognizable shift in *mentalité*.

Michel Vovelle has identified the shift that appears to have occurred sometime around 1760 as a *"tournant des mentalités."*[19] The work of Vovelle and others suggests that shortly after the middle of the eighteenth century ordinary French people manifested a congeries of new attitudes and new forms of behavior. Among the more significant of these changes there figured a decline in formal religious observance for at least some men; the beginnings of a feminization of domestic service; a growth in literacy in urban and developed regions, especially a more rapid growth in the rate of literacy of women relative to men; an increase in the habit of letterwriting among the urban, notably Parisian, population; an increase in the number of unwed mothers, again particularly in urban areas where such births were registered; a growing insistence, at least among the well-to-do, that women should nurse their own children; a related emphasis on the special role of women as mothers and on the importance of proper mothering for the development of children; a dissemination, again primarily among the well-to-do, of new ideas of the family as an affective unit; a new interest in marriage for love; and even, as Robert Darnton has shown, a dissemination of the ideas of the *Encyclopédie* among the middling urban population.[20]

Although social history provides insight into the function of belief and collective life among social groups that normally do not leave autograph evidence of their concerns and perceptions, it provides little direct evidence of the subjective perceptions of discrete individuals. Yet the social changes point in the direction of what is known as modernity, to the emergence of a modern personality. In very different ways, they contribute to the social and cultural relations that would encourage at least some, still primarily men, to think self-consciously of themselves as individuals. But in important ways these various changes remained tendencies which, as such, might have been reversed before the Revolution. Only the political and institutional changes of the Revolution grounded the tendencies on solid foundations that could shape their future development. And even thereafter they jostled with contrary tendencies. The ideology of motherhood doubtless penetrated the urban petty bourgeoisie which, at least in Paris, was close to totally literate, which habitually corresponded, and which had access to the latest books. But among the members of that class the practice of putting children out to wet nurses actually began to increase during this period.[21] As Du Pont states in his autobiography, the mother's work at a trade or craft was necessary to the economic position of the family: her valuable time could not be spared for the nursing and intimate care of her children.

Du Pont's autobiography offers marvelous vignettes of the topics that concern social historians and historians of *mentalité*. Readers should be especially grateful for the picture he offers of his mother's life. He permits us to glimpse an accomplished craftswoman as a young wife: sending her children out to nurse, losing some of them to that dangerous practice, working all day at her workbench with her child playing at her feet, keeping her own earnings and contributing them to the maintenance of the household or to her charitable causes. In passing, we are even offered glimpses of distinctive female relatives: the Norman grandmother; the scorned young lover who dressed as a man to pursue her faithless swain and challenged him sword in hand when she caught him; the determined young Protestant who defied her family and joined a convent in order to be able, after several years, to marry the Catholic suitor of her choice. Du Pont's account of his own adolescence—not merely his education, but his pastimes—vividly enhances our picture of eighteenth-century life.

Du Pont's autobiography, in this respect and others, can be recognized as an invaluable document for social history, but its reading must be subject to all the caveats that govern the reading of such documents and even the reading of literary texts. For Du Pont, writing in 1792, shaped his representation of his life in the 1750s and 1760s according to values he had acquired after the events he describes. The text, like all such texts, must be read as itself an exercise in interpretation. To stress the interpretive quality of the autobiography is not to invalidate it as a document, but merely to underscore its quality as a subjective document in which adult concerns mingle with childhood memories. If we cannot rely upon some putative absolute accuracy, we can trust to essential veracity. But its truth is that which Du Pont considered significant after the fact. The autobiography must be read with attention to what Du Pont, in his fifties, believed to have been decisive in his life and with attention to the model he wished to offer to the sons whom he was addressing. If these considerations occasionally led him to modify the facts, however slightly, his modifications only enhance our understanding of what he took to be significant. In this respect, the autobiography becomes an outstanding chronicle of the making of a bourgeois individual.

II

Du Pont's life, which has been ably recounted several times, cannot be identified with a single career or accomplishment.[22] In this respect, his biographers have faced a difficult task. The best general scholarly biography, that of Ambrose Saricks, has the unavoidable quality of a shopping list. All those interested in Du Pont and, indeed, in eighteenth-century France are deeply indebted to Saricks's accomplishment. But in facing the responsibility to provide a comprehensive history of Du Pont's life, Saricks accepted the structure of the life as the structure for his own work. And from the perspective of scholarship and historical significance, the life lacks a sense of overriding purpose: no specific events or accomplishments stand out as so important as to make the closure of death a kind of anticlimax.

Biographers of Du Pont who have begun their task with some extrinsic sense of purpose have had an easier time in providing a sense of unity. Gustave Schelle's pioneering work, *Du Pont de Nemours et l'école physiocratique* derives its unity and coherence from Du Pont's relation to physiocracy. Schelle's strategy disregards many of the details of Du Pont's career and especially his personal life, but permits the integrated quality of an essentially intellectual biography. Bessie Gardner du Pont implicitly takes her organizing principle from her ex-husband's ancestor's mission as founder of the family. Pierre Jolly presents Du Pont as a "soldier of liberty" and integrates his various activities and some of his writings into this theme. Marc Bouloiseau concentrates on the decade of revolution, 1789–99, and presents the history of the Du Pont family during this period as exemplary of the experience of the bourgeoisie during the Revolution.

The specifics of Du Pont's public career can be followed in any of these biographies. Born in 1739 to a Protestant couple, he grew up in Paris, where his parents practiced their trades as clockmakers. The autobiography provides the only source for his life until his meeting with Méliand and then Quesnay in the early 1760s, after which his relations and accomplishments can be documented from other sources, including his own publications. The public record thus begins at about the time the autobiography breaks off.

At that point, Du Pont has just received an assignment from Méliand to take a kind of agricultural census and survey of the intendancy of Soissons, and he has just published his first physiocratic work, *De l'exportation et de l'importation des grains*. These accomplishments launched him, but they did not provide sufficient regular income for him to marry his betrothed, Marie-Louise Le Dée. An offer from the publishers of the *Gazette du commerce* to assume editorship of their new journal, the *Journal de l'agriculture, du commerce et des finances* in 1765 finally assured him that income. In 1766, he and Mlle Le Dée married. In 1767, their first son, Victor, was born. He was followed in 1769 by a second son, Paul-François, who died of smallpox as an infant, and in 1771 by their third son and last child, Eleuthère-Irénée.

The early years of marriage proved something of a struggle for the young Du Ponts. Du Pont rapidly lost the confidence of his publishers and the editorship of the journal. Almost immediately thereafter, he inherited the editorship of another journal, *Les Éphémérides du citoyen*, from Baudeau.[23] His initiative and militant advocacy of physiocracy rapidly brought him to the attention of foreign princes and tightened his ties to the circle of enlightened administrators around the Trudaines and Turgot. From the mid-1760s until the Revolution, Du Pont served as secretary to government administrators, especially Turgot; as correspondent to foreign princes, particularly the Margrave of Baden and Gustavus III of Sweden; as tutor to the son of Prince Czartoryski; as inspector general of commerce; as councillor of state; as elector for and then delegate to the Estates General of 1789. His trip as tutor to Poland permitted him to purchase the modest estate of Bois-des-Fossés near Chevannes (Loiret), the family property to which he refers in the autobiography. And, in 1783, the Comte de Vergennes, the minister of foreign affairs for whom he was working, obtained a *lettre de noblesse* for him from the king. Significantly, at the time of preparation for the Estates General, Du Pont chose to represent the third rather than the second estate.

As a delegate to the third estate, Du Pont sat in the Constituent Assembly in which he served on the standing committees of agriculture and commerce, National Treasury, examination of accounts, public assistance, public taxes, examination of the Caisse d'Escompte (discount bank), imposts, ecclesiastical affairs, finances, alienation of the national domain, and tithes. In 1791, the decision of the Constituent Assembly to disbar its members from election to its successor, the Legislative Assembly, forced Du Pont's retirement to private life. With his personal income from governmental positions depleted, he determined to buy a printshop. His friend, the renowned chemist Antoine Laurent Lavoisier, advanced the money in return for a mortgage on Bois-des-Fossés. As publisher and editor during 1792, Du Pont clearly expressed his growing disagreement with the course of the Revolution. In August 1792, at the head of a small band of militia that he had organized and that included his son Irénée, Du Pont helped to defend the royal family as the Paris crowd thronged into the Tuileries in an attempt to topple the monarchy. According to family legend, Louis XVI, crossing the courtyard on his way to place himself and his family in the custody of the Assembly, paused to acknowledge his service: "Ah, M. Du Pont, one always finds you where one has need of you."[24]

Du Pont's final act of service to the monarchy proved his practical and symbolic break with the Revolution. Immediately, he went into hiding in the Observatory with the help of its custodian, the astronomer Joseph Jérôme Lefrançois de Lalande. Philippe Nicolas Harmand, the tutor of his sons and a loyal family friend, brought him food during his period of concealment. But the arrangement was dangerous for all concerned. On September 2, when the gates of Paris were opened and briefly left unguarded during the beginning of the September prison massacres, Du Pont fled the city. For the next two months he found refuge in Harmand's country house at Cormeilles-en-Parisis. There he wrote the draft of the autobiography. In November, he was able to make his way back to Bois-des-Fossés, but being on the list of the proscribed he could not risk a trip to Paris. In the fall of 1793, he made brief trips to Rouen, where the authorities were accusing him of the crime of emigration because of his failure to appear with the proper certificate of residence. It took some effort to convince them that he was in fact residing in the kingdom, but not at Rouen. Then, in July 1794, political realities intruded on Du Pont's retirement: on 25 Messidor (13 July), the Committee of General Security ordered his arrest and incarceration in the prison of La Force in Paris. By

August of the same year, his family and friends had managed to secure his release.

The Constitution of the Year III, which established the Directory, permitted Du Pont's reentry into public life. In October 1795 he was elected to the Council of Elders, from which, for the next two years, he defended the virtues of social order and moderate revolution. But during the coup d'état of 18 Fructidor An V (4 September 1797), he once again suffered arrest and imprisonment in La Force, this time with Irénée. He almost immediately obtained his release, under circumstances that remain unclear but may include a deal with the authorities. In any event, on 27 Fructidor (13 September), the Directory delivered to the Council of Five Hundred his formal letter of resignation from the Council of Elders. On the same day, his name was at last formally removed from the list of *émigrés*. Du Pont emerged from the Revolution still identified with those who had supported the monarchy, but ready for a fresh start. By 1799, his plans bore fruit, and he, together with his entire family, removed to the United States of America, the land whose time had come. "The temperate, moderate, judicious, and republican government of the United States offers almost the only asylum where persecuted men can find safety, where fortunes can be rebuilt through work, where the prudence of heads of families may invest their last savings, the last portion of the subsistence of their children."[25]

By the time of this transplantation, Marie-Louise had been dead for fifteen years, and Du Pont had married in 1795 Françoise Poivre, the widow of Pierre Poivre, a colonial administrator and author who had been a friend. Both of his sons, Victor and Irénée, had married. In 1794, a year after his return from a diplomatic mission in Philadelphia, Victor married the aristocratic and devout Gabrielle Joséphine de La Fite de Pelleport, who always remained deeply hostile to the Revolution. Irénée, the younger, married Sophie Madeleine Dalmas in 1791.[26] Du Pont had opposed the marriage because of the youth of the couple, but rapidly became devoted to Sophie who stayed at Bois-des-Fossés to keep house for him while Irénée ran the printshop in Paris. At the time of the family's departure, the two young couples had five children between them. The nucleus of what would become the Du Pont dynasty existed in miniature.

For Du Pont himself, the emigration did not prove permanent. He returned to France in 1802 and remained until 1815, continuing his writing and his various political and intellectual activities. The specifics of his career during these years, which can be followed in other accounts, have their own interest, not least for their additional perspective on the emergence of the intelligentsia of the Ideologues and their allies, to which Du Pont never strictly belonged but with which he was associated.[27] Nonetheless, the first emigration to the United States in 1799 marked a natural culmination of Du Pont's varied careers under the *ancien régime* and the Revolution. In his sixtieth year, he had reached a maturity and consistency in his own views that would not alter significantly thereafter. Many of his opinions had persisted since his early commitment to physiocracy, but events had modified them and had led him to emphasize some themes over others. His assessment of the potential of the United States in the third edition of his *Philosophie de l'univers* (1799), cited above, clearly enunciates the concerns dearest to his heart.

For if Du Pont inaugurated his career with political economy and remained engaged with its theory and practice until the end of his life, he grew ever more committed to the importance of a few fundamental concepts. As he grew older and his children grew up, as he experienced firsthand the tumult of social change, he reflected on the purpose of human existence and the possibilities for progressive but reasoned change in the human condition. Firmly committed to a republican government, he insisted that it be moderate and judicious, by which he meant that it reflect the interests and engage the responsibilities of property holders. Property itself, that cornerstone of social order, would normally constitute the reward of work, a concept he valued as highly as any other zealot of the work ethic. Families constituted the basic unit of society and its microcosm. And education, which he did not mention in this passage, increasingly became his primary preoccupation as the only means through which to transmit acquired values and to promote measured change. For Du Pont, that wonderful science of political economy, the "science of natural law applied, as it should be, to civilized societies," extended to the very boundaries of the philosophy of the universe.

Du Pont had acquired his first lessons in natural law at Quesnay's feet, and he never abandoned those early convictions. In his correspondence with Jefferson in the early years of the nineteenth century, he refers to Quesnay's brilliant, if largely forgotten, article on natural law.[28] Du Pont, following Quesnay, could never accept the idea of a social contract that either restricts or augments man's natural rights. Property, man's inalienable right to the enjoyment of that which belongs to him, must be understood as a presocial right that no legitimate society can restrict in any way. The entire point of society is to facilitate the individual's enjoyment of his property. If for Quesnay the idea of property closely resembled an abstract economic concept, for Du Pont it gradually had acquired social substance. From the mid-1770s, when he first started working with and for Turgot on the *Mémoire sur les municipalités*,[29] he envisaged property as literally a piece of the realm. In his and Turgot's work, property ownership should entitle the king's subjects to a consultative voice in the affairs of the realm, but not to any sovereign share in decisions. Only during and after the Revolution did Du Pont come to understand the legitimacy of representation. And throughout his life, he retained a deep horror of votes for nonproperty holders. "I have developed not merely disgust, but horror, for barroom electors," he wrote to Jefferson in 1816. Everyone has an inalienable right to express his thoughts, provided they do not contain insult or calumny of others, but this right in no way implies that of "*deliberating*, of *voting*, of *pronouncing* on the affairs of others . . . for society is only made to conserve for each *that which he has*, and the faculty of improving *that which he has* without attacking the liberty or the property of whomsoever." Those who can only eat thanks to a wage and who can only lodge themselves by means of a contract cannot be considered the full equals of those "from whom they have solicited the roof and the bread, who shelter them and who nourish them. . . ." Such people have no material stake in society; they can always go elsewhere, whereas proprietors are effectively "co-sovereigns" of the country.[30]

The continuity and development in Du Pont's idea of property and of the political consequences of property ownership can stand as proxy for his political ideas in general. A fuller study could reveal the subtle, step-by-step evolution of his thought, but would not alter the general contours.[31] For Du Pont, property provides one of the more important links between the objective and subjective circumstances of the individual. His attitudes toward property reveal both his persisting authoritarianism and his flirtation with democracy. For him, property literally constitutes the anchor of the self, of his self. He relies upon the idea of property to justify his rebellion against his own father, even as he implicitly draws upon it to justify his authority over his sons. In both cases, his concern remains the material foundations of his subjective sense of himself as an individual, the external manifestation of his rights and his work.

As Du Pont grew older, especially as he himself became a

father, the role of the family in society and the polity became a growing preoccupation. He never specified his ideas about the family; one must piece together hints from different places. The autobiography suggests that Du Pont moved from one concept of the family to another. The shift is elusive, but there can be no doubt that when he considers the family from his mature optic of *père de famille* he sees it as the cornerstone of society. Writing to Jefferson of possible questions for discussion about the nature of government, he queries: "What are the natural laws of the good government and the good administration of a family isolated in a desert . . . how can they be applied and extended to the five hundred million families that will one day populate America."[32] Overall, in his mature writings, both public and private, he regards the family as the social unit that corresponds to the political and economic unit of property, and he regards the father as the head of the family. At the same time, he breaks decisively with the patriarchalism of the *ancien régime* in presenting families themselves as "little republics." And he always appreciated the skills of women as workers, managers, and full contributors to family fortunes.[33]

Again, his letters provide important indications of the personal feelings that underlie his public attitudes. At the time when Irénée wanted to marry Sophie and Du Pont opposed their intentions, he wrote Irénée:

> It is hard that your studious, affectionate father should be asked by you to live with no family or to be destroyed by a family whose wants will exhaust his powers; of whom the customs, habits, life, principles, standards, plans can have nothing in common with mine and can give me no happiness . . . My son is dying to me. . . . If I remain firm I shall be helpless, lonely, slandered in my own family.[34]

In 1782, when the boys were still young and when he had been absent in Paris for five months, he had written:

> And while it is important that I should see to my harvests, it is still more so that I should see what work my children have accomplished with their tutor, and by going over it with them show them the practical use of it—a part of the education of children of which only fathers realize the necessity; for scientific knowledge deserves only the second place.[35]

These letters and others like them reveal Du Pont's deep identification with his family of procreation. He may well offer an unconscious clue to his perception of a break between his family of origin and the family he made for himself when he writes, of his second wife, to Jefferson: "The scriptures say: Man will forsake his *Father and his mother and attach himself to his wife,* these ties which have been voluntarily assumed are the most sacred."[36] Du Pont's complex intermingling of feelings about himself and his family, most particularly his sons, dominate the autobiography. But it is worth underscoring here how deeply his thoughts on education permeate his thoughts about his sons. Away from home for long stretches, he corresponded with them about their studies, corrected the errors in grammar and spelling in their letters, and in general attempted to shape their young minds. The miracle remains that, notwithstanding struggles over Victor's adolescent rebellion and extravagance, he seems to have been remarkably successful. Almost more than by any self-conscious statements, one is struck in reading his sons' letters by the off-hand comments that betray his influence, e.g, Victor's request that Irénée send him some books: a grammar, a dictionary, "and the first volume of Grandison," that is, Samuel Richardson's novel, *Sir Charles Grandison,* which had long been his father's favorite.[37]

In Du Pont's mind, education, like property and family, constitutes an important aspect of individualism. Procreation and property alone will not suffice to perpetuate himself. Education must shape the consciousness of the next generation, and formal education must be solidly grounded in the internalization of worthy values. In this respect, preparing his sons to be his heirs resembled preparing society to accept enlightened leadership and to defend legitimate order. As early as 1800, Du Pont was pressing Jefferson to make haste on the translation of his work on education so that it might help to consolidate republican values in America. He says of education, revealing his understanding of bourgeois individualism and his purpose in writing an autobiography:

We ignore the language of the multitude that is stupid or heedless; we do not know how to penetrate brains that have little breadth and aptitude; we know even less the means with which to dispose the intelligence of children to listen to our own. It has been so long since we were children that we have forgotten; and young men, in their pride, in their passions, do not have sufficiently sustained thoughts to remember well and with a sufficiently deep philosophy that beautiful and interesting period of their life; moreover, they are occupied with ambition and pleasure, a great work with little glory is not their thing.

We must therefore carry ourselves back to the age of our childhood, seek carefully in our memory how and why we understand, and how we were humbled, in order not to repulse this youth that succeeds us, to make it understand and wish, and to render it as enlightened, as happy as the median condition of our species permits.[38]

Du Pont's pamphlet on education, *Vues sur l'éducation nationale par un cultivateur ou moyen de simplifier l'instruction, de la rendre à la fois morale, philosophique, républicaine, civile et militaire, sans déranger les travaux de l'agriculture et des arts aux quels la jeunesse doit concourir* (Paris, An II, 1794) belongs to the same period of his writings as the autobiography and the *Philosophie de l'univers.*[39] In my judgment, they all derive from a common impulse, from the attempt to make sense of his life in historical context. The political exigencies of the *ancien régime* had imposed distinct limits on the conclusions that might be drawn from his physiocratic principles. The Revolution did not significantly alter Du Pont's interests, but it did permit— indeed force—him to rethink and reformulate them. The prospect of being guillotined wonderfully concentrated his mind, as Dr. Johnson had assumed it would. His thoughts, in those dark days, did not turn to reaction or cynicism. He remained wedded to what he had always taken to be the basic truths of natural law. The absence of a sympathetic audience for his political views, which had been altogether distasteful to the Jacobins, may have provided an added incentive for him to reflect upon broad social and philosophical questions as well as narrowly personal ones. But both the broad and the narrow questions concerned his view of the relations of men in society—political, social, and economic organization—and his views on education and the universe concerned his understanding and representation of himself.

The *Philosophie de l'univers* likely constitutes a kind of conclusion or coda to the autobiography.[40] Apparently written between December 1792 and June 1793, it follows directly on his first draft of the autobiography. Although the work admittedly lacks intrinsic philosophic interest, it establishes the context of the autobiography and provides a valuable perspective on Du Pont's attitudes. Overwritten, rhapsodic, undisciplined—everything that Quesnay would have hated—it gives vent to Du Pont's frustrated poetic aspirations. But under the romantic gloss the reader can recognize a deep optimism far removed from facile romanticism. The avowedly irreligious Du Pont here expresses his conviction that things do occur for the best in the universe, and according to plan. Quesnay's tough-minded materialism and Du Pont's own displaced authoritarianism emerge clearly from his insistence that nothing, not the least throw of a die, occurs by chance. This determinism, which corresponds to such a deep strain in Du Pont's personality, never appears pessimistic. The human capacities to know and to love help to soften the implications of the determinism, although he never admits that they contravene it. In essence, human agency and responsibility operate within a predetermined context. It is as if impersonal natural laws establish the conditions of human existence, which humans themselves can improve or undermine. Human action will not change the Creator's plan for the universe, but human love and knowledge can realize the full extent of human potential. In this work then, Du Pont tries to make some sense of the relation between objective conditions and subjective perceptions and possibilities; if the world obeys incontrovertable laws, what do my feelings, intentions, and actions matter? What difference can they effect? If his answer lacks philosophic rigor, or even intellectual force, it nonetheless demonstrates how much the question of objective conditions informs his attempt to understand himself.

III

The *Mémoires de Pierre Samuel Du Pont adressés à ses enfans*, written by Du Pont between September and November 1792 at the age of fifty-three at Cormeilles-en-Parisis, represents a kind of closure, an attempt at a final summation, although its author would live for another quarter century. Events cut short Du Pont's project, but not in the manner he feared. When it became possible for him to make his way back to the seclusion of his country property, Bois-des-Fossés, he apparently abandoned his manuscript, or so those who have used the autobiography always imply. Saricks, for example, asserts that Du Pont "never found time to complete it beyond the point at which it breaks off abruptly—just before his first marriage early in 1766."[41] Such passing remarks aside, the history of the autobiography as a manuscript has received little attention, although since Schelle first received the Du Pont family's permission to consult their ancestor's papers in the late 1880s it has served as the basic source for all biographies of Du Pont.

The manuscript is preserved at the Eleutherian Mills Historical Library in Wilmington, Delaware. There also can be found Betty-Bright Low's in-house history of the Du Pont collection, which includes manuscripts, papers, correspondence, and books. Mrs. Low's splendid account makes possible as full a reconstruction of the history of the manuscript as available evidence permits.

Throughout his adult life, Du Pont had manifested an intense, self-conscious concern with the documentation of his career. As early as the period at which he drafted the *Mémoires*, he was making a sustained effort to preserve and organize his papers, which were in fact seized and sealed by the revolutionary authorities at least once in 1793, and at least one box of which was buried at Bois-des-Fossés, presumably to forestall seizure, during the same year. In his autobiography, Du Pont occasionally refers to papers that his sons will find among his things. The remaining traces of his own organization of the papers suggest that he had followed the procedures used by the French government during the final years of the *ancien régime.* It is also possible that his projected edition of Turgot's works, for which he had begun collecting material as early as 1787, had led him to consider seriously the organization and preservation of his own papers.

In 1799, when he and his family left for the United States, he requested Irénée's wife Sophie to pack up his papers and manuscripts to be taken with them. And upon his return to France in 1802, he took them home. When he went back to the United States in March 1815 upon Napoleon's return from Elba, during the Hundred Days, the haste of his departure prevented his taking the precious collection with him. He left it packed in boxes in his Paris apartment, in the keeping of his second wife, who was too ill to travel with him. His letters to her and to others about his desire to return to her side during the remaining years of his life dwell on the fate of those archives. He recommends that she have his papers bound so that, looking like books, they will escape the detection of the police. He worries constantly about the loss or destruction of those materials—the raw materials for the conclusion to the history of his life. He died in Delaware in 1817 without being reunited with either his papers or his wife.

The subsequent history of Du Pont's manuscripts and papers constitutes a detective story in its own right. Only in 1847 did Irénée's daughter, Eleuthera du Pont Smith, retrieve the papers from the heirs of Francoise Poivre du Pont. She brought the core of the present collection back from France and, during the succeeding half to three quarters of a century, she and other members of the Du Pont family worked at sorting, binding, organizing, cataloguing, and editing them, in part with the assistance of Helen Austin. The rich collection permitted Gustave Schelle first to complete his study of Du Pont and then his massive edition of Turgot's works and papers. Bessie Gardner du Pont drew upon them not only for her biography of Du Pont himself, but also for her life of Irénée reconstructed through contemporaneous letters. Du Pont's fixation on the creation and preservation of his archives has yielded rich returns for scholars and has served his memory well, largely thanks to the devoted and determined efforts of his own descendants. And the collection is still yielding up hidden treasures, most recently the celebrated and long-lost "third edition" of Quesnay's *Tableau économique* unearthed by the distinguished scholar of physiocracy, Professor Marguerite Kuczynski.[42]

The history of the manuscript of Du Pont's autobiography has inevitably been submerged in the larger history of the collection as a whole. Sometime after Mrs. Smith had brought the entire collection back from France, she and her sister Sophie (Mrs. Samuel Francis Du Pont) made a transcript of it. Bessie du Pont subsequently made a typescript, from which Pierre S. du Pont (1870–1954) made a translation, still available for consultation at the Eleutherian Mills Historical Library. And in 1906, Henry A. du Pont published an annotated version, *L'Enfance et la jeunesse de Du Pont de Nemours racontées par lui-même*. Alterations of and omissions from the original text make this edition unreliable, although the annotations provide valuable information. In fact, the private typescript and translation also suffer from omissions, although less seriously. Du Pont's descendants seem to have wished to draw a veil over *Bon Papa's* remarks on his mother's sexuality and his religious views, and they excised his reference to having taken a shot at the lottery. But both internal evidence and what is known of the family's deep reverence for Du Pont's every word suggest that none of them ever deleted anything from the original manuscript itself.

If it is possible to reconstruct the history of the manuscript with reasonable accuracy for the period following Du Pont's death, its history during his lifetime is much less clear and has never been seriously explored. The date of the original draft cannot be disputed: Du Pont explicitly sets his memoirs during his hiding, and he dates them. Subsequent scholars have assumed that he simply abandoned the manuscript when it became possible for him to return to Bois-des-Fossés. In support of that supposition, one can advance the internal evidence that at the end of the existing manuscript Du Pont has received his first paying assignment and announces: "I was very happy." But in essential respects, that closure violates the apparent purpose and dynamic of his account. There are innumerable and commanding reasons to assume that, with or without the return to Bois-des-Fossés, the autobiography would have ended at roughly this period in Du Pont's account of his own life. But those very reasons, more extensively discussed below, insistently suggest that, all things being equal, he would have brought his narrative to a close with his appointment to the editorship of the *Journal de l'agriculture* in 1765 and, above all, with its most important consequence, his marriage in 1766.

The cogency of the narrative-cut-short-by-external-events theory depends upon Du Pont's having abandoned the manuscript for good with his departure from Cormeilles-en-Parisis in November 1792. Yet the manuscript we now have itself suggests that he did not. The hand—indisputably Du Pont's—in which the text is written betrays the author's return to his initial draft sometime after he returned to Bois-des-Fossés. The existing manuscript was visibly written in stages, possibly at different times, and probably not in sequence. The first chapter differs from all the others in being written in a small, cramped hand and riddled with cross-outs and corrections. In particular, the first four pages of that chapter contain the roughest writing, the largest number of cross-outs, and are written on different paper than the remainder of the chapter and the rest of the text. Beginning on page 5 of the first chapter, the hand becomes more regular and the characters appear to have been traced with a different pen. Beginning with the second chapter, the hand becomes more open and the paper again appears to change, although the text still includes more corrections than the subsequent chapters. In the main body of the text, there are occasional corrections, notably two entire leaves and sixteen lines in Chapter 10, and two lines in Chapter 7 have been excised or overscored. According to Saricks, these excisions were the work of subsequent hands.

He may be correct, and we may never know for sure. But in my judgment, Du Pont was his own editor and was probably editing with a view to publication.

With respect to the evidence of handwriting, Du Pont's editorship can hardly be questioned. In at least one place, there is clear evidence that an additional paragraph was added at the bottom of a page with a thinner nib and in a smaller hand, between two paragraphs written with a larger nib and in a larger hand.[43] There are many other instances in which he appears to have crossed out a name and substituted another above it, as if correcting his memory. At least for Chapter 3 and those that follow, this visible editing appears to have been imposed on a clean copy, probably already a revision of the manuscript he drafted in the fall of 1792.

The first and second chapters present more complicated problems. The first chapter differs from all the others both with respect to paper and to handwriting, and differs within itself. The first four pages may well belong to the initial draft of the manuscript, but there is good internal evidence that the pages from five on were written during the winter of 1793–94, the most plausible date for his having revised the manuscript as a whole. The second chapter presents other problems: more legibly and boldly written than either part of the first, it nonetheless bears more crossings-out than any of the others, with the exception of only those few places in which the overscorings affect two or more lines (Chapters 7 and 10) and are done in a regular, bold hand in the form of linked circles, much as children are taught to practice when learning to write. In contrast, the crossings-out in the second chapter, like those in the first, take the form of horizontal lines drawn through a word or group of words.

This internal evidence initially led me to suspect that sometime after Du Pont's return to Bois-des-Fossés—probably during the winter of 1793–94, when he was effectively cut off from communication with the outside world—he decided to copy or to rework the manuscript with which he had occupied his hours in hiding. The winter of 1793–94 appears to be not merely the most likely date because of what we know of his seclusion during that period, but also the earliest probable date, for in the existing manuscript (Chapter 1, p. 6), he writes of how strange it would be, should he be accused of having emigrated, when all the time he was hiding right at the center of the kingdom. Du Pont indeed was accused of emigrating because of his failure to confirm his residence in Rouen, where he owned property; but this was only in the fall of 1793, almost a year after he had supposedly written the first draft. This fact, together with the apparent sequence of composition of the existing manuscript, strongly suggests that if anything remains of Du Pont's original manuscript—on the assumption that he wrote a manuscript in September 1792—it can only be the first four pages of the first chapter. But that assumption does not adequately help us to account for what appears to be two (or possibly three) other stages of composition of the existing manuscript.

In my judgment—a serious word for best guess—the existing manuscript of Chapter 1, following page 4, and Chapter 2 probably was drafted during the winter of 1793–94. But the remainder of the manuscript probably represents yet another reworking at a later and unknown date, at a point at which Du Pont was thinking of publication. By the time he had completed an initial draft or had reworked an initial draft during the winter of 1793–94, he presumably had recognized the possibility of writing a modern autobiography in the mode of Rousseau, and even more of Franklin, but was uncertain about whether to launch his account with information for his sons and from the familiar convention of a family history: what I know of my ancestors. This hypothesis receives some external confirmation from the existence at the Eleutherian Mills Historical Library of a few manuscript pages concerning the autobiography, which are reproduced in the Appendix.

The pages include a slightly revised version of Du Pont's dedicatory note to his sons and synopses of the first two chapters of the existing manuscript. In the synopses, he writes of what "the author" includes in these chapters and presumably is writing for a potential publisher. Unfortunately, one of the pages is torn off at the bottom, but the words that remain at least open the possibility that Du Pont was leaving to a publisher's discretion whether the two chapters on family history would be of the same interest to a general audience that they would be to his own sons. Perhaps, therefore, the pages were to accompany the reworked version of the manuscript beginning with Chapter 3.

If this assumption is valid, Du Pont probably recopied, and may even have reworked, the discretely autobiographical sections of his manuscript. For beginning with Chapter 3, the text becomes a structured narrative rather than a stream of reminiscences and bits of useful information about the families. It seems that Du Pont came to envisage the possibility of a finished work, in contrast to a chatty letter to his sons, as he wrote and rewrote. At the same time, he also clearly grasped the charm that the personal dimension might lend to his autobiography as an official work. For not merely did he retain the direct and intimate asides to his sons from what appears to be his final copy, but he rewrote the dedicatory note to them for the prospective publisher. Thus even as he contemplated downplaying or dropping altogether the theme of family as official history, he clung to the idea of family as personal relations: the emphasis on family as genealogy receded; the emphasis on family as affective unit, as the appropriate setting for the individual, or self, persisted or grew.

This reading of the possible history of the manuscript leaves open the possibility that the present text is incomplete in another way: not because it was hurriedly abandoned, but because a final chapter or two may have been lost; or that the original draft, beginning with Chapter 3, has been lost; or that he was waiting to rework the final chapters until he heard from the publisher and, not receiving a positive response, moved on to other projects. On this assumption, Du Pont would have temporarily retained the original Chapters 1 and 2, not having decided how finally to write the beginning of his autobiography; would have worked at revising the main body of the text; and would have been interrupted in this work of revision by his imprisonment in La Force.

Even as he was revising the *Mémoires*, Du Pont would have begun work on *Philosophie de l'univers* and *Vues sur l'éducation nationale*, which should be recognized as the sequels to the autobiography of his early life—the substitutes for a continuation of the autobiography devoted to his adult years and public career. There can be little doubt that Du Pont never intended to write a full account of his life. But considerable doubt persists concerning his intentions for the manuscript that we have. Additional random notes in Du Pont's hand demonstrate that he continued his attempt, captured in Chapters 1 and 2, to reconstruct as precisely as possible the histories of his parents' families, especially that of his father. Yet, as suggested above, it appears that he harbored doubts about whether to begin his own autobiography with those histories. Franklin had begun his autobiography with a history of his father's family and proceeded to a personal account of his own life. Du Pont might have intended to follow his model, but we cannot be sure. We cannot even be sure that he intended the recopied version of Chapters 3–15 for publication, although it seems highly likely. The recopied version includes running asides to his sons that suggest that at least some part of him remained wedded to a private communication rather than a public self-revelation. Yet Rousseau had demonstrated the possibilities of self-revelation, of a confessional mode. And the recopied text reflects a higher degree of craft and self-consciousness than one would expect from some random recollections jotted down to occupy his time in a period of hiding.

Du Pont, in his *Mémoires*, suggests to his sons that should something untoward befall him, they will be able to complete the story from his letters. He informs them in effect that beyond the point he has reached in his narrative, his story becomes a matter of public, or semi-public, record that can be documented from sources other than his own memory. In this respect, the autobiography constitutes a kind of long prefatory letter to his subsequent correspondence with Turgot, Lavoisier, and Madame Lavoisier. Yet the correspondence with Turgot does not really assume the proportions of sustained documentation until after the period when the present text breaks off. So we have another hint that the original draft of the autobiography may not have ended until his first marriage.

Whatever the precise point of closure of the original draft of the *Mémoires* or the point of closure toward which Du Pont was working, they signify the point in his life at which he had become a writing being who leaves a record of his thoughts, actions, and relations, and who figures in the documents of others. Du Pont surely intended, in the innumerable pages of his letters, to create a record of himself. From the period at which the autobiography ends, well before the period at which it was drafted, Du Pont had come to identify himself and his accomplishments with those pages of words. Words served a double purpose for him. First, they fixed his thoughts, feelings, and personality: they gave him some semblance of permanence. Second, he confirmed himself through the response of others. By writing letters rather than keeping a journal, he sought to validate himself through the imagined confirmation of others. He by no means sought only agreement or so needed approval that he could not register the responses of others when they were critical. He by no means had so little ego that he could not give credence to his own feelings without external confirmation. Yet he always needed to test himself, always needed an interlocutor, and always sought some affirmation of self from those whom he respected and whose recognition could enhance his recognition of himself.

The autobiography reveals that Du Pont saw Quesnay as a father figure, as the legitimate authority his own father had failed to provide. He suggests that Quesnay's conversation shaped the final formation of his character. Quesnay, he recounts, sternly opposed his wasting his talents and spreading his personality around through mindless and compulsive letterwriting. And, following these admonitions, he resolved henceforth to restrict his letterwriting to a single privileged correspondent: first Turgot, then the Lavoisiers. Now in hiding, he is writing what may be the final and most important letter to the fruits—perhaps, as he says, the only *net product*—of his labors. The epistolary format, which Du Pont may have borrowed from Franklin, cannot be dismissed as a mere convention. In the autobiography (itself a letter), Du Pont pointedly evokes Quesnay's opposition to his letterwriting. He also suggests in the text and by the very form of the text-as-letter, his own pleasure in and need for letterwriting. Quesnay occupied a special position in Du Pont's internal world and represented something akin to the final form of the paternal superego. We shall return to Du Pont's attitudes toward paternal authority, but here it suffices to note that Quesnay, the custodian in Du Pont's mind of objective knowledge, seemed to embody objective standards: the laws of accomplishment, worth, and truth. Du Pont thus pits his self against the explicit prohibition of that (legitimate) authority.

Du Pont distinguishes between the respective merits of Quesnay and Turgot. The latter, he writes, had a gentler, more yielding disposition and a more flexible intelligence. Du Pont does not choose between these two heroes, but his differentiation suggests that he found Turgot more human and approachable. The voluminous correspondence between them, in which Turgot proved to be a genuine if not equally prolific partner, confirms their enjoyment of close personal relations. For Quesnay Du Pont wrote political economy; to Turgot he wrote letters. He worked with and for Turgot and expected Turgot to know him in a way he did not expect from Quesnay. It is tempting to suggest that Turgot invited love while Quesnay invited reverence. The distinction is too sharp, but indicates a tendency. Turgot balanced Quesnay's role as the embodiment of a demanding and prohibitive superego with one as an ego ideal, with perhaps a hint of maternal acceptance. Whatever the explanation, which cannot approach clinical precision since adequate evidence does not exist, Turgot permitted Du Pont some measure of self-revelation and offered him an opportunity to be valued for what he thought himself to be, as well as for his performance.

Du Pont thus acquired the habit of seeking and getting a sense of self-acceptance and identity through correspondence. No longer promiscuously spreading himself around, seeking approval and identity in all corners, he concentrated on a few special relations in which he invested heavily. The psychological support he gained from this correspondence rested on more than the words of his correspondent; it also rested on his own feelings in writing. His having cast his autobiography in the form of a long letter to his sons must be seen in this context for, passing direct remarks to the sons notwithstanding, the text we have is an autobiography, not a letter.

Du Pont's internal representation of his relations with his sons pervades and structures the autobiography. We must take him at his word when he describes his sons as his abiding legacy. He had already invested heavily in their education and had participated intimately in shaping their personalities. Now they had moved beyond his formative influence, although his life continued to be intertwined with theirs. In his letter to Irénée, written when Irénée was proposing to marry Sophie immediately, Du Pont protested that his son was dying to him. In June 1789, he had previously written to him:

> Why had I no news of you? When you saw that I did not arrive on Thursday at six o'clock in the morning and you could have come and you still can today. You might at least write to me. It seems as if we were dead to each other. That should grieve you. It distresses me. *Vale et me ama.* Your friend and father Du Pont.[44]

The fear that his son is dying in relation to him and the fear that they are dead to each other may be translated as a fear that he is dying to his son and thus ceasing, at least in part, to exist. Conversely, Du Pont deeply believes that he lives through his sons. But his sense of living through them cannot be reduced to some parasitical living off their accomplishments. To the contrary, at this time and long thereafter he had every reason to assume that his accomplishments and reputation would far outstrip theirs. His living through them reveals his abiding need for recognition; his plaintive tone suggests the child's desperate need to be smiled at: the universal need so poignantly captured in the Biblical verse Numbers 6:25, "And the Lord make his face to shine forth upon you."

Du Pont, who betrays no wish to look into the void, thus shapes his autobiography as a letter to his sons. Writing in a period of violent revolution with the world, not to mention his own accomplishments, tottering around him, he seeks some understanding of who he is, of how he became who he is, of what he has accomplished. Both the events of the Revolution and his own gnawing suspicion that he never equaled the stature of a Quesnay or a Turgot account for his not wishing to stake his worth on his public career. He bets instead on his private self and especially on his identity as a father, which accounted not merely for his reproduction, but for his *"net product."*

The problems of assessing honestly his own public role help to account for Du Pont's restricting his autobiography to his youth and adolescence. Had he written fully of his adult career he would have had to reduce himself to observer, chronicler, and aide of the great—and thus transform the autobiography into memoirs—or to lie about his own importance. Du Pont never shied away from claiming the maximum significance for his own role, but it would have stretched even his generous interpretation of his influence on others, not to mention the credulity of his readers, to claim that he alone had authored the policies of Vergennes or Charles-Alexandre de Calonne.[45] The autobiography testifies that he might have wished to do so: he categorically affirms that, contrary to received opinion, he did not serve many ministers, but made many ministers serve him, or at least the truths that he himself was serving. But that interpretation of the politics of the 1780s would not have played well in Paris, where too many knew the story even after the beginning of the Revolution.

Du Pont might have continued his autobiography as an account of his private life during his mature years, but his vision of his relation to his sons foreclosed that option. He teases them with the great secret of his relations with their mother. To continue beyond his marriage would have meant to break that secrecy or to fail in essential candor. It would also have forced him to talk of himself at the age his sons had already reached and would have seriously jeopardized his seniority as father. It was one thing to share his own childhood in empathy with theirs. It would have been quite another to admit them into his fraternity of adult men and thereby to risk their judgment and competition as equals. Far better to let them finish, if need be, the account from his correspondence.

Both these reasons combined in Du Pont's strategy of completing his adult legacy in the more impersonal writings on the philosophy of the universe and education. His philosophy of the universe permitted him simultaneously to affirm a belief in the ultimate beneficial outcome of human affairs—a comforting antidote to the chaos he saw around him—and to affirm the beneficent, if omnipotent, character of authority against that which he seems to have experienced as the punitive aspect of his father and of traditional Christian doctrine. The writing on education permitted him to perpetuate his values and to affirm his faith in the possibility of worthy successors to his life's work. The realms of philosophy and of practical education effectively bracket the problematic terrain of his own impact on the course of history and his own standing among great men.

The works, therefore, that Du Pont wrote as he was completing or possibly revising his autobiography constitute both a coda to and a context for it. In addition, they implicitly confirm the specific purpose of his autobiographical project: his determination to provide a narrative or a history of himself.

IV

Autobiography as a genre has generated heated debates in recent years. According to a minimal consensus, autobiography consists of a first-person narrative in which the author, the same as the narrator of the text, writes about his or her own past experience in conformity with some accepted standard of veracity. Beyond that minimum lies deep disagreement about the character, significance, literary standing, and historical specificity of autobiographical texts.

Each autobiography privileges a specific narrative: I became myself.[46] In this respect, autobiography might be considered the ego's—or author's—history of himself or herself. To write one's autobiography is to confer meaning on one's life, to protect that life in some measure against the dissolvent effects of time, against oblivion. Yet autobiography as a history can exist only in or through time. So the effort of preservation belongs precisely to the medium it is trying to defend against. And like all history, autobiography constitutes an act of interpretation. Moments of being in time are ordered, from the perspective of a specific moment in time, with a view to creating a meaning that will survive the further passage of time.

The related issues of time and history govern any understanding of autobiography and are invoked not merely as an aid to the understanding of specific autobiographies, but also to provide a precise understanding of the genre in contrast to other forms of first-person narrative. Philippe Lejeune especially has insisted that autobiography be recognized as a distinctly modern phenomenon. By modern, he means that pivotal second half of the eighteenth century. Like those who share his perspective, he would take the posthumous publication of Rousseau's *Confessions* in 1782 as the inauguration of autobiography in the strict sense.[47] In this view, autobiography departs decisively from older forms of first-person narrative, especially such didactic religious texts as Augustine's *Confessions* and various forms of memoirs. This view of autobiography emphasizes its character as the individual's interpretation of his or her self as an individual and without reference to determining external values or communities. Autobiography, in this sense, requires the disembedding of the individual from the surrounding social, cultural, and ideological terrain. The author of a true autobiography assumes the primary responsibility of constructing a self—an interpretation of the self—as an end in itself, not as illustrative of the life of a community or the truth of a doctrine. In stark contrast to memoirs, an autobiography addresses the consciousness of its observing subject, not the swirl of life and personalities around him or her. In contrast to a journal or a diary, an autobiography presents the sequence of a life from the perspective of a specific moment in time and as a whole, not as a sequence of impressions and responses.

The insistence upon the intimate links between individualism and autobiography invites a variety of challenges. It is child's play to recognize authoritative and flamboyant individuals in the Middle Ages, not to mention the Classical period and the Renaissance. Georg Misch's massive history of autobiography documents the prevalence of first-person accounts throughout history and around the world.[48] Western culture alone has been characterized from its origins by first-person accounts of persons and events, including the life of the author. It is not merely absurd, but ethno- and temporo-centric as well, to claim the individual as the splendid and unique product of modern Western culture. But to claim a special relation between systematic individualism and that culture is something altogether different, and probably accurate.

In the most general sense, this association means simply that autobiography constitutes a distinct genre, a historically and stylistically specific way of presenting and understanding the individual under conditions in which the individual is taken to constitute the fundamental unit of truth and of consciousness. The necessary historical, psychological, and ideological conditions for autobiography in this specific sense include assumptions about the primacy of the individual over the group, the possibility and authority of self-knowledge, and the dominance of rationalism over tradition. Historically, the growth of these assumptions as a coherent, or at least plausible, picture of society accompanied the triumph of capitalism and constituted the essence of bourgeois individualism. Lejeune apparently has these or analogous considerations in mind when he defines autobiography as a "retrospective narrative in prose that a real person makes of his own existence, when he places the accent on his individual life, in particular on the history of his personality."[49]

No discussion of autobiography has managed to avoid entirely some emphasis on the self or the personality of the autobiographer, if for no other reason that autobiographers, from Rousseau on, have been mesmerized by their own personalities. There is no small irony in bourgeois culture's having so dramatically privileged the notion of the self in this sense, for the underside of the promise of self-realization inherent in bourgeois individualism has been the growing interchangeability of bourgeois individuals. The possibility of escaping external social and ideological definitions of one's self results inescapably in the possibility of confusion among all selves; thus, it should not cause surprise that the rise of bourgeois individualism has prompted a gnawing concern with the self as distinct from the external and uniform condition of the individual.

It is understandable that concern with self—in Rousseau's formulation, that one is different but no better or worse than others— has plagued autobiographers who try by that very act of writing to distinguish themselves from the throng of their competitors. Also understandable, but much less justifiable, is the preoccupation of scholars of autobiography with that same self. Many have apparently experienced an overwhelming temptation to view the self as in fact essential, if not eternal, and immune to time. In the most extreme cases, they offer autobiography as a window on the true self hidden beneath the imposed mask of the historical actor. Georges Gusdorf, a leading and usually insightful scholar of autobiography, has argued that autobiography subordinates the truth of facts to the truth of the man, that it can be called a theodicy of the individual, that it attempts to construct an eschatology of the individual life.[50] Gusdorf's remarks remain ambiguous: he does not commit himself to the notion that there exists a truth of the man independent of the life of the man or his account of it. And elsewhere he allows that the significance of autobiography lies less in its "literary function" than in its "anthropology."[51]

Other commentators have shown less caution. Even Roy Pascal, in a generally fine, sensitive account, writes that autobiography is "inspired by a reverence for the self, . . . the self in its delicate uniqueness," and informed with the "consciousness that the self escapes definition. . . ."[52] James Olney and others yet more warmly embrace the idea of a self distinct from other selves and the world, a presocial self that resists the incursions of time and events and embodies its own truth.[53] These and other critics have established the claims of autobiography as a genre, but they accept uncritically this myth of the self which autobiographers have promoted as a defense against insecurities and anxieties—against their own lives in history. Recent criticism, especially deconstructionist, has treated the infatuation with the self harshly.[54] But the indisputable importance of understanding the historical and psychological dynamics that informed the concept of the eternal or essential self should not lead us to dismiss the value that autobiographers placed upon that self. The compelling question remains that of how, when, and why autobiographers attempted to substitute a concept of identity for one of location. As Janet Varner Gunn has written, the "real question of the autobiographical self then becomes *where do I belong?* not, who am I? The question of the self's identity becomes a question of the self's location in the world."[55]

Whatever their differences, all critics of autobiography concur that the genre poses a special case of the problematic relation between truth and fiction. Historians may profitably read autobiography for information about an individual or even about a social class or a historical epoch, but woe betide the reader who expects an autobiography to rest entirely upon verifiable fact. Memories fail. Authors deceive. Making a point sharply seems to require some tampering with facts. There are those who, impressed by the elusiveness of facts, would identify all narratives with fictions. The complex and fascinating issues which directly engage the most compelling problems concerning the nature of texts, truth, and reality far exceed our present concerns. But the general problem of truthfulness affects autobiographies in two important ways.

First, there is the question of accuracy of information. The autobiographer asks the reader to accept the narrative as an accurate record of events and people. We should be offended by flagrant departures from a verifiable history. And autobiography, being inherently referential, demands a plausible relation to its purported setting. But occasionally an autobiographer like Du Pont can be shown to have altered verifiable facts. If, as with Du Pont, the alteration does not invalidate the essential meaning of the narrative but reinforces a central theme or psychological influence, we need not take offense. For example, Du Pont writes that his mother gave him a book she could not have given him. The book, Richardson's *Sir Charles Grandison,* became his favorite novel, its hero his model. By having her give it to him, he overdetermines its emotional significance to him and establishes a link between her influence and his own ideals. The liberty he takes is all the more interesting for *Sir Charles Grandison's* corresponding more closely to the values she instilled in him than many of the books we can be fairly certain she did read with him. This slight violation of strict truth—and it is always possible that he misremembered, that he came to believe that she had given it to him—does not destroy our confidence in his narrative and underscores one of its most important themes. The lapse in historical accuracy does not justify a charge of general untruth. The autobiography is not identical to what happened: it is a subjective account of what happened, and thus an interpretation. But it should not, for this reason, be classified as fiction in the normal sense of the term.[56]

Second, we have the problem of the truth of the autobiography as a narrative. Earlier critics of autobiography coped with this problem by falling back on the idea of the self. The autobiography embodies the truth of the self, against which standard lapses in accuracy count for little. But surely we need not accept the individual's feelings, aspirations, fantasies as the truth of autobiography unless they are identified as such. And the moment they are so identified, others, society, and history return through the back door, if only because the identification of fantasy implies an acknowledgment of the reality from which it departs. We do not, in fact, have very good standards for a reasoned level of truth in auto-biography. If we accept *a priori* the absolute primacy of subjective experience over external conditions, we abandon the tension of the individual-in-history, which presumably accounts for the sense of the self in the first place. Yet we can hardly require a personal history to cast itself purely as a function of objective conditions. The truth of the autobiography would seem to depend in the first instance on the authenticity of the picture of the self as an individual-in-history, in the second on the plausibility of the relation of the present self who is writing to the earlier selves who are being evoked and interpreted.

Critics of autobiography increasingly argue that the truth of the autobiography depends upon the relation between the text and its reader. This criterion for truth solves little, for the recognition of the reader's importance can be taken to mean anything from the most sophisticated hermeneutical relation to the simplistic and unacceptable proposition that each reader creates his or her own text. Obviously, succeeding generations read texts through different lenses and for different purposes. But the changing response to texts cannot alone suffice as a standard of truthfulness for the author of the text. Currently, some try to solve that problem by banishing the author from the discussion entirely. The text must stand on its own. Let us grant the salutory effect of this insistence on the integrity of the text, which, after all, the New Criticism of the 1950s had forcefully reminded us of. But to focus exclusively on the reader while denying the author means arbitrarily to destroy the dynamic tension of the text as a mediation between two consciousnesses. The intractable problem of the relation of author to text permits no easy solution. Lejeune proposes the concept of "autobiographical pact" to ease it. If, he argues, autobiography can be defined by "something external to the text, it is not towards the interior, by an unverifiable resemblance with a real person, but beyond, by the type of reader that it engenders, the credibility that it secrets. . . ."[57] Yet even this proposal does not allow sufficient weight to the role of the author who produced his or her text, at least in part, to attract or engender certain kinds of readers.

Du Pont preselected his readers and never entrusted his text to a larger audience. Paradoxically, the narrowness of his choice lends credibility to his autobiography today. Since he wittingly would not have confronted his sons with a man they could not recognize, his choice of readers contributes to the psychological plausibility of his account. The modern reader has confidence in his text because it was addressed to those who presumably knew him best. To argue for the credibility of the text in this sense is to do more than suggest that it offers a recognizable portrait which refers implicitly and explicitly to a specific context and a specific set of personal relations.

Du Pont's letter to Jefferson on education suggests that he had made a self-conscious effort to remember his own childhood in order to be able to understand and, consequently, to influence his sons. Empathetically watching them must have revived his own memories, doubtless long buried. For example, when he discusses his feelings of rivalry for his sister in a passage of extraordinary charm, he doubtless has in mind Victor's response to Irénée's birth, as well as his own more distant experience.

Although Du Pont explicitly addressed his autobiography to his sons, it seems likely that he had another reader in mind as well—one who would never fulfill the role—his father. The entire autobiography constitutes an extended exploration of Du Pont's precarious balance between the role of father and that of son. That tension, too, contributes to its credibility. For even in his fifties he has not completely laid that old ghost. And yet, in his fifties, a father of grown sons himself, he needs to understand the ways in which his father had been correct and had been meeting paternal responsibilities and the ways in which he had been unjust. The role of father, the personality of different men, and the historical conditions all come into play. He seeks to reassure himself that he can assume the prerogatives of fatherhood without assuming the attributes of tyranny. He seeks to make his own authority legitimate, even as he seeks to make himself loved and understood by his sons.

The decisive historical moment for any autobiography is the moment at which it is written. The remembrance of things past, in the memorable phrase of the Scott Moncrieff translation of Marcel Proust's title, is, like the original of that title, the search for lost time. That enterprise bears the stamp of the hour of remembering more clearly than that of the hours the rememberer is seeking to recover. The moment of remembering shapes the choice of feelings and events to be recorded as it shapes the choice of the elements of the personality that are to be emphasized. In this respect the moment of closure that the moment of writing inescapably represents is also the moment of beginning. For the life represented in the autobiography cannot be given from the outset: it is, in Roy

Pascal's words, "not simply the narrative of the voyage but the voyage itself. There must be in it a sense of discovery, and where this is wanting, and the autobiography appears as an exposition of something understood from the outset, we feel it is a failure, a partial failure at any rate."[58] Pascal seeks to underscore the creative dimension of the act of remembering. His insight can be pushed further, for the writing and remembering self, in effect, produces a history of the self at a particular moment in time. To recognize this process of self-creation must be to acknowledge that the self cannot be considered an ahistorical, absolute entity. It not merely exists in history, its self-consciousness is doubly historical: it has existed in a succession of specific historical moments, and its recollection of its own history, and hence its identity, occurs under specific historical conditions.

Gunn has argued that autobiography as a form could only emerge "when men and women began to experience what Mircea Eliade has called 'the terror of history'."[59] She means in essence that autobiography results from people's experience of their finitude. The absence of absolute transcendent values or of defining communities exposes the self to its own mortality, without protection or mediation. Facing that void can spur the mind to make sense of apparently random events and to endow one's life with meaning. If it can engender a feeling of nothingness, it can also generate a quest for authorship and agency.

In a general way, Du Pont, like many of his peers, experienced that terror of history which resulted from the systematic questioning of established authorities, that spirit of criticism of revealed truths and established institutions which characterized the Enlightenment. Far more immediately, he experienced the terror of history that resulted from the Revolution. If its early phases had seemed to promise the realization of reforms for which he had long worked and even new opportunities for his own career, by August 1792 it appeared more dangerous. The threat of violence hung like the guillotine over the writing of his autobiography. No abstract or metaphysical shadow, this terror assumed the concrete form of mobs who were rampaging in the streets, overrunning the citadels of legitimate authority, killing his friends, and seeking to kill him.

That terror drove Du Pont to capture in words, to review, and to find meaning in his own life. Mortal danger initially prompted the writing of his autobiography, and its shadow hangs over his pages. Yet the autobiography returns to an earlier private life; it does not directly confront his present crisis. It exudes a feeling of preparation, or taking stock, but the cloud of impending judgment does not darken its mood. In the face of danger, Du Pont proved capable of calm and of resolution.

The threat of impending execution might lead to a denial of reality and an escape into fantasy. Not for Du Pont. His return to his childhood cannot be dismissed as a retreat to idealization or pastoralism. Significantly, his account lacks those evocations of the sights and sounds and smells of rural life, those evocations of flowers that bloomed brighter or of food that although simpler tasted better. Here is no enclave of country-fresh milk or flavorful bread. Marmontel would indulge in such idealizations of his childhood in the Auvergne; writing after the Revolution had spent its fury, he was seeking to evoke the special charm of the *ancien régime*, albeit without directly celebrating its hierarchical institutions.[60] Du Pont avoids such displacements, just as he avoids romanticization of the old order. He fears the current course of the Revolution and regrets its excesses, but he never repudiates its moderate and legitimate goals. If he turns to the personal, he does so in part because of his pressing concern about his relation with his sons—his own identities as son and as father—and in part because he seeks the personal roots of his own identity as a mature political man.

Du Pont's autobiography remarkably blends the personal and the political as they intertwined in the lives of men and women of his generation. He draws upon the language of politics—of bourgeois individualism—to make sense of his own early life and even to justify his rebellion against his father. Political terms and categories help him to make sense of personal feelings and to evaluate the influences on his life. He invokes the concept of property to label as unjust his father's harsh discipline. He reproves the restrictive privilege of the rector of the university who prohibited his second public performance as a learned child. But, perhaps most tellingly, he explores and criticizes the privilege and the ideology of nobility. He brilliantly evokes the hegemony of nobility as it penetrated the life of the *ancien régime*: from the right to wear a sword, to the lure of a military career, to his mother's claims of noble descent and her attempt to inculcate in him noble values. He succeeds in sketching the transition of a world in which nobility of soul essentially followed noble status—at least in ideology—to one in which nobility of soul can be recognized as the attribute of the character and work of the individual and in which pretensions to nobility must be dismissed as mere smoke.

We know from extratextual sources that as late as the 1780s Du Pont remained imprisoned by the self-inflating claims of nobility. He valued highly his own patent of nobility as well as the distinctions he had received from various foreign princes. More significantly, he could still write in this period to the Marquis de Mirabeau, by then a friend, "you who are noble. . . ." He remained, in short, awed by nobility. And we can safely assume that he still responded to the allure of his mother's noble descent. It seems likely that his thoughts about nobility remained conflicted. He seems to have resented covertly that to which he was also drawn, and on some level he must have experienced its abolition by the Revolution as a release. Certainly, he mentions the disappearance of noble status in his autobiography. He even counterposes noble descent to natural descent when he writes that his claims to nobility through the female line had been worthless, since women did not transmit nobility "although their descent is much more certain." But if personal resentments and political events encouraged his growing criticism of nobility, its more destructive illusions must already have been painfully impressed on him by his son Victor's extravagant pursuit of a leisured, noble life, for which he expected his father to pay the bills. Du Pont's correspondence with Victor during this period, and even passing references in the autobiography, reveals his difficulty in disciplining and restraining his son. That experience must have led him to reconsider not merely noble pretensions, but also his own relations with his father. His treatment of nobility in the autobiography would appear to reflect his serious thinking on all these matters and his attempt to weave his thoughts about himself, about Victor, and about the political implications of noble status into a coherent interpretation.

The language and values of bourgeois individualism permit Du Pont to reinterpret his past in a way that simultaneously affirms legitimate authority, including the authority of fathers, and validates responsible individualism. Work and property emerge as the principal anchors both for authority and for the self. Via work, the individual internalizes authority and acquires property which becomes the external manifestation of the self. By insisting upon the presocial character of property and upon its role as the foundation of any legitimate social order, Du Pont provides a material anchor for the sense of self. In this respect, it appears that his sense of himself, which grew in his conflicts with his father before he had encountered physiocracy or other writings on political and social theory, doubtless informed his appropriation of those theories. His personal experience led him to embrace a theory that stressed the sanctity of property as external confirmation of himself and, when the time came to write his autobiography, the theories that were already informed with his personal feelings helped him to interpret and to name his own development.

Du Pont, like all other autobiographers, drew for his narrative of his life upon what Michael Polanyi has called the "system of acceptances."[61] He formulated his sense of himself from the language and concepts his culture offered him. His choice among the alternatives available in the culture at large reveals much about both his early history and his subsequent interpretation of it. Used with caution, his autobiography permits us to reconstruct something of the possible education of a child and young man of his class and generation. Yet the achievements of his adult life, compounded by the upheaval of the Revolution, forced him to reassess those early acceptances. Du Pont's use of political language provides the best example of how he reinterpreted the past in the light of his more recent past and his present. Other choices reveal both stages and disjunctures in his personal and intellectual development that resulted at least in part from changes in the culture at large.

Like Franklin, Morellet, and Marmontel, among other early bourgeois autobiographers, Du Pont emphasizes the importance of books in his development and even uses the titles of books he assumed would be generally familiar as signs of his own interests. The books he mentions include the obvious milestones in the development of eighteenth-century liberal thought: Rousseau's *Discourse on Inequality, Social Contract,* and *Emile*; Montesquieu's *Spirit of the Laws*; and Defoe's *Robinson Crusoe*. He also treasures classics, like Caesar's *Commentaries*. But his intellectual references, especially for the period of his struggle with his father when he has begun to launch out on his own, bear little relation to the system of references in which he was enmeshed prior to his mother's death. For her examples of greatness—the models she offers to his emulation—derive from a noble and military tradition; she appears to have read and to have spoken to him of Turenne's *Mémoires,* and perhaps also those of the Duc de Rohan and Montecucolli.[62] The autobiography strongly suggests that his early models of greatness derived from military careers, and his early castles in Spain all concerned military renown.

Du Pont may have tried to cope with this disjuncture when he wrote that his mother, shortly before her death, gave him three books—*Robinson Crusoe, Sir Charles Grandison,* and Montaigne's *Essays*—and bade him ponder and emulate them. The books share a concern with the education of a man and with responsible individualism. They clearly represent an alternative to aristocratic notions of heroism and grandeur. Since Du Pont's mother could not have given him *Sir Charles Grandison,* she may not have given him the others either, but he seems to be using those books as a way of transforming his mother's legacy—of transforming nobility of condition into nobility of soul, military daring into solid bourgeois accomplishment.[63] In the autobiography, he will show his own consciousness to have been lagging behind her new message, or the message he attributes to her. But he draws upon the culture of his time to point the new direction he will take as he comes to maturity.

Du Pont's use of the culture offers us a privileged view of the shaping of a mind in a period of changing *mentalité.* He grows up with the legacy of seventeenth-century heroism and matures to preromanticism, anglomania, and affective domesticity. It is uncommon to see those values shading into each other. Yet for those of Du Pont's generation it appears to have been so. If different individuals interpreted their relation to that transition differently, most literate people apparently experienced it. Raising his sons can only have sharpened Du Pont's awareness of his own experience, his awareness of the continuities and differences between the system of acceptances that dominated his childhood and theirs.

The contrast between the world as it was and the world as it had become at the moment of his writing must have heightened Du Pont's sense of self. Confronting momentous changes and risk of death, he attempts to distinguish between the permanent and the contingent in his own life and personality. He does not fall into the trap of postulating an essential self, but he does seek and find constancies—primarily traits of personality. He regularly reminds his sons of his own obstinancy and opinionatedness, which he calls a family trait. We Du Ponts are a stubborn lot, he reminds them, and cautions them to monitor the failing in themselves. He takes comfort in one of his ancestor's having sired children when in his seventies. That inheritance augurs well for his own advanced years. The individual, he recognizes, comes into the world with the legacy of his forebearers. But Du Pont does not restrict the constant self to genetic inheritance. His mother, he recounts, had said to him after he had fallen for a young married lodger in their house, "my son will be transparent like a lantern throughout his life." And he complacently acknowledges that she was correct. "I am too free, too proud, too frank, too assured in my conscience for any evil principle to sway me." In this instance, under the guise of gentle self-mockery for lack of sophistication, Du Pont is congratulating himself. His face invariably betrays his soul. He is essentially honest.

Throughout the autobiography he periodically refers to such constant character traits. But he balances them against the role of events, even accidents. His self emerges from this interplay of character and contingency. And he does not dwell more heavily on introspection than on assessment of the external world. In this respect, Du Pont's autobiography more closely resembles that of Franklin than that of Rousseau, although he may offer a more sensitive picture of the social world of childhood and adolescence than either. He surely recognizes that his history and his success depend upon his relations with and ability to understand the world. His self-knowledge exists in direct relation to his knowledge of others, of the world, and his possible place in it. He would have applauded, even if he could not himself have formulated, Goethe's wise observation:

> I must confess that I have always been suspicious of that great and so fine-sounding task, 'Know Thyself,' as something of a stratagem of a secret conspiracy of priests who wanted to confuse men by making unrealisable demands of them, and to seduce them from activity directed towards the outside world to an inner and false contemplativeness. Man knows himself only in so far as he knows the world, and becomes aware of the world only in himself and of himself only in it.[64]

Du Pont's autobiography can be read as an exercise in growing self-knowledge, but not self-knowledge in the service of itself. Written under the sword of history, it constitutes an effort of recollection and self-understanding in the service of future generations, especially his own sons. For modern readers, the autobiography offers a special view of a culture in transition, of the making of a bourgeois individual, and of the interplay of the personal and the political—of society and ideology—in the transformation of *mentalités* and the period of the Revolution. Roy Pascal has written that the true purpose of autobiography must be " 'Selbstbesinnung', a search for one's inner standing. It is an affair of conscience. . . ."[65] He adds that the true quality of an autobiography ultimately depends on the quality of the spirit of its author. Du Pont receives high marks on both counts. His autobiography depicts a man of generous spirit who holds himself accountable to others.

V

Near the close of the middle third of the autobiography, when he is forming the plan that will permit him to free himself of his father, Du Pont writes:

> I have been thought to have been *born* for many disparate things, because to a sustained will, I joined a fairly easy talent. But do you want to know why I was really born? To want to *do well* whatever it might be and above all what is useful to others independent of all praise and at the risk of blame; to desire, nonetheless, glory; to be affected by praise but even more by the pleasure of deserving it; to adore a wife, cherish my children, love more than my life one or two friends. Give those qualities to a courageous man who is not stupid and you will make him do anything that pleases you.

The passage more closely approximates a general judgment of his own character and purpose than any other. It represents him as profoundly honest, worthy, and loyal, while it betrays conflicting attitudes that pervade the autobiography as a whole. The "I have been thought to have been *born*" evokes innate characteristics—an essential self—that are undercut by being attributed to the thoughts of unnamed others rather than to nature. The combination of his will and his facility—an easy rather than a commanding talent— has led others to read many purposes into him. He corrects that external view, but only by enunciating that he had been born to want to do certain things, to love certain people. The text substitutes his desires or intentions for the idea of an innate nature. It explicitly evokes his relations with others, to which it subordinates his accomplishments: he wanted praise, but even more he wanted the pleasure of deserving it. Finally, in an extraordinary twist, the text substitutes the reader, the authority, the unspecified "you" for his own agency. Rather than affirming that if you give a man those qualities he (I) can do anything, he affirms that you can do anything with him. This purported malleability must be set against Du Pont's repeated references to his pride. This is the same man who was never "able to suffer that anyone in the world assume an air of superiority with me."

The text never clarifies the identity of the you that can make a man such as its narrator do anything. But the complex psychodynamics that this strange phrasing evokes pervade it. Du Pont's autobiography offers a compelling psychological portrait of a struggle between father and son over a son's identity, of an oedipal struggle. A number of subordinate conflicts shadow this central confrontation between Du Pont and his father: the struggle between the father and the mother for the soul of the son; the struggle between Du Pont and his sons for the mysteries of sexuality and generation; the son's struggles with real and fictive siblings for his mother; his struggle with his father for his mother; and more. But the basic oedipal struggle dominates the narrative and structures Du Pont's account of his life. The text so nakedly exposes this conflict that we are tempted to speculate about the secrets that lie behind Du Pont's explicit account. His transparency cannot be accepted at face value, for what he writes shields as well as reveals himself. His secrets do not lend themselves to easy disclosure, but evidence of his unarticulated concerns can be unearthed from the silences of his text.

The autobiography can be read in many ways, and its tone suggests possibilities. Du Pont oscillates between identification with and distance from the narrator.[66] A disarming self-mockery of an earlier self appears in many places and, like his account of his early sibling rivalry, seems to result from two distinct, if interrelated, attitudes. He uses mockery first to establish distance between his mature (writing) self and his youthful self; and second to sustain the distance between his present (paternal) self and his sons. For it appears plausible that he identifies his youthful self with his sons, that his attempt to influence and educate his sons offers him a fresh perspective on himself. The instances of such teasing abound. In Chapter 10 he describes how, following the fight with St. Yriex, he thought he was dying and "even composed, in honor of this hasty end, some fairly beautiful verses, harmonious, sentimental, philosophical—and you will find them in some corner." The final prosaic note permits his sons to understand, if they have the wit, that for some time he thought those verses worthy of preservation. It even permits them, and us, to understand that the verses still merit preservation, but for their documentary rather than their intrinsic value.

This passage is important for other reasons that illuminate the central themes of the text. The theme of dying shadows and sets off two other occasions on which Du Pont faced death. But unlike the others in which the danger of death was real, here it is only a fantasy, a self-dramatization. And that fantasy itself relates to the unreality of the duel in which he had engaged. We know that a fascination with military glory dominates much of Du Pont's boyhood and adolescence. He first shows himself carrying a little toy sword at about age five; he records his admiration for his father's right to bear a sword. When an adolescent, he takes fencing lessons. He allows that his father enjoyed and was adept at swordplay. Having been prohibited by his father from carrying a sword during the worst of their quarrels, he acts in private theatricals that the father enjoys and that require the son to wear a sword. And if for rehearsal and performance, why not between? These very theatricals lead to his acquaintance with St. Yriex and to the duel that simultaneously realizes and ends his ambitions as a swordsman. The irrelevance of swordplay to his real goals or purpose is underscored by his learning, after his unexpected and quasi-accidental victory over St. Yriex, that the lady whose honor he had fought to defend in fact confessed to the rather loose morality that St. Yriex had tarred her with. Du Pont's romantic adolescent fantasies become the principal casualty of the encounter, less because he recognized their unreality at the time than because the text effectively undercuts them.

Comparable if more grandiose versions of the same fantasies open the succeeding chapter, which recounts Du Pont's beginnings of his real career. The whimsical opening contrasts dreams and accomplishments and provides a kind of threshhold to maturity. The text mocks rather than assaults the swan song of the adolescent dreamer. It also binds his experience to that of his son, especially that of Irénée who had so recently insisted on marrying Sophie against his father's admonitions of their youth and lack of visible means of support. "In truth," the chapter opens, "I had advanced with confidence and boldness, following the vague and very inconclusive reasoning that a man who had conceived the means to attain a crown certainly would know how to provide bread for himself and his companion." And in a didactic and probably unnecessary gloss, he adds that "the deduction was unsound." But faced with the need to provide a living for his fiancée, the young Pierre Samuel turns his thoughts to warfare, "the science in which I was the most learned and in which success could, it seemed to me, be the most rapid." He thinks of "taking Gibraltar." Again, the mocking tone provides distance, although even the mature Du Pont, in whom the temperament that spins romantic dreams demonstrably persists, also provides a straightforward account of the plans he drew up, one of which he refuses to reveal even now because it might still be used.

Throughout the text, the interplay of humor and seriousness, of mockery or distancing and identification, spin a web of self-revelation and self-concealment, of continuity and disjuncture both within Du Pont's own personality and between him and his sons. But his observation that "you" can do what you want with a man of his qualities also invokes his father, the authority, that could have shaped and legitimated him.

The titles of the succession of chapters that structure the autobiography suggest that the text simply records a succession of events. Nothing in Du Pont's explicit organization and labeling of his memoirs suggests any particular emphasis. One thing seems to follow another. In this respect the shopping-list character of the organization conceals the deep structure of the enunciated themes. The chapters can be grouped according to distinct phases in Du Pont's life.

The first two chapters, devoted to the families of his father and his mother, stand apart as a kind of introduction to or background for his own life, but can be grouped with the third chapter on his father and mother.[67] Chapters 4 through 6 carry the narrative from Du Pont's birth to his mother's death and depict his early education, his passionate attachment to his mother, and the struggle that pits mother and son against father over the question of the son's future. Chapters 7 and 8, the center of the text we have, chronicle the most intense phase of the struggle between father and son, no longer mediated or confused by the presence of the mother, and they terminate with Du Pont's repossession of his liberty. Chapters 9 through 11 recount Du Pont's tentative and erratic efforts to find a career that will adequately define, remunerate, and realize him. In Chapters 12 through 15, he inaugurates his rural studies, arrives independently at some first principles of political economy, is adopted by Quesnay, and takes the first steps in what will be his adult career.

The structure reveals a tension between formal organization and covert message throughout. The complex treatment of his father and his mother must be treated separately, but the transition between his late adolescent flirtations with various careers and his young adult commitment to administration and political economy provides an excellent example of his strategy. Chapter 10 introduces Marie-Louise Le Dée, who would become his wife or rather, as he writes to his sons, would become their mother. Du Pont describes his growing interest in the young woman as almost a matter of chance. He never claims the love or infatuation for her that he claimed to have felt for Mlle Van Laan, who caused his great confrontation with his father. He allows that, happily, he and Mlle Le Dée never made the mistake of taking each other for brother and sister—thus hinting at sexual love, for only such a love could have been branded incestuous. But he insists that he only proposed to marry her in order to save her from the unmerited fate of being married off to a dotard. In short, he casts his growing attachment and commitment to her in negatives. We look in vain for anything that resembles Irénée's impassioned letters about his love for Sophie and her virtues. There can be no doubt that Du Pont's text, for whatever reasons, minimizes the importance of Mlle Le Dée in his internal life. Having engaged himself to her, however, he assumed the responsibility of providing for her: she represented the external embodiment of his new-found purposefulness.

Du Pont appears to have decomposed—literally deconstructed—his fiancée. When writing of his childhood triumph, when he performed publicly at M. Viard's school, he informs his sons that he had known only one moment of greater happiness in his life, and, "my friends, I shall not tell you which." The reference to his first sexual relations with his wife, their mother, seems clear enough. After he has become engaged to Mlle Le Dée, he goes to see her when he has the opportunity, fights her family's attempts to keep them apart, resorts to all the conventional stratagems of pebbles thrown against a window for a secret meeting. The autobiography chronicles affection for her. She never dominates the text or his expressions of emotion, but there is indirect evidence that his love for her provided the essential bedrock of his growing maturity. External evidence suggests that they were devoted to each other and that she constituted the very foundation of his life.

He meets her when he is twenty-two, five years after his mother's death. Their meeting follows closely on his freedom from his father. Although his protracted battle with his father has its own logic, it should not be separated from his period of mourning for his mother; presumably, the end of the two processes depended on each other. Du Pont, for his own reasons, distracts our attention from that relation. He never emphasizes the impact of his emotional attachment for Mlle Le Dée on his future development. Earlier in the text, he had written that he had sought his mother in every woman with whom he fell in love, and that he had normally been disillusioned. All these hints suggest that Du Pont transferred to his fiancée at least some of his feelings for his mother. It seems entirely plausible that that transference, combined with and indeed confirming the end of his mourning for his mother, helps to explain the growing purposefulness in his own career. His persisting castles in Spain—the taking of Gibraltar—attest that the transformation did not occur in a flash; nonetheless, shortly after the engagement, Du Pont did begin to write. His writing seemed to bring together his dreams of glory and his obligation to earn a living, albeit an as-yet precarious one. But the way had been opened. And whatever credit Du Pont gives Quesnay for setting him on the correct path, the text shows that he had started on that path before meeting Quesnay.

Du Pont's claim that he had, to all intents and purposes, worked out the correct principles of rural economy before ever meeting Quesnay betrays a sneaking desire to claim Quesnay's genius for himself, to validate his native brilliance. But if that self-inflation may take liberties with what Du Pont worked out for himself and what he learned from his master—with what was intrinsic to him and what derived from a paternal legacy—it entirely obscures the role of his wife-to-be in anchoring and solidifying his personality, in grounding his public self in secure internal feelings.

Du Pont's reasons for not crediting precisely his wife's influence on and importance to him remain a matter for speculation. Du Pont was no misogynist. He visibly liked and respected, as well as depended upon, the women in his life, but he may have shared with many of his peers a desire to define himself against women.[68] His open acknowledgment of his deep attachment to his mother thus paradoxically helps to screen his dependence upon other women, for in presenting her death as an absolute he seems to deny the persistence of his own feelings and their subsequent attachment to other objects. Conversely, Du Pont's attachment to his fiancée may have resolved feelings about his mother, for against Du Pont's bald affirmation of adoration for his mother must be set the text's clear recognition of her mixed influence on him. The critique of nobility, like the more gentle critique of romantic dreams of glory, must be understood as criticisms of his mother—of his mother in him. But beyond this admirable putting-in-perspective lies Du Pont's representation of the outcome of his oedipal struggle with his father.

According to the autobiography, Anne Alexandrine du Pont died of her attempt to protect her son from his father. In an explicit passage excised by the family, Du Pont writes that when he was fourteen, as the efforts to postpone the workbench were faltering, his mother, who had not given birth for ten years, suddenly bore two children in quick succession. Du Pont wants us to believe, as he obviously did, that his mother had avoided sexual relations with his father for a decade because she feared pregnancy. We can afford to leave Du Pont's fantasies about which of the two men in his mother's life she preferred in the oblivion to which he consigned them, but he explicitly ascribes her being in his father's bed to her desire to permit his own spirit to range as freely as possible. "Excellent woman!" he applauds her. "But more excellent Mother!"

Du Pont's interpretation of the cause of his mother's death offers him something less than a perfect oedipal victory, or even unambiguous consolation; for if she had yielded to her husband's sexual demands for the sake of her son, she had also thereby confirmed the father in his role as possessor of the mother's sexuality. And if she had sacrificed herself for that same son, he thereby inherited a heavy burden of guilt. Her actions on his behalf had cost her her life, had left him unprotected, and may even, if his reading is correct, have made him doubly the object of his father's wrath.

Du Pont's reinterpretation of his mother's death must have been occasioned by his thoughts and feelings at the death of his own wife. If he preferred to see his mother's highest destiny in her role as mother, did he feel the same about Marie-Louise? The autobiography does not cover the period of her motherhood, but it refers to her as the mother of his sons and to the purpose of their union as the conception and rearing of those sons. Du Pont spent long periods away from home during his first marriage. He and his wife had only three children, the second of which died.[69] Had Marie-Louise also withdrawn from conjugal sexual relations? Had her emotional loyalties vacillated between husband and sons? To represent the wife as primarily the mother of sons—a favorite son—is implicitly to strengthen the identification of Du Pont with his own father as the man who loses his wife to his son. To represent the wife as primarily the lover of her husband is to ensure Du Pont's victory over his own sons, but to cast his father as equally victorious over him and to threaten his interpretation of his mother's having loved him to the point of sacrificing her life.

Marie-Louise did not die in childbirth. The events in the two cases do not parallel each other, and the family dynamics surely differed. Yet, Du Pont casts himself as pivot in the three-generational father-son relation: he looks both ways. And his feelings about his family of procreation betray unresolved feelings about his family of origin. The point is not to solve a set of equations, but to indicate the kinds of conflicts that shadowed Du Pont's text.

Du Pont's struggle with his father dominates the autobiography. The text pits father against son in a bitter contest the stakes of which, from the narrator's explicit perspective, are the self-determination and freedom of the son—his property in himself and his liberty to realize it. In that battle, the father is shown as narrow, frightened of change and of being abandoned, selfish, and hot-tempered to the point of being irrational. The unthinking rigidity of his prejudices permits his wife to manipulate him with ease. He can see no further than the goal of having his son follow precisely in his trade—the only kind of validation he can imagine—and to be able to support him in his old age. This view of the father derives from Du Pont's representation of his own feelings at the time of their battles. It also represents a harsh caricature of the most noxious forms of paternal authority and bigotry of the *ancien régime*: it is tyranny in the personal sphere as well as in the political.

But the father in the autobiography emerges as something more than arbitrary despot and foolish man. His failings are shown to derive from his character and from his historical position. They also are shown to mingle with an accurate perception that transcends both. For the Du Pont who is writing, and is himself the father of sons he has been pushing to earn their livelihood, recognizes that his father had a legitimate goal, even if he tried to impose it in the wrong way and through the wrong form. Du Pont evokes himself as adolescent, confusing, at least in part because his father confused, the specific workbench with the general responsibility to work. And he hints that his own opposition to his father might not have been simply a refusal to become a clockmaker, but an attempt to avoid work. His father conflates prescriptions to become a clockmaker and to do something useful; Pierre Samuel conflates his reaction against them. Looking back, he perceives the magnetism of his mother's romantic dreams and chimeras of nobility that, he is now prepared to admit, may have set his mind against any kind of work with his hands—any honest labor at all.

But the issue remains confused for historical reasons. Du Pont himself avers that the only plausible careers open to him as a Protestant were doctor and minister. His mother's tales have drawn him to visions of military glory, but there had been no great Protestant military figures since the taking of La Rochelle under Richelieu in the early seventeenth century. And the Duc de Rohan was never a plausible choice of career for a Protestant youth of petty bourgeois and peasant descent. The autobiography depicts him as attempting to tailor these dreams to realistic options, but the gap between reality and imagination remains large, as Du Pont is the first to point out. In fact, Du Pont the narrator offers yet more deflating perspectives on the dreams of the young Du Pont. For example, in Chapter 6, shortly after stating the limited possibilities for Protestants, he provides a sketch of the career of Bosc d'Antic who became both doctor and minister in a picaresque and dilettantish career. He offers proof, should it be needed, of how Du Pont himself might have been expected to turn out at this stage in his life, and under the *ancien régime,* had he followed his fancy. Later in the same chapter, he inserts a description of the group of cabalists around Madame d'Urfé and his and his mother's relations with them. He stresses the high social standing of the guests, including foreign princes. He recounts Madame d'Urfé's promises of the advancement he could expect if he concurred in the reality of the undines. Here, Du Pont himself pronounces the emperor to have no clothes and thereby assumes a hint of moral (male) leadership over his mother who, although she no longer sees, still believes she saw previously. He, perceiving the illusion, flatly declares that he never saw. This incident, which constitutes such an important milestone in his depiction of his own emerging solid instincts, also offers an implicit critique of the probable results of his more grandiose fantasies. It is simultaneously a lesson in self-worth and integrity and in the illusory character of his most cherished projects.

Here as elsewhere, Du Pont the narrator thus adds support to paternal authority even at the moment that he is depicting his own worst conflicts with it. But when he depicts himself as reading beneath the hated workbench to which he has been figuratively, if not literally, chained, he offers a more complex message. For reading would ultimately provide the path to his adult success. His father wrongly opposed it. Well, something was wrong in his opposition, although Du Pont the narrator admits that the father also was on to something. For the adolescent Du Pont reading is shown to have signified a poorly differentiated collection of feelings, dreams, and escapes. If reading could include mathematics, Restaut's grammar, the Logic of Port Royal, and other solid works, it could also include the memoirs of great generals interlaced with his mother's unrealistic ambitions; it could include that poetry which Quesnay would so sharply reprove; and it could include works of political theory that, as the narrator knows, would provide the impetus to and rationale for violent opposition to constituted authority. If Rousseau had attained the status of respectability by 1792, his standing in 1760 had been another matter altogether, as Du Pont's evocation of his letter to Christophe de Beaumont implicitly acknowledges.

Du Pont does not fully develop these tensions, to which he alludes, but they constitute important strands in his account. They weave his struggles with his father into the political confrontation that the narrator knows was brewing. On the personal level, Du Pont achieves only partial resolutions in his conflict with his father. In the early scene of his triumphant school performance, his father is shown as appreciating his son's success. In Du Pont's account, the honorable completion of a public exercise constitutes a beautiful day for a child, nourished as he had been "on the cookies of self-love"—maternal nourishment indeed. He writes of having experienced unutterable pleasure as he was carried over the heads of the crowd to the place where his "Father and my Mother melted in tears of joy. My Father also wept despite his repugnance for literary glory and work. Oh! How happy he made me! I believed that he loved me more than he had up till then; I believed that I had vanquished him." The triumph proved of short duration, but the juxtaposition of "he loved me" and "I triumphed over him" is revealing. Presumably, Du Pont should have expected his father to love him for his submission to the paternal will. The reversal testifies to Du Pont's success in putting himself back into the head of a child. It also signals the intractable knot of confusions that will pit him and his father ever more desperately against each other to the point, much later, at which Du Pont finally offers his submission and is thrown out.

Du Pont identifies his own coming of age with his decision to make a perfect watch and to present it to his father. He accomplishes his intention and in handing over the tribute due to paternal authority repossesses his own liberty. That act, he suggests, accomplishes his internalization of legitimate paternal values and his legitimate rejection of his father's false claims. But the story of his wrestling with the angel does not terminate at that point. For in his final symbolic departure from his father's house, he carries with him two things: first, the ability to earn a living and, more important, a dawning understanding of work and self-reliance; and second, a persistent quest for a father and a persistent ambivalence about paternal authority.

Du Pont never specifies what makes paternal authority legitimate. At times he seems to suggest that it must rely on love rather than on coercion, that the ways in which it is imposed matter. At other times, he suggests that the content of its requirements determines its legitimacy: Quesnay was simply smarter than his father and had more worthy goals. Finally, he seems to believe at the time of writing that the status of father in and of itself confers legitimate authority but that, like political authority, it must not be abused. Whatever his precise meaning, and it likely included all of the above, his relations with Quesnay complete the narrative of his relations with his own father.

Du Pont states categorically that in Quesnay he found a true father. He emphasizes the love and consideration that Quesnay showed him, and the reader gets the distinct impression that Quesnay's selection of him as a disciple was a kind of intellectual ennoblement, a legitimation. He also emphasizes the discipline that Quesnay imposed on him. Under his tutelage, Du Pont tells us, "I became a man." By explicitly identifying Quesnay as the good father, the text implies Du Pont's own submission to his authority, but that submission would have required relinquishing much that his own father had ordered him to relinquish: poetry, chimeras, all the remains of his mother's romanticism. In truth, Quesnay had little more patience with Du Pont's independent subjectivity than his father had had, although he displayed less direct hostility.

According to Du Pont himself, Quesnay had the authoritarian personality of a tough-minded, independent man who believed that he had discovered an important truth. And Du Pont shows himself as deeply attracted to precisely those qualities that he had so sharply rebelled against in his own father. The pattern is hardly uncommon, but it is also uncommon for all impulses to rebellion to disappear entirely. Casting the autobiography as a letter itself reflected a gentle flirtation with Quesnay's prohibition, all the more since Du Pont himself records it. Extratextual evidence confirms that Du Pont's covert testing of Quesnay's authority extended further than his letterwriting or his indulgence in his abiding love for poetry. In 1767, Du Pont had published an edition of Quesnay's collected writings under the title of *Physiocratie*.[70] As editor, he was perfectly fulfilling his self-appointed role as son and disciple, but he also indulged in a little self-expression. He omitted Quesnay's celebrated *Tableau économique*, which Du Pont in fact had never fully understood and which he preferred to transform from numbers into words. So the "Maxims of an Agricultural Kingdom," which he mentions in the autobiography, replaced the *Tableau*. And the sin of omission was compounded with one of commission: in Du Pont's hands, Quesnay's twenty-four maxims became thirty.

Du Pont's behavior appears to have obeyed two imperatives. Substantively, his additions to Quesnay's work stressed the sacred character of private property and the need for certain changes in the structure of marketing; they reflected his own special political concerns and pushed Quesnay's abstract analysis in the direction of reforms realizable under the *ancien régime*. In this respect, Du Pont was helping to develop the doctrines of physiocracy into a plausible political language, and he probably had a better intuition than Quesnay of how to cultivate a broader audience for the truths of physiocracy. His own experience would have been a legitimate guide for strategies that could mobilize the identifications of people more concerned with what they took to be the real world than with abstract and absolute truths. But psychologically, Du Pont himself seems to have been driven to appropriate and tamper with Quesnay's truth. Even as he acknowledged and celebrated Quesnay's authority, he could not resist putting his own stamp on it. The rebellion—covert, perhaps unwitting—was rebellion nonetheless. Du Pont could not deliver himself entirely over to the hands of a master and could not will himself putty in the hands of authority, however legitimate he perceived that master or that authority to be.

Du Pont's account of his relations with his natural and acquired fathers, whom it is tempting to identify as the bad and the good father, marks the contours of his relations with his own sons. The conflict reduces to one between authority and freedom, between the law and the individual. Du Pont makes heroic efforts to unite the two: both his image of the beneficent, impersonal Creator in his philosophy of the universe and his concept of property conflate authority and freedom. The Creator's authority bestows freedom on humans by granting them the power to know and to love; property transforms the freedom of the individual into authority, manifested as the law of society. To resolve the contradictions, Du Pont falls back on essentially abstract qualities. Property especially creates ubiquitous possibilities for conflict. That recognition, however, did not much help Du Pont personally, for he proved himself an abyssmal politician. For a man with his sensitivity to others he displayed a staggering inability to understand and to negotiate the conflict of interests.

The political language of Du Pont's mature years helps him to describe his adolescent conflicts with his father. In a particularly memorable scene shortly after his mother's death, his father throws him out of his room for having already sneaked out at night to visit Mlle Van Laan. Du Pont flies into a rage: his father had already "exceeded his powers" and imposed "tyranny" in forbidding the visits to Mlle Van Laan. Now he was banishing him from his room, which—and there ensues a litany of its attributes—"was for me a property of an inestimable price." Du Pont is careful in this passage to underscore that those were his views at the time. He neither endorses nor repudiates them. The reader is left uncertain as to whether he believes that the application of political categories can be justified in the context of the relations between a father and an adolescent son. Du Pont the narrator, mindful of Victor and Irénée, may now doubt whether a room under the parental roof subsidized by parental labor constitutes a son's property in the full sense of the term. He remains, as we have seen, scornful of the ideas that those who depend upon others for their food and lodging should vote. They are not proprietors. He himself would have to complete his work, the watch for his father, and make his own "primitive advances" before he could walk away free as both individual and proprietor.

Du Pont admits to his desire to see his father exceed the bounds of legitimate authority, to place himself incontrovertibly in the wrong, so that Du Pont's own rebelliousness will be justified. Du Pont the narrator thus endows the young Du Pont with gnawing doubts. Under the force of the anger, questions about legitimacy percolate. The simple desires to realize his own will, to repudiate that of his father, need not necessarily be legitimate; legitimate order and individual impulse do not inevitably converge, but then established authority and the natural order do not necessarily converge either.

By the end of the *ancien régime,* many persons believed that established authority departed radically from natural order. Among the many streams of criticism of the abuse of royal power figured a deep current of resistance to its patriarchalism, which was seen to have assumed the character of illegitimate authority. The more sophisticated critics of the crown were beginning to question patriarchalism as an appropriate model for government and for the relations between the king and his subjects. A more popular current fastened on the arbitrary use of *lettres de cachet* as emblematic of royal abuse.[71] The possibility of sending someone to prison by the simple issuing of a royal command seemed to violate all protection for the freedom of the individual. But *lettres de cachet* were also especially associated with the power the king could grant to the father of a family to have his wife or children confined at his will. In this respect royal and paternal power met and reinforced each other in an aberrant patriarchalism. The Revolution abolished patriarchalism, not merely by abolishing *lettres de cachet* and related abuses, but by abolishing nobility, the vestiges of serfdom, and feudal tenures. By the time Du Pont was writing, the guilds had been abolished; labor had been freed, henceforth to be subject only to the free play of the market; and the successive legislative bodies had been attempting to subject the will of the king himself to the wishes of the elected representatives of the sovereign people.

Du Pont on the whole approved these changes, many of which he participated in making and most of which corresponded to his own prerevolutionary views. But the confrontation between the king, the members of the Legislative Assembly, and the Paris populace mounted during 1791 and 1792. The king, by his flight to Varennes, betrayed his untrustworthiness and, by his use of the royal veto, affirmed his desire to remain in command. The revolutionaries came to believe that patriarchalism would have to be violently extirpated in its embodiment: the king would have to go.[72] Du Pont, with his attraction to authority, did not accept this conclusion. He sought to defend the king against the rabble and legitimate monarchy against its detractors. He was writing the first draft of his autobiography during the period between the imprisonment of the king and his execution. Political events, however distant from his retreat, must have pressed upon his reinterpretation of legitimate and illegitimate political authority. His text confirms, as few first-person accounts do, the interlocking of the role and perception of fathers in the public and the private spheres.

Du Pont would come to favor a conservative republic and the view that the family, which constituted the fundamental unit of any society, should embody the same republican principles as the larger polity. The autobiography itself probably should be read as a subjective exploration of the personal implications of political principles. In it, Du Pont demonstrates a gut rejection of patriarchy, but also a deep longing for legitimate parental authority. He seems to be seeking confirmation of his own paternal authority over his sons together with a guarantee of a general, beneficent paternalism in society. The old order is breaking up around him; his own youthful rebellion is being confirmed in society at large. But the price of such change includes a certain measure of anxiety.

Twice during the autobiography Du Pont recounts how he was given up for dead: the first time, he had succumbed to a fever and had been shrouded; the second, he thought he had drowned. He writes that on both occasions he learned that although dying—the struggle to stay alive—is terrifying, death itself is nothing. As he wrote, he had every reason to fear for his life. The repetition of the lesson that death is nothing was surely intended to allay those fears and to reassure him that the worst would not be anything at all. Should the plot terminate before the conclusion of the story, he writes to his sons, you will know what to do; you will be able to finish the story for yourselves. The story itself thereby protects him against the plot and locates him in relation to his sons; it affirms a continuity that will outlive external upheaval. But the historical changes of Du Pont's lifetime, violently confirmed by the political events of the Revolution, dictated a new way of interpreting the continuity of families and the succeeding relations between fathers and sons.

The two chapters on the families of his father and mother which open Du Pont's autobiography seem almost to belong to a different text than the rest. Contained within the letter to his sons, they themselves contain many references to the present location of individuals and family papers, but in other respects they mesh poorly with the sustained narrative of his own life. Franklin in his autobiography, also cast as a letter to his son, similarly evokes his ancestors, and Du Pont may have borrowed the idea of the beginning from him. But precedents for his strategy could also be found in the tradition of family history and *livres de raison* that had, as Natalie Davis has argued, become increasingly common among middling sorts of people toward the end of the "early modern period."[73] Such accounts testified to a growing self-consciousness about the family and history—the growing impulse to locate the family in time and to record its continuity.

In this perspective Du Pont's autobiography, as a text, can be seen to encompass the transition from that early modern consciousness of family identity and history to the modern, postrevolutionary consciousness of the individual. Within the text, the individual emerges from the familial context as the locus of the narrative. But the earlier roots are not mindlessly jettisoned, for the individual alone cannot bear the entire weight of the narrative and its purpose. The individual himself acutely poses again the question of family, of the process of generation and history. Authority, especially paternal authority, had brooded over, shaped, and perhaps distorted the natural course of history, the true history of the individual. Now it is repossessed and literally internalized, but the repossession, rather than abolishing the conflicts between authority and freedom, ensconces them at the core of the individual's own identity.

The families of Du Pont's parents constituted microcosms of the history of the *ancien régime*. His father's Norman ancestors, in his view, had collectively amounted to no more than honest peasants, with an occasional successful merchant thrown in. The artisans, sea captains, idiosyncratic women, and others constituted no more than variations on that central theme of the *ancien régime*—the peasantry on which both monarchy and nobility rested. The one-time, legendary nobles of his mother's family appear as no less typical of general trends. Whether through improvidence or bad luck, the family had failed to sustain its position and had been obliged to work to survive. It is surely an indictment of the *ancien régime* that noble status and honest labor be taken to contradict each other. But under that regime the experience of worthy, upstanding labor alone did not suffice to contravene the dominant social values. To the contrary, the loss of noble status appears to have cultivated the fantasies of noble identity, the dreams of noble glory. Du Pont himself becomes the battleground for the conflict between the different values that his father and his mother had inherited. And, as he tells it, that battle results in a synthesis: he combines in himself the work and the dreams, the solidity and the imagination. But if the conditions of the late *ancien régime* do permit Du Pont to forge a career and achieve considerable success, they do not readily permit the institutionalization of his accomplishments, do not ground them in absolute property, and do not provide for the transmission to his sons of a responsible individualism based upon work. Only the Revolution appears to guarantee that the dreams of nobility will be repudiated, that careers will be genuinely open to talent, and that bourgeois property will receive the protection and respect it deserves. Yet that same Revolution threatens life itself.

Du Pont's autobiography constitutes an affirmation of his legacy to his sons, which consists essentially in his self. His life history legitimately may be seen as a synecdoche—that special form of metaphor and metonymy, the act of taking together, of substituting the part for the whole—for the last generation of the *ancien régime* itself. Not that he presents his life as typical, although in some respects it may have been. But implicitly, he presents it as emblematic, as containing within itself the most important tendencies and the most fundamental conflicts that characterized the emergence of bourgeois individualism. And we would do well to accept his assessment.

Notes

[1] Jean-Jacques Rousseau, *Oeuvres complètes*, ed. Bernard Gagnebin and Marcel Raymond, vol. I, *Les Confessions: autres textes autobiographiques* (Paris: Gallimard, 1959); Leonard W. Labaree, et al., eds., *The Autobiography of Benjamin Franklin* (New Haven and London: Yale University Press, 1964). In both instances, the editors' introductions provide histories of the texts and their publication.

[2] Jean-François Marmontel, *Mémoires*, 2 vols., ed. John Renwick (Clermont-Ferrand: G. de Bussac, 1972); *Mémoires inédits de l'Abbé Morellet, sur le dix-huitième siècle et sur la Révolution*, 2nd ed., 2 vols. (1822, repr. Geneva: Slatkine, 1967). For a preliminary list of autobiographies, see Philippe Lejeune, *L'Autobiographie en France* (Paris: Armand Colin, 1971), pp. 106–19.

[3] Valentin Jamerey-Duval, *Mémoires: enfance et éducation d'un paysan au XVIIIe siècle*, ed. Jean Marie Goulemot (Paris: Le Sycomore, 1981); Jacques-Louis Ménétra, *Journal de ma vie*, ed. Daniel Roche (Paris: Montalba, 1982).

[4] Betty-Bright P. Low, "Memorandum on the Past Use and Provenance of the Papers of Du Pont de Nemours," The Longwood Library (May 1958).

[5]Gustave Schelle, *Du Pont de Nemours et l'école physiocratique* (Paris: Librairie Guillaumin et Cie., 1888); and his *Oeuvres de Turgot et documents le concernant*, 5 vols. (Paris, 1913–23, repr. Glashütten in Taunus: Verlag Detlev Auvermann KG, 1972).

[6]The most comprehensive, scholarly biography is that of Ambrose Saricks, *Pierre Samuel Du Pont de Nemours* (Lawrence: University of Kansas Press, 1965). For Du Pont's correspondence, the indispensable source is the collection of his papers at the Eleutherian Mills Historical Library, Wilmington, Delaware (hereafter cited as EMHL), especially Winterthur MSS, Group 2.

[7]Letter of 12 December 1787, EMHL, Winterthur MSS, Group 2.

[8]Ronald Meek, *Social Science and the Ignoble Savage* (Cambridge: Cambridge University Press, 1976), for the development of the theory of stages. Among the many works on the Scottish Historical School, see Gladys Bryson, *Man and Society: The Scottish Enquiry of the Eighteenth Century* (Princeton: Princeton University Press, 1945); William C. Lehmann, *John Millar of Glasgow 1735–1801: His Life and Thoughts and his Contribution to Sociological Analysis* (Cambridge: Cambridge University Press, 1960); Anand Chitnis, *The Scottish Enlightenment: A Social History* (London: Croom Helm, 1976); Ian Simpson Ross, *Lord Kames and the Scotland of his Day* (Oxford: Oxford University Press, 1972); N. T. Phillipson and Rosalind Mitchison, eds., *Scotland in the Age of Improvement* (Edinburgh: University of Edinburgh Press, 1970).

[9]See in particular John Stuart Mill, *The Spirit of the Age*, ed. F. A. von Hayek (Chicago: University of Chicago Press, 1942), and for a general view Walter E. Houghton, *The Victorian Frame of Mind* (New Haven: Yale University Press, 1957), esp. Chapter I, "The Character of the Age"; Ferdinand Tönnies, *Community and Society (Gemeinschaft und Gesellschaft)*, trans. and ed. Charles P. Loomis (New York: Harper & Row, 1963).

[10]Max Weber, *The Protestant Ethic and the Spirit of Capitalism*, trans. Talcott Parsons (New York: Charles Scribner's Sons, 1930).

[11]See for example Alex Inkeles and David H. Smith, *Becoming Modern: Individual Change in Six Developing Countries* (Cambridge, MA: Harvard University Press, 1974).

[12]See for example Lloyd de Mause, ed., *The History of Childhood* (New York: Psychohistory Press, 1974). For a critique of the application of the neo-Freudian theories of Erik Erikson to the historical study of personality, see David Hunt, *Parents and Children in History: The Psychology of Family Life in Early Modern France* (New York: Basic Books, 1970), esp. pp. 11–26. For a fine example of the use of psychoanalytic theory in historical biography, see Arthur Mitzman, *The Iron Cage: An Historical Interpretation of Max Weber* (New York: Grosset & Dunlap, 1969).

[13]For a fuller development of my views on the history of the French Revolution, see Elizabeth Fox-Genovese and Eugene D. Genovese, *Fruits*

of Merchant Capital: Slavery and Bourgeois Property in the Rise and Expansion of Capitalism (New York: Oxford University Press, 1983), esp. Chapters 8 and 11.

[14]On physiocracy, see my *The Origins of Physiocracy: Economic Revolution and Social Order in Eighteenth-Century France* (Ithaca and London: Cornell University Press, 1976); Ronald Meek, *The Economics of Physiocracy* (Cambridge, MA: Harvard University Press, 1963); Georges Weulersse, *Le Mouvement physiocratique en France (de 1756 à 1770)*, 2 vols. (Paris: Félix Alcan, 1910, repr. 1968); and Marguerite Kuczynski's introductions to her editions of Quesnay's economic writings, François Quesnay, *Okonomische Schriften 1756–59*, 2 vols. and *Okonomische Schriften 1763–67*, 2 vols. (Berlin: Akademie Verlag, 1971 and 1976), and Institut National d'Études Demographiques, *François Quesnay et la physiocratie*, 2 vols. (Paris: INED, 1958). All of these works contain references to the vast literature on physiocracy.

[15]On the debate over the grain trade, there is also a voluminous literature. See for example Weulersse, *Mouvement physiocratique*; Steven L. Kaplan, *Bread, Politics and Political Economy in the Reign of Louis XV*, 2 vols. (The Hague: Martinus Nijhoff, 1976); Georges Afanassiev, *Le Commerce des céréales en France au dix-huitième siècle* (Paris: Alphonse Picard, 1894); Léon Cahen, "La question du pain à Paris à la fin du XVIIIe siècle," *Cahiers de la Révolution française* 1 (1934): 51–76; Guy Lemarchand, "Les troubles de subsistance dans la généralité de Rouen (seconde moitié XVIIIe siècle)," *Annales historiques de la Révolution française* 35 (1963). Among the voluminous physiocratic writings in favor of the freedom of the grain trade, see Louis-Paul Abeille, *Faits qui ont influé sur la cherté des grains en France et en Angleterre* (Paris, 1768); Nicolas Baudeau, *Avis au peuple sur son premier besoin . . .* (Amsterdam and Paris, 1768); J.A.N. de Caritat, Marquis de Condorcet, *Du Commerce des bleds* (Paris, 1775) and his *Lettres sur le commerce des grains* (Paris, 1774); Guillaume-François Le Trosne, *La Liberté du commerce des grains, toujours utile et jamais nuisible* (Paris, 1765); and Pierre Samuel du Pont, *De l'exportation et de l'importation des grains* (Paris, 1764, repr. ed. Edgard Depitre, Paris, 1911).

[16]See Weulersse, *Mouvement physiocratique, passim*.

[17]Cf. the career of Roederer: Kenneth Margerison, *P.-L. Roederer: Political Thought and Practice during the French Revolution* (Philadelphia: American Philosophical Society, 1983).

[18]Ibid. See also the figures discussed by Keith Michael Baker in his article, "Politics and Social Science in Eighteenth-Century France: the *Société de 1789*," in John F. Bosher, ed., *French Government and Society 1500–1850* (London: Athlone Press, 1973).

[19]Michel Vovelle, "Le Tournant des mentalités en France 1750–1789: la sensibilité pré-révolutionnaire," *Social History* 5 (1977): 605–30.

[20]Michel Vovelle, *Piété baroque et déchristianisation en Provence au XVIIIe*

siècle (Paris: Plon, 1973); Cissie Fairchilds, "Masters and Servants in Eighteenth-Century Toulouse," *Journal of Social History* 12 (1979): 368–93; J. P. Gutton, *Domestiques et serviteurs dans la France de l'Ancien Régime* (Paris: Aubier, 1981); Claude Delasselle, "Les Enfants abandonnés à Paris au XVIIIe siècle," *Annales. Économies. Sociétés. Civilisations.* 30, no. 1 (January–February 1975): 187–218; François Lebrun, "Naissances illégitimes et abandons d'enfants en Anjou au XVIIIe siècle," in *loc cit.* 27, nos. 4–5 (July–October 1972): 1183–89; Cissie Fairchilds, "Female Sexual Attitudes and the Rise of Illegitimacy: A Case Study," *Journal of Interdisciplinary History* 8 (1978): 627–67; François Lebrun, *La Vie conjugale sous l'Ancien Régime* (Paris: Armand Colin, 1975); J.-L. Flandrin, *Families in Former Times,* trans. Richard Southern (Cambridge: Cambridge University Press, 1979); François Furet and Jacques Ozouf, *Lire et écrire: l'alphabétisation des français de Calvin à Jules Ferry,* 2 vols. (Paris: Editions de Minuit, 1977), I, pp. 9–115, *passim*; Daniel Roche, *Le Peuple de Paris* (Paris: Aubier, 1981); George Sussman, *Selling Mothers' Milk: The Wetnursing Business in France 1715–1914* (Urbana: University of Illinois Press, 1982), esp. pp. 19–35; Robert Darnton, *The Business of Enlightenment: A Publishing History of the ENCYCLOPÉDIE,* 1775–1800 (Cambridge, MA: Harvard University Press, 1979).

[21]Sussman, *Selling Mothers' Milk,* pp. 36–72.

[22]Saricks, *Pierre Samuel Du Pont de Nemours,* includes an excellent bibliography of works on Du Pont; Gustave Schelle, *Du Pont de Nemours et l'école physiocratique* contains an excellent bibliography of Du Pont's writings which Saricks did not attempt to surpass; Pierre Jolly, *Du Pont de Nemours, soldat de la liberté* (Paris: Presses Universitaires de France, 1965) draws upon archival sources but contains neither footnotes nor a formal bibliography; B. G. du Pont, *Du Pont de Nemours,* 2 vols. (Newark: University of Delaware Press, 1933) draws extensively upon family papers; Marc Bouloiseau, *Bourgeoisie et Révolution: Les Du Pont de Nemours* (1788–1799) (Paris: Bibliothèque Nationale, 1972) also makes extensive use of the papers at the EMHL. See also James J. McLain, *The Economic Writings of Du Pont de Nemours* (Newark: University of Delaware Press, 1977).

[23]Earle E. Coleman, "Éphémérides du Citoyen, 1767–1772," *Papers of the Bibliographical Society of America* 56 (1962): 17–45, provides a skillful history of the complex history of the journal and its various editors.

[24]Saricks, *Pierre Samuel Du Pont de Nemours,* p. 214.

[25]Pierre Samuel du Pont de Nemours, *Philosophie de l'univers,* 3rd ed. (Paris, 1799), p. 326.

[26]B. G. du Pont, ed., *Life of Eleuthère Irénée du Pont from Contemporary Correspondence 1778–1791,* 5 vols. (Newark: University of Delaware Press, 1923), I.

[27]On the Ideologues, see Sergio Moravia, *Il pensiero degli Ideologues: Scienza e filosofia in Francia, 1780–1815* (Florence, 1974); Emmet Kennedy,

A Philosophe in the Age of Revolution: Destutt de Tracy and the Origins of "Ideology" (Philadelphia: American Philosophical Society, 1978); Martin S. Staum, *Cabanis: Enlightenment and Medical Philosophy in the French Revolution* (Princeton: Princeton University Press, 1980).

[28][François Quesnay] "Observations sur le droit naturel des hommes réunis en société" first appeared in the *Journal d'agriculture* in September 1765, while it was under Du Pont's editorship. It has been reprinted in INED, *François Quesnay et la physiocratie*, II, pp. 729–42.

[29]For the *Mémoire sur les municipalités*, see Schelle, ed., *Oeuvres de Turgot*, IV, pp. 568–621.

[30]Gilbert Chinard, ed., *The Correspondence of Jefferson and Du Pont de Nemours* (Baltimore: Johns Hopkins University Press, 1931), pp. 12–14.

[31]See the collection, *The Economic and Political Writings of Pierre Samuel Du Pont de Nemours* (KTO Press and Kraus Reprints, 1980).

[32]Chinard, ed., *Correspondence*, p. 268.

[33]See his remarks on his mother in the autobiography. This attitude is confirmed by his letters to his first wife who ran Bois-des-Fossés for him, managed his finances, and assisted him in every way. For example, as he wrote in 1782, "It would be a great pleasure also to me to spend a few days with my wife, who is amiable, estimable, worthy, sure to succeed and to please in any society and who willingly spends her life in the country for the sake of economy and because of her devotion to our children and to me." B. G. du Pont, ed., *Life of Eleuthère Irénée*, I, p. 23. The unpublished correspondence can be found in the EMHL, Winterthur MSS, Group 2, Series B. His attitudes reflected the emerging ideal of bourgeois domesticity. See E. Fox-Genovese and E. D. Genovese, *Fruits of Merchant Capital*, Chapter 11, "The Ideological Bases of Domestic Economy."

[34]B. G. du Pont, ed., *Life of Eleuthère Irénée*, I, p. 194.

[35]Ibid., pp. 23–24.

[36]Chinard, ed., *Correspondence*, p. 267.

[37]B. G. du Pont, ed., *Life of Eleuthère Irénée*, I, p. 90.

[38]Chinard, ed., *Correspondence*, pp. 12–14.

[39]See Marc Bouloiseau, "Du Pont de Nemours et l'éducation nationale," in *Histoire de l'enseignement de 1610 à nos jours. Actes du 95e Congrès des Sociétés Savantes, Reims, 1970, histoire moderne et contemporaine*, I (Paris, 1974), pp. 171–84.

[40]Saricks also expresses this view; see *Pierre Samuel Du Pont de Nemours*, pp. 222–24.

[41]Ibid., p. 360, note 2.

[42]Marguerite Kuczynski and Ronald Meek, eds., *Quesnay's Tableau économique* (London and New York: Macmillan Press and Augustus M. Kelley, 1972).

[43]The added paragraph is in Chapter 3 of the autobiography and is identified by note 5.

[44]B. G. du Pont, *Life of Eleuthère Irénée*, I, p. 113. The salutation could be translated as "Go in health and love me."

[45]Saricks handles the intricacies of Du Pont's claims and his actual accomplishments very well; see *Pierre Samuel Du Pont de Nemours*, esp. pp. 63–144, *passim.*

[46]Ménétra, *Journal de ma vie*, Daniel Roche's introduction, p. 12.

[47]Philippe Lejeune, *Le Pacte autobiographique* (Paris: Éditions du Seuil, 1975), his *Autobiographie en France*, and the discussion among him, Georges Gusdorf, and others in *Revue d'histoire littéraire de la France* 75, no. 6 (1975): 931–35.

[48]Georg Misch, *A History of Autobiography in Antiquity*, trans. E. W. Dickes, 2 vols. (Cambridge, MA: Harvard University Press, 1951). Only vol. 1 of the original German has been translated; for the remainder, see his *Geschichte der Autobiographie*, vols. 2–4 (Frankfurt-am-Main: G. Schulte-Bulmke, 1955–69). See also Karl J. Weintraub, *The Value of the Individual: Self and Circumstance in Autobiography* (Chicago: University of Chicago Press, 1978).

[49]Lejeune, *Pacte autobiographique*, p. 14.

[50]Georges Gusdorf, "Conditions and Limits of Autobiography," in James Olney, ed., *Autobiography: Essays Theoretical and Critical* (Princeton: Princeton University Press, 1980), pp. 24–48, *passim*, and his "De l'autobiographie initiatique à l'autobiographie genre littéraire," *Revue d'histoire littéraire de la France* 75 (1975): 974. See also his *La Découverte de soi* (Paris: Presses Universitaires, 1948).

[51]Gusdorf, "Conditions and Limits," pp. 33–34.

[52]Roy Pascal, *Design and Truth in Autobiography* (Cambridge, MA: Harvard University Press, 1960), p. 181.

[53]See for example James Olney, *Metaphors of Self: The Meaning of Autobiography* (Princeton: Princeton University Press, 1972), and his "Autobiography and the Cultural Moment: A Thematic, Historical, and Bibliographical Introduction," in Olney, ed., *Autobiography*, pp. 3–27.

[54]For a recent critical review essay, see Candace Lang, "Autobiography in the Aftermath of Romanticism," *Diacritics* (Winter 1982): 2–16. The issues are extremely complex and the debates heated. See also Michel Foucault, "Qu'est-ce un auteur," *Bulletin de la Société Française de Philosophie* 63, no. 3 (1969): 75–104.

[55]Janet Varner Gunn, *Autobiography. Toward a Poetics of Experience* (Philadelphia: University of Pennsylvania Press, 1982), p. 23.

[56]Cf. Albert E. Stone, *Autobiographical Occasions and Original Acts* (Philadelphia: University of Pennsylvania Press, 1982), and William C. Sengemann, *The Forms of Autobiography: Episodes in the History of a Literary Genre* (New Haven: Yale University Press, 1980).

[57]Lejeune, *Pacte autobiographique*, p. 46.

[58]Pascal, *Design and Truth*, p. 182.

[59]Mircea Eliade, *Cosmos and History: The Myth of the Eternal Return*, trans. William R. Trask (New York: Harper & Brothers, 1959).

[60]Marmontel, *Mémoires*; see for example I, p. 18.

[61]Michael Polanyi, *Personal Knowledge: Towards a Post-Critical Philosophy* (Chicago: University of Chicago Press, 1974), p. 267.

[62]On Du Pont's reading, see especially Chapters 6, 7, and 8 of the autobiography and accompanying notes.

[63]See Chapter 6, note 7, of the autobiography.

[64]Cited by Pascal, *Design and Truth*, pp. 46–7. The passage is from Goethe's *Maximen and Reflexionen*, vol. VI.

[65]Pascal, *Design and Truth*, p. 182.

[66]Chapter 4 offers a good example of Du Pont's alternating tenses and points of identification to convey different perspectives on and degrees of identification with himself.

[67]Chapter 3 offers an interesting contrast with his treatment of his parents once he has been born. In Chapter 3, he presents them as young people whom he is trying to understand from their own point of view and somewhat objectively.

[68]Despite his passionate attachment to his mother, he is quite prepared to admit to himself that she may have cultivated vanity and a passion for glory in him, that his father's view of the world may have been more responsible. Moreover, he always allows a slight emphasis to father and the status of fatherhood. The misogyny of Enlightenment thinkers is still hotly debated, but there are strong grounds for believing that even those who liked women did not believe them to be the equals of men and that many covertly or openly mistrusted and feared women. See Samia Spencer, ed., *French Women in the Age of Enlightenment* (Bloomington: Indiana University Press, 1984), my introduction and chapters by Pauline Kra on Montesquieu, Blandine McLaughlin on Diderot, and Gita May on Rousseau. See also Eva Jacobs, et al., eds., *Woman and Society in Eighteenth-Century France* (London: Athlone Press, 1979), especially chapters by Sheila Mason on Montesquieu and Robert Niklaus on Diderot. See also Nancy K. Miller, *The Heroine's Text: Readings in the French and English Novel 1722–1782* (New York: Columbia University Press, 1980).

[69]It is worth noting that Du Pont's family of origin, as well as his family of procreation, provide specific examples of that precocious French tendency toward family limitation. See Etienne Van De Walle, "Alone in Europe: The French Fertility Decline until 1850," in Charles Tilly, ed., *Historical Studies of Changing Fertility* (Princeton: Princeton University Press, 1978), pp. 257–88.

[70]*Physiocratie ou constitution naturelle du gouvernement le plus avantageux au genre humain*, 2 vols. (Pekin & Leyde [Paris]: 1767). On the date of publication, see Luigi Einaudi, "À propos de la date de publication de la 'Physiocratie,' " in INED, *François Quesnay et la physiocratie*, I: 1–9.

[71]See Claude Quetel, *De Par le Roy. Essai sur les lettres de cachet* (Toulouse: Privat, 1981).

[72]See Michael Walzer, ed., *Regicide and Revolution: Speeches at the Trial of Louis XVI* (Cambridge: Cambridge University Press, 1974), and David P. Jordan, *The King's Trial: Louis XVI vs. the French Revolution* (Berkeley: University of California Press, 1979).

[73]See Natalie Zemon Davis, "Ghosts, Kin, and Progeny: Some Features of Family Life in Early Modern France," *Daedalus* 106, no. 2 (Spring 1977): 87–114.

MEMOIRS

of
Pierre Samuel Du Pont
addressed to his children

Rectitudine Sto

September 1792

Memoirs of Pierre Samuel Du Pont addressed to his Children

from Cormeilles   4 September 1792

Uncertain, my dear children, if I shall ever have the happiness of seeing you again, or in what fashion I shall leave my current retreat, I think I should profit from it by giving you some necessary information concerning your family; and also an account of my life that will at least be pleasurable for you. I myself will enjoy the sweetness of writing you a very long letter.

It will be divided into chapters, which I shall have delivered to you successively.

If the outcome were to occur before the end of the story, you will fill in the gaps as you can.

1

What I know of my paternal family.

Our family is protestant and Norman. I have found it established opinion that it was originally from Brittany; and the same opinion obtained in the family of MM Du Pont from the area around *Vire*, who are today bankers in Paris and who are allied with us through Madame Le Dée, the daughter of a Du Pont. It is not impossible that we are their distant relatives, but I have no documents to prove it.

I know of no other presumption of relationship with any other Du Pont family. Our name is extremely common in all countries and in all languages: *Pontius* among the Latins; *Pontio*, which we translate *Ponce*, among the Spaniards and the Portuguese; *del Ponte* among the Italians; *Von Brucke* among the Germans; *Van Brugh* or *van Breughen* among the Dutch and the Flemish; *Bridge* among the English; *Mastowski* among the Poles. All these names also apply to families that descend from a *warrior* so-called because of his defense of a bridge, of a *Master of a castle* charged with guarding a bridge, of an *architect* celebrated for having built a bridge, of a *collector of tolls*, holding a rights of passage over a bridge, of a child found on a bridge. Everywhere, there have been a large number of men in one of these five cases and especially in the last two, from which it follows that there are many Du Ponts in all professions and in all ranks, but most in the least illustrious class.

As for those from whom we are descended, I can only trace back to my great grandfather who was called *Abraham Du Pont*. The first document I have that concerns him is the contract for the acquisition of two small houses that I own in Rouen, and which are consequently very old. In it, he is designated by the qualities of honorable and wise merchant. The commerce in which he was engaged in Rouen and in the fairs of Normandy dealt particularly with copper boilers and cooking utensils.

He apparently had a brother named *Jean* or *Jonas* who established himself in Rotterdam and from whom descended through the male line:

1. M. *Jonas Du Pont*, like Abraham a merchant or producer of copper boilers at *Rotterdam*, who returned to Paris in 1742 or 1743 where, for a long time, he lodged with my Father. M. N. Du Pont, his son, today the First Physician of the city of Rotterdam, completed his medical studies in Paris. He is four years older than I am: he is a man of merit, small, well-made, with an agreeable face which entirely resembles that of my Father and my Sister. He was much in love with the latter and failed to marry her. I no longer remember what interfered with this marriage, which would have been perfectly suitable in all respects. I think that my Sister was not rich enough.

I followed some studies in anatomy with M. Du Pont, the doctor. We like each other very much, and we have remained in correspondence from time to time.

2. MM Du Pont, who moved from Holland to London and who are jewelers in London. One of them was a jeweler for the King of England in 1756. I do not know their descent. MM *Du Pont* of Holland, who have retained continuous relations with them know of this.

Through the female line.

1. M. Mesnil, jeweler in Rotterdam, son of a young lady Du Pont, the aunt of *Jonas*, of whom I have just been speaking. M. Mesnil came to France with M. *Jonas Du Pont* and also lodged with my Father. He had one or two sisters. He has a son and a daughter. The son came to see us about fifteen years ago, and you may remember him. He spent a month at Bois des Fossés. He is a very fine child.

2. M. Pierre *Fouquet*. Painter and dealer in paintings in Amsterdam, Son either of a young lady Du Pont or of the sister of M. Mesnil, the father. M. Fouquet enjoys a large fortune; he has

made three or four trips to France during the first of which I was very close to him. He is married and has several children. His correspondent in Paris is M. *Toline*, a banker of the rue Quincampoix.

The reason I believe that MM *Du Pont* and *Fouquet* descend from a brother of my ancestor is that their kinship to us is not in doubt; it is recognized by a sustained correspondence and the respective visits during voyages to our country and the others by the Du Ponts of France and those of Holland; and that I cannot find any specific tie since my great grandfather. From this I conclude that the common ancestor was my thrice-removed great grandfather, and that MM Du Pont of Holland descend from a son of *Abraham Du Pont* of Rouen.

It will be necessary to write to them to establish the degree of kinship; to know who are those of our other relations of whom I knew nothing; and finally to know what is the filiation of MM *Du Pont* of England, who are descended from the branch with whom we have never had direct relations.

My great grandfather had two sons. The elder, *Jean Du Pont*, who was my grandfather, remained in Rouen, and continued to practice his father's profession there. The second, *Abraham Du Pont*, left France after the Revocation of the Edict of Nantes. He moved to America, in Carolina. As a result of his immigration and of his share of the rights to the paternal inheritance, the Administration of the goods of fugitive Protestants took possession of the income of *forty livres* from one of the two houses that belonged to the family. This rent was delivered to me by an order of the counsel under the ministry of M. *de Malesherbes* shortly before the general law, rendered by the archbishop of Sens, that was intended to restore all such goods to their families.[1] The law did not impede the national constituent assembly from issuing a decree to the same effect and the national legislative assembly from renewing the same order. That which abounds does no harm, and easily demonstrates on this occasion that laws have always been made with much light-heartedness and negligence. The constituent assembly did not wish to listen to me when I told its members that they were decreeing that which had already been ordered two years before by a declaration of the King. Thus we have four titles instead of one to enjoy our income of forty livres. It would be a nuisance to lose it under the pretext that I had emigrated when, in fact, I am in the center of the Kingdom.

My great Uncle *Abraham* got married in Carolina. I do not

know the name of his wife nor the number of his children nor what has become of them. I only know that one of his daughters married M. *May*, a Swiss from Berne, from one of the two hundred sovereign families of Berne, and that during my childhood I saw their son, *Rodolphe May*, who had been sent from Carolina to Berne where, it was said, their fortune was assured by the leases that the lords of Berne give exclusively to their Relatives.[2] He was a little bit older than I and should, if he is still living today, be between *fifty-eight* and *sixty years old.*

My Father was the uncle, in the manner of Brittany, of *Rodolphe May;* I am his first cousin; you are his second cousin. This relationship could be of some use in Switzerland, if from revolutions to revolutions the government of Berne is not overthrown, as it is likely that it will be. In any event, it is always good to know our relatives. One never knows from where one may *collect* inheritances, nor whom one may have to assist. I reproach myself that I never informed myself about what could have happened to my cousin *May* since I spent an entire day with him.

My grand Father, *Jean Du Pont*, attained some success in his commerce, but toward the end of his life he lost a part of what he had gained when he suffered an attack of apoplexy, after which he was struck with paralysis of the tongue for several years until his death.

In addition to the two houses in Rouen, he left a small farm of about one hundred *arpens** of land, meadow, and woods, which was called *la Robinette,* lay about two leagues from Rouen, and can be found on the map of Cassiny. He also left another small house with a bit of land, meadow, and wood as well as some watercress beds which are said to yield a good profit in the village of *Fontaine sous Préaux*, which is the Parish in which *la Robinette* falls.

My grand-Father did not reach old age. He was, I have been told, a gentle man of great kindness. He had married *Marie de la Porte*, who died as a result of a fall from a horse at eighty-five years of age. She was a beautiful woman, of medium size, who had good sense, was very active, and had a decisive spirit, resolution, and courage. Through my grand-Mother *Marie de la Porte* we are cousins of MM *du Bucq* and *Le Maignan*, whom I saw in my youth. The first was a merchant and shipbuilder, the second a diamond merchant.

---

*Seventy or eighty acres.

Both were taken to be wealthy. Through her, we are related to MM *Tassin* and *Cottin*, both bankers. But I do not know the genealogies that establish these relations and distant cousinships. It would be fitting and useful if you investigated them.

Jean Du Pont and *Marie de la Porte* had eight children, of whom six were boys and two girls.

The oldest of the boys, called *Jean Du Pont* like his Father, continued the latter's commerce, but died fairly young. He had married *Marie du Bucq*, his cousin, whom he left a widow and who remarried a M. Boullenger. She had no children with my uncle, and the branch of *Jean Du Pont* died out.

The second, *Pierre Du Pont*, who was my Godfather, had a likeable face, much vivacity, intelligence, and what is known in English as *humor*. He told good tales, played the flute well, rode horseback with grace. He was a clever clockmaker and had accumulated a large fortune in England where he had established himself. But he invested it all wildly. In the same fashion he sold my father one of the two houses in Rouen which had been at once his share of the paternal legacy and that of his brother Jean. Having thus doubled his income, he then spent it all, so that although he loved me particularly, he left me only fifty guineas and a diamond worth roughly fifteen louis, which I still have. It is the larger of the two in the desk.

My uncle *Pierre* was married, survived his wife, and left no children. Second branch extinguished.

My third Uncle, *Jacques Du Pont*, was only a poor *Village Artisan*.[3] He established himself on a piece of the land at *Fontaine sous Préaux*, which was encumbered with a payment to one of his brothers. He was litigious, like a Norman, and slightly quarrelsome. He never could get along with his mother, nor with his brother, nor with his neighbor of whom I shall speak to you. He ate up a part of his slim fortune in litigation. Finally having become wise at the age of fifty, he exploited his small piece of land and lathed chairs and spinning wheels. I do not know the name of his Wife: she is dead and he is too. He left a son whom I went to see in 1778. He is married to a pleasant enough woman by whom he has three children. To me he appeared a handsome, gallant man, with the physiognomy of a Du Pont, which is not at all like mine, nor like yours, my children, and which in our branch only your Aunt has. I and you have taken that of the Monchanins, which you have somewhat combined with that of the *Le Dées*.

I found *Jacques Du Pont* in the small house, which is worth a little more than my house at one rue des Bordes, but not much. It has slightly more apparent spaciousness than that of the *des Mures*, whom you know, and is about at the same level of that of the *Le Jays*, at the very most. Thus this branch of your family is frankly composed of peasants and has little hope of becoming anything else.

My fourth uncle was called *Nicolas*. He was an excellent man, a good son, a good brother, and a man of extremely gay temperament. He never wanted to marry as long as his mother was alive, and he worked the farm of *la Robinette* for her. It was due to be his share of the inheritance.

Since the death of my grand-mother, my uncle, at the *age of sixty-nine*, has married the housekeeper and had two children: a boy who died and a girl who is living and whom her mother married off very young to a butcher named, I believe, Potier.

Our Rouen Relatives were very much displeased with the marriages of my uncle and his daughter. Where will vanity implant itself? I, who am a great partisan of the freedom of marriages, was enchanted to have an uncle who had sired children when he was seventy; that, joined to the vigor which I saw my grandmother retain when she was eighty-four, gives me a happy attitude toward my own advanced age, if it does advance, and if I do not leave my head at the end of this narrative. I went to see my uncle on his farm, which I had already seen in my childhood and which had appeared admirable to me then. The small house of the Master is composed of a kitchen and three rooms. The rest comprises buildings necessary to work the farm. It is situated in the middle of one of those vast apple orchards that are called *masures* in Normandy. Residing there would not displease me if there were any other water than swamp water: as it is, when one wants drinkable water it is necessary to go half a league to get it from the watercress growers of Fontaines. The people of the Country say that an honest man should only drink cider when he does not have wine.

The fifth son of my grand Father is *Samuel Du Pont*, my Father, who well deserves a chapter for us.

The sixth was named *Abraham Du Pont*. My Father, who loved him above all the others, introduced him to clockmaking. *Abraham* became a very good workman and, having heard that his brother *Pierre* had been very successful in London, he moved there. He worked for the renowned *Graham* and contributed to the reputation of this great English clockmaker who invented the cylindrical escapement. But my uncle *Pierre* married a rich woman with whom he had no children; my uncle *Abraham*, to the contrary, quickly married a poor one who was in poor health, and he had many children, several of whom died in their early years and one of whom lived for a long time impotent. He was never able to raise himself above his misfortune. To cap these woes, the two wives quarreled and estranged the two husbands: so *Pierre*, although rich, offered no help to *Abraham*, who was poor. I have frequently heard my Father blame him for this; and my Father preached by example; he regularly sent money to his brother.

I shall tell you, with respect to the hardness displayed by my uncle Pierre, who was in other respects a very good man, that there has always been a failing in our family against which you should protect yourselves: it is an opinionatedness, a rigidity of character that renders us very steadfast in friendship, but very implacable in enmity. I have seen examples of this in my own Father, who disapproved of this same disposition in his older brother. I have also frequently been attacked by it. Your Aunt is the only one I have known to forgive great wrongs. For too long, I have retained animosities against M. *Brac de la Perrière*, against the *archbishop of Sens*, and against M. *Magnien*. The first was only impertinent to me, which a man of good sense should consider altogether tolerable. The second was unjust, the third was an ingrate: but I nurtured too much bitterness for these trifles. One must cultivate gentle passions in oneself and reject the rancorous ones.

My uncle Abraham's impotent son is dead. He had another son who went to sea more than twenty years ago and of whom there has been no news. He left two daughters. The elder, *Marie Magdelaine Du Pont*, married a Swiss clockmaker named M. *Rochat*, a very honorable and sensible man. He died. *Madame Rochat* has remained a widow with two little girls, one of whom is now almost grown and is said to be rather amiable although somewhat spoiled. I think she is called *Mary* and the second *Betsy*.

The Mother lives in some poverty and keeps a school for little girls to whom she teaches French, although not very well. You should find her address in the letters I receive from her. I normally write to her in care of my excellent friend *James Hutton Pimlico*, but he is very old and I fear does not have long to live.[4]

Anne Du Pont, the Sister of Madame Rochat, had an extremely negligent education. She was twenty when she began to write. She married a locksmith named *John Bourne* with whom she moved to *New York* in the United States of America where they remain and where *Victor* had some services to render them.

I also always had to perform services for Madame *Rochat*, and not long ago I sent her eight guineas, for which I owe close to fifteen louis to M. *Grand* since the charges are so heavy. Pay them as soon as possible.

Madame *Rochat* and Madame *Bourne* between them are entitled to an income of *one hundred and fifty livres*, or thereabouts, on the property of *Fontane sous Préaux*, which belongs to the branch of M. *Jacques Du Pont*, and also, I think, something from *la Robinette*, which belongs to the branch of M. *Nicolas Du Pont*, or to *Madame Beaufort*.

My uncle *Nicolas du Pont* had rights as much in his own name as through his status as the heir or legatee of *Pierre Du Pont*, in the houses of Rouen that had remained in or been acquired by my branch. I bought back this right for a fixed income, the exact amount of which I do not remember. I have, I believe, a counter interest in *la Robinette*. We have always spoken of exchanging them, and I do not know if that has been completed. I do not have a very clear idea of this part of my affairs.

I had some desire to have la Robinette put up for auction and to buy it; before my uncle was married, he was willing to sell it to me. But we have no need of property in the department of the Seine Inférieure when the basis of our landed fortune forms a rather considerable and almost contiguous mass in the department of the Seine et Marne and that of the Loiret. On the contrary, our interest is to liquidate as rapidly as we can all of our affairs in the erstwhile Normandy, to sell our houses in Rouen as soon as they attract buyers, and to sell off entirely, or to improve, or to extend our property in the erstwhile Gâtinais.

I should note, in speaking of the houses in Rouen, that they are mortgaged at a fixed interest of *three hundred livres* without deductions, on the basis of a capital sum of *six thousand livres*, which I created for my sister from what remained to her of the succession of my Father.

We cannot sell the houses without the expense of reimbursing my Sister; and we would do well to reimburse her ahead of time if we have the money.

The houses are rented together for either 500, 520 or 550 livres. I no longer remember: the correspondence with M. *d'Ailly* will say. I shall speak of him shortly.

It is time to speak of my Aunts and their branches.

The elder was called *Marie*; she was married to M. *Jacques Oulson*, he came of a family that was originally English, was the captain of a merchant vessel, and I saw him in my early childhood. Captain Oulson had merit and fortune. He lost the latter, with his life, in a wreck off the coast of *Labrador*, from which his son, who was with him at the time, returned after having undergone more extreme misery than that to which the captain succumbed. He held the principal interest in his ship. Madame *Oulson* remained without any property, with her son who arrived naked and two daughters.

The elder of the daughters, *Maria Oulson*, was very beautiful; she greatly resembled Madame *La Motte* except that she was kinder. She fell deeply in love with M. *d'Ailly* who was employed by the customs and who was waiting to inherit a sizable fortune from his Relatives, who were wealthy merchants in Rouen, but it did not materialize. M. *d'Ailly* was, and still is, Catholic. My Aunt *Oulson*, my grand-Mother, my uncle *Nicolas*, my Father, all the grand Parents, good Huguenots of God, were horrified that Mademoiselle *Oulson*, whose only worldly possessions were her beautiful eyes, her tall figure, her Norman skin and throat, and whose seventeen or eighteen years did not make her very mature, could be tempted to marry a suitor who presented himself and who had the irremediable fault of being catholic. My mother, who was more intelligent, would have been more indulgent, but, for the same reason and because she was more educated, she was the Theologian of the family. They took advantage of her weakness and had her write a beautiful letter to her niece. M. *d'Ailly*'s Family did not find it any more tolerable that he dared to think of marrying a Protestant. Finally, someone said to the young woman that *in becoming a catholic she would be showered with the favors of the court, and would be able to marry her lover despite her family.*

Mademoiselle *Oulson* took herself off to the convent for new Catholics. There, touched by the *grace* of the holy spirit and by that of M. *d'Ailly*, whom today you would never suspect of having had graces, she abjured the errors of the *pretended reformed Religion*: but that did not yield the consent of her Relatives, nor did it dispose them to give it. It was hoped that she would become a Nun: she was only faithful to her lover. She remained in the convent for six years and emerged at twenty-five with a pension of *one hundred francs* on the bursary, since reduced to *seventy-two francs*: such was the price of her conversion.[5] But having come of age, and being protected by my mother, who was deeply touched by enduring love, she married her gentle friend and made peace with her Relatives.

My mother helped her, with advances of money, to open a

shop in Rouen as a fashion Merchant. At that time she came to Paris to get stock, and I saw her for the first time. She was not yet *twenty-six* years old, and she made my poor heart beat rapidly. I deemed M. *d'Ailly* a very happy man.

So long as Mme *d'Ailly* was beautiful, her shop prospered. Finally, she became ugly, like Mlle *Cunnagonde*; the yield of the shop diminished with her charms.[6] For young women, much less the friends who advise them, old-fashioned Merchants never appear to understand new tastes. In the last years, everything that had been gained in the beginning was eaten up. Madame *d'Ailly* died two years ago. Her husband did not inherit from his parents as he had expected; a very poor little haberdashery business and the expectation of a pension, never given, in return for forty-two years of service in the office of the *controller of the tax of the fourth* in Rouen, were his entire fortune.[7] He broke with his Director during the period of the revolution over having *saved the Registers* at the risk of his life. This director, who would have preferred to have the Registers lost, engaged in odious quarrels with him. He would have been destitute, despite long and pure service, for having had courage and probity, if I had not protected him with M. *Necker* and M. *de Lessarts*.

He manages my affairs in Rouen with much care and intelligence, but good sense dictates that I help him, *all the more since he* has never asked me for anything because he is as embarrassed as he is honest. And you can see from that how, in aiding Mme *Rochat*, Mme *Barre*, M. *d'Ailly*, and your Aunt *Gudin*, whose income also is not adequate, it happens that my property in the department of the Seine inférieure is an altogether negative quantity in my fortune.

I have told you that the captain *Oulson* had a son who was a bit younger than Madame *d'Ailly*, and whom he had taken on all his voyages. The horror of a shipwreck and the miseries of *Labrador* had greatly disgusted the young man with seafaring. He came to *la Robinette* and worked there for several years exploiting the farm under the orders of my uncle *Nicolas*. Then he married and took a lease on another farm. But the dowry of his wife, which had served to set it up, proved to be insufficient; he lacked advances; he was reduced to making carts; he lost his dungheaps; at the end of his lease, leaving agriculture, he returned to the sea.

When he had completed several voyages the Family got together to build and outfit a small ship for him. I contributed three eighths, M. *Pouchet* a quarter, M. *d'Ailly* a sixth, etc. This practice is very common in seafaring regions; a whole family subscribes, outfits a

Vessel, and confides it to a poor Relative who is a sailor.[8] The Captain has a small interest in the ship and passes for the Proprietor; this status gives him confidence and credit in commerce. He handles his own affairs and those of his relatives and associates.

The others deferred to me in the honor of naming the ship, for I had already become the man of importance among our relatives: they wanted it to carry *my name*; I preferred to endow it with the mark of my principles, and I named it *The Freedom of Commerce*. It was used throughout the war for the King's Service. Solomon *Oulson* commanded it with the commission of *Lieutenant of Frigate* for the duration of the war. The small craft was an excellent sailboat. In the fleet of Brest its name was removed and replaced with that of the *Diligent*, which its performance merited. Three months after the peace it was shipwrecked; and the captain, with sorrow, found another ship.

He had a son, *Jacques-Guillaume*, or *Jacques-Antoine*, or *Jacques-Louis Oulson*—I do not remember the name exactly—who was a ships' captain like him. He also had two daughters whose names escape me, both pretty, and whom I went to see in Dieppedale in 1778.

The elder married around the same time, in 1781, a M. *Picquefeu* who was employed by the general farm in the salt depot.[9]

The second has since married, and I do not remember the name of her husband, who I think was also in the transport of salt. You will find the name in M. *d'Ailly's* correspondence. Both girls should have children, who are your second cousins.

In the *Oulson* branch, there is also a Madame *Vaudry* who was named *Marianne Oulson* and who, at the death of the captain, was comforted by my Mother to whom she caused some sorrow; since then, she has caused me much more, but that is part of my personal memoirs. Madame *Vaudry* was the universal legatee of my Father. She is the widow of *Pierre-François Vaudry*, clockmaker, from whom she had a son and a small piece of land at *Evêquemont* on the road to Rouen. At sixty, she is still annoying, stupid, and coquettish; but the young *Vaudry is nonetheless your cousin once removed*.

Through the *Oulsons* we are allied to MM *Boullard*, merchant shippers of Dieppe. They and my Father treated each other as cousins, although they are linked to our male and female cousins of the *Oulson* branch.

The last daughter of my grand-Father was named *Anne du Pont*. She married a merchant from *Bolbeck*, a rich and intelligent man named *Abraham Pouchet*. They had two children.

A daughter was taken from them by order of the King, as a

huguenot, was placed in a convent, raised a catholic, and became a Nun in an abbey near Rouen, under the name of *Madame de Ste Colombe*. She was beautiful and spirited. I saw her in 1778; already she was no longer young, and I do not know what became of her during the Revolution.

Her brother, *Abraham Pouchet Belmare*, my second cousin, is a man of sense, of virtue, and of talent, who married a woman of his family and of his name, and who had established at *Bolbeck* one of the first manufactures of cotton velvet. It was accidentally burned down. He rebuilt his fortune, his work, and his merit; and established at *Eauplet-les-Rouen* a new manufacture of painted cloth, which has been very successful. It is now run by his older son, my nephew-in-the-manner-of-Brittany, whom my son Irénée knows and who is a young man worthy of his Father. He has just married one of his cousins, also of his name, and who has at least five or six brothers and sisters.

Of all our family, MM *Pouchet* are the men who are the best educated, the most suited for business, and of the strongest character. It is, in every sense, agreeable and honorable to belong to them.

They form in Rouen, in the surrounding area, and in the Pays de Caux, a kind of tribe of relations of the same name who willingly marry among themselves, and who are all intelligent and enlightened. Among others, we can distinguish M. *Louis Pouchet*, brother of my cousin *Pouchet Belmare*, and, I think, also Father of the wife of your cousin, the young *Pouchet*. To the skill of a great merchant and a first-class manufacturer he joins the zeal of an excellent citizen and the views of a Statesman.

Notes

[1]By the Edict of Fontainebleau of 17 October 1685, Louis XIV revoked the Edict of Nantes of 1598 which had granted distinct rights and a corporate personality to the Protestant communities in France. Among the various provisions of the revocation was one that forbade Protestants to leave the country or to send their property out on penalty of being sentenced to the galleys for men or of being imprisoned and having property confiscated for women. Those who left were allowed four months to return, at which point their property could be restored to them. The second half of the eighteenth century witnessed mounting pressure for greater tolerance in France and the restoration of civil rights to Protestants. The

Edict of Versailles of 19 November 1787, for which Lamoignon de Malesherbes, who became keeper of the seals in the government of Loménie de
Brienne, had worked, restored civil rights to Protestants and, specifically,
the right "to enjoy all the possessions and rights that may now or in the
future belong to them as property or inheritance, and to carry on their
business, crafts, trades, and professions without being disturbed or dis-
quieted on account of their religion." Roland Mousnier, *The Institutions of
France under the Absolute Monarchy 1598–1789: Society and the State*, trans. Brian
Pearce (Chicago: University of Chicago Press, 1979), p. 408, and pp. 393–
402.

[2]In the eighteenth century, Bern featured a highly aristocratic government. Citizenship had become purely hereditary, with no new citizens
admitted between 1651 and 1790. In 1651, those among the citizenry who
qualified for membership in the town council had been designated as
"patricians." At that time, eighty families held offices; in 1787, only sixty-
eight. Collectively the members of the governing council were known as
LLEE, Leurs Excellences. Office could prove very lucrative to those who
held it, since the town governed the surrounding countryside, and members of the government who were responsible for the rural "subject districts" could, it was said, make enough to live on for life through governing
one of those districts, such as the Vaud, for only six years. See Robert R.
Palmer, *The Age of Democratic Revolution: A Political History of Europe and
America, 1760–1800*, vol. I, *The Challenge* (Princeton: Princeton University
Press, 1959), p. 35.

[3]Specifically, he was a *tourneur*, or a craftsman who worked by hand
on a lathe.

[4]James Hutton was a London bookseller, a leader of the Moravian
Brethren in England, a friend of Benjamin Franklin, and a correspondent
with Du Pont on matters literary, philosophical, and political between
1772 and 1778. See Ambrose Saricks, *Pierre Samuel Du Pont de Nemours*
(Lawrence: University of Kansas Press, 1965), p. 77, and note 62, p. 380.

[5]The royal government frequently paid the expenses of Protestant
girls who converted and entered convents, although by the middle of the
eighteenth century, the controller general was asking for assurances that
the girls really were Protestant and that their conversion could be expected
to promote conversions of others; in short, that girls were not just claiming
to be Protestant in order to have their expenses paid in a convent.

[6]"La belle Cunégonde" was a character in Voltaire's *Candide* (1759).
Beloved by the hero, she becomes more and more ugly during the course
of the story.

[7]*Controlleur du droit du quatrième*, in French. He was an official charged
with the administration of the tax so-called "of the fourth," but in fact of
one fifth of the price that was imposed on wines, ciders, and brandies in
certain regions. The *quatrième* was one of the *aides*, or sales taxes. See

Marcel Marion, *Dictionnaire des institutions de la France aux XVIIe et XVIIIe siècles* (1923; repr. Paris: A. & J. Picard, 1969).

[8]The practice was common in French ports; see Paul Butel, *Les Négociants Bordelais: l'Europe et les iles au XVIIIe siècle* (Paris: Aubier, 1974); Charles Carrière, *Négociants Marseillais au XVIIIe siècle: contribution à l'étude des économies maritimes* (Marseille: Institut Historique de Provence, 1973), 2 vols.; Jean Meyer, *L'Armement Nantais dans la deuxième moitié du XVIIIe siècle* (Paris: SEVPEN, 1969).

[9]For an explanation of the *ferme générale* and its administrators, see Chapter 13, note 2.

2

What I know of my maternal family.

You have seen that my Father's family was composed only of Peasants, merchants, sailors, or craftsmen, and that the most successful of My Paternal Relatives was a Manufacturer of painted cloth.

In my mother's Family, to the contrary, they were what was then called *noble*: and they were very proud of it, although in my time almost all of those I knew had derogated.[1]

MM *de Monchanin*, or *de Montchanin* (for the two spellings were used, and in one of the papers of my grandfather I found that the manner of writing the name varied constantly from one generation to another) had, in effect, originally been very good gentlemen of the Charollais and the Mâçonnais. One part of their distant genealogy may be found in Father *Anselme's* book on the great officers of the crown.[2]

This family had a crest of gules with a gold chevron and three silver stars, placed two and one.

It is divided into three branches.

The older, according to father Anselme, ended with a daughter who married into the house of *Damas.*

This branch was also allied to the Amanzé. The Amanzés and the Damases are allied to the Condés. You see how vanity gallops.[3]

It is true that MM *de Monchanin,* of the branch to which my Mother belonged, did not establish, at least according to the papers I have seen, their precise relation to the first branch, of which they call themselves the younger and which had made these beautiful alliances. But that is not important. It was the pretension of the family to be the second branch of that which I have just cited.

This second branch, or that which claims as much, added a second chevron to the coat of arms. I have made a genealogy of the smaller number of generations of this branch, for which I have been able to find titles through my Grand Father and my uncle *Pierre de Monchanin.* It is in the hands of his Son, as is a Bible that had come to my Mother and that I returned to my uncle. It is bound together with a notebook that for several generations my maternal ancestors used to inscribe the births of their children.[4] This bible comes from the family of my grand-Mother and reveals that in the female line you descend from *Le Grain* who wrote a *décade* on the history of France. You may consult these two pieces.[5]

The third branch, or that which also claimed to be such, had, it claimed, taken three chevrons, thus adding one more chevron than the second branch, just as it had added one more than the first. The existence and the pretensions of this third branch consolidated those of the second by a strong analogy in the absence of proof.

I believe that this last branch ended with the person of the *Chevalier de Monchanin,* one-time reformed aide-major of the Regiment of Condé's cavalry. You saw him during your childhood. He directed the equestrian Academy under M. *du Guast,* subsequently became Equerry of the *Duc du Bouillon,* and bequeathed me his swords.

The chevalier *de Monchanin* and I *called each other cousin* with all our hearts, for he was a very gallant man. We wrote each other as the red cousin to the green cousin, the red chevalier to the green chevalier, or the green to the red; and we could not establish our kinship except on the identity of name, of Province, of coat of arms, and of pretensions. But the chevalier was truly noble and poor; I was ennobled, and was tied through women to a noble family, I appeared rich and of sound credit, and I had a decoration superior to that of the chevalier: the two vanities shored each other up.

You can thus see, my dear children, (1) that I am not answering for the certainty of any branch; (2) that it all matters little to us since nobility has been abolished; (3) that even if hereditary nobility still existed, we *Du Ponts*, descendants of a very estimable brazier—as was *Colin d'Issoire*, immortalized by *Voltaire*—would have nothing to claim from this puff of smoke which women do not transmit, although their descent is much more certain. But I must tell you of the family of my Mother, what I told you of that of my Father, namely *what I know of it*, and with comparable ingenuity. And it seems sure to me that MM *de Monchanin* were what were then known as *good gentlemen*, in extreme poverty. They were, in addition, very zealous Protestants.

My Grandfather, *Héléodore de Monchanin*, had several brothers, one of whom moved to Prussia; another of whom died in Switzerland after having served in England; a third brother, who apparently converted to catholicism, died in Paris, at Les Invalides, as a captain and a knight of St. Louis.[6]

Héléodore had himself served in a Regiment of French Refugees in the pay of the Republic of Holland during the War of the Spanish succession. He left me the holster pistols that went through that war.

Having returned to the Charollais to collect some crumbs from the inheritance of his Parents, my Grandfather claimed the protection of the Marquis of *Jaucourt-Epénilles* to whom he was related by marriage. Or such is the pretension of the MM *de Monchanin* of my branch. MM *de Jaucourt*, who have always shown a great deal of interest in me and mine, have never mentioned the alliance to me, and I have no title of it. The derogation of the majority of the MM *de Monchanin*, and indeed my kinship to them, have always deterred me from asking the MM *de Jaucourt* whom I have known if this opinion of my family had any foundation. Since it is proven that one *Monchanin* woman married a *Damas*, another could quite possibly have married a *Jaucourt*. The *Jaucourts* and the *Monchanins* were Huguenots, which contributes to the plausibility, for much importance was attached to marrying in one's own Religion; and protestant gentlemen being rarer than catholic, it happened that the lords of the greatest houses, who did not wish to misally with respect to blood or opinions, married simple demoiselles. And they even did just as well when these young women were beautiful and good: one finds greater domestic bliss in making the fortune of one's wife than in receiving one's own from her.

M. *de Jaucourt* offered to assure my grandfather a situation by making him the steward of his lands in the Nivernais, the Charollais, and Burgundy. He gave my grandfather *six hundred francs* of the time, which today would be worth *thirteen hundred*; lodging; and the pleasures of life in the Château of *Brinon-les-Allemands*, the capital of the administration.

It is there that my Grandfather married Alexandrine du Rousset, the daughter of a doctor and herself knowledgeable in medicine, which enabled her to provide assistance to the inhabitants of the estate and, thus, made M. and Mme *de Monchanin* beloved. My Grandfather, moreover, was a good and just man. M. *de Jaucourt* had the same character. They were both blessed in the Region.

I know that through the *Pinette* we are allied to a family of the same name as one among the wood merchants that has a branch of rich Financiers. On the same side, we are also distant cousins of MM *Gudin*, who themselves by their Mother are distant cousins of M. *Le Noir*, and who have since become very closely linked to us through the marriage of *Gudin de la Ferlière* and my Sister. There is a bit of everything in Families: but one must know their relations. The foregoing account is based only on traditions concerning which MM *Gudin* and *de Monchanin* should have more information than I. I have not seen proofs of filiation.

My grandfather *de Monchanin* had four boys and two girls.

The oldest, *Louis de Monchanin*, who was said to be a man of intelligence, died young, as a medical student. This branch is extinguished.

This Family had no fortune at all. M. *de Jaucourt-Epénilles* was himself burdened with children and was not very well off. His protection had been exhausted in giving my grandfather the position of Steward. The MM *de Monchanin* were obliged to bend their pride and place themselves in apprenticeships to learn trades and to live from them.

The second of my uncles, *Alexandre de Monchanin*, was an engraver for clockmakers and mediocre at it. He nonetheless lived fairly honorably from this art. He was a most amiable man. In conversation he had grace and sparkle, was easy and noble: what was then called *to feel one's worth*. He married a pretty enough Widow, very small, who survived him and with whom he had no children. This branch is extinguished.

At the time, clockmaking and the arts that depended on it must have been taken to be very lucrative, for I see that both families to which I belong, confounded by numerous children, threw them into clockmaking and its subordinate professions. It is also natural that an art which requires instruction, artifice, intellect, ability, and which allows a certain luxury, should especially please young people who, obliged to work for a living, nonetheless retain some recollections of vanity and ambition. My third uncle, *Pierre de Monchanin*, became a clockmaker who specialized in making watch cases—a specialization that is closer to the goldsmith's craft or jewelry making than to true watchmaking.

M. *Pierre de Monchanin* was one of the most virtuous men I have known, and in my Memoirs I shall give you proofs of this virtue. He had little sparkle, but a great deal of judgment, wisdom, and solidity. The family proverb held that *my Mother had all the intellect and my uncle Pierre had all the good sense.* His brothers called him *the man of good sense,* and he justified the name: I should have called him *the man of good,* and the name would have been yet more justified.

When he was forty-two, he married *Marie Angélique Besnard* from an Orléanais family. Mlle *Besnard* had a brother who was a theatrical entrepreneur in Nancy and elsewhere and who used Fleury as his stage name. He is the Father of *Fleury* of the Comédie Française who is the nephew of my Aunt-in-Law, whom I have sometimes called my cousin out of courtesy, although he is not; for, since my attaining fortune, I have feared being accused of denying my origins: in addition, he is a very estimable fellow and actor.[7]

My uncle *Pierre* had a large number of children of whom there remains only *Pierre-Héléodore de Monchanin,* whose Patrimony consists of a thousand écus of income, who is employed in the national liquidation, and whom you know perfectly well.[8]

My fourth Uncle, *Etienne-Auguste de Monchanin,* had also been placed in clockmaking, but, less wise than his brother, he did not stick to it. He has been a man-at-arms, a gambler, and very much a libertine: that was called *sustaining nobility.* He lost an eye from a wound received in a quarrel. Finally, he went to England, placed himself in the service of the British East India Company, and was killed by the explosion of a bomb at the siege of Madras undertaken and lifted by M. de Lally.[9] At the time he was Captain aide-major. He was the worst rogue, or to be more precise, the only rogue of the family; and he is the only member of the family who may be said not to have derogated. You see what a strange institution *nobility* was.

Etienne-Auguste had much intellect and a brilliant quality but extreme immorality. He took an abominable pleasure in setting all his Relatives against each other and, having exercised this talent with respect to my Father and Mother, he caused such violent pain to the latter that, since she told me of her pain as I was growing up, I remember more than once, in my chivalric ideas, having conceived the ambition of going to India to fight my uncle.

In Switzerland, he had betrayed a large, beautiful, and vigorous girl from the region of Vaud whose name I do not recall. Disguised as a man, she followed him to England, forced him to take up his sword, wounded him, and got herself married. She was *formidable*; I knew her and I assure you that it could be said of her, as of Armide, *she was yet more lovable*.[10] As she grew older, she lost her very beautiful eyes; she went blind, and I fear that she has died. She lived at *Southwarck* with an intimate friend, Miss *Inkle*.

With her, my uncle had a son, *Etienne Louis de Monchanin*, who inherited some of the vices of his Father. He moved to Jamaica more than twenty-five years ago, and we have heard no mention of him since. His mother sought information about him in vain. It is likely, although not certain, that this branch is extinct.

The Family thus seems reduced to the branch of *Pierre de Monchanin*, which includes only one individual, *Pierre Héléodore*, and to our own, which is only a female branch.

The older of the *de Monchanin* Daughters was also the oldest child of *Héléodore de Monchanin* and of *Alexandrine du Rousset*. She was named *Françoise*. She was my Godmother. You saw her die at a very advanced age, having long outlived all her brothers and sisters. She was goodness, piety, economy, and generosity themselves. The poorest member of the family, she alone always assisted all the others, and she alone was capable of making substantial gifts: Stingy for herself, generous for others.

She did not have much intellect: like all the *Monchanins* and like all the *Du Ponts* (ponder this in order to fear it and correct it in yourselves, my children), she was extremely and unbearably opinionated; but she was one of the noblest hearts that Heaven has created.

After she had served as a second Mother to all her brothers she was without situation, without beauty, with a heavy Burgundian or Comtois figure, two enormous cheekbones, a square face, a snub nose, with the mediocre education that could be acquired in *Brinon-les-Allemandes*. So my Grand-Father again consulted M. and Mme *de Jaucourt-Epénilles*. He was told to send his oldest daughter to Paris, where the youngest was already; and, after mature deliberation, the lot of this daughter was to become *lady's maid* to Mademoiselle *de Jaucourt*, with whom her sister had been raised.

This sister, *Anne Alexandrine de Monchanin,* the youngest of the family, was my Mother. I shall speak to you of her at length in the following chapter.

Now, except for more detailed information that you may wish to obtain from your cousin *de Monchanin* about the family of my Mother and its filiation—a matter of small import to you today— you know as much as I about my two families and the individuals who belong to them.

When I get to your Mother, I shall write two parallel chapters on her two families, after which you will know all your Relatives. But you do not want me to get married yet; I am not yet born.

Notes

[1]To derogate was to forfeit nobility by entering retail trade or otherwise disgracing the noble estate, which originally had been that of bearing arms and which remained, in principle, untainted by such demeaning practices as working for a living or sullying one's hands with petty trade. On noble status, trade, and derogation, see Marcel Reinhard, "Élite et noblesse dans la seconde moitié du XVIIIe siècle," *Revue d'histoire moderne et contemporaine* (1956); H. Lévy-Bruhl, "La noblesse de France et le commerce," *Revue d'histoire moderne,* NS 8 (1933): 209–35; R. J. Grassby, "Social Structure and Commercial Enterprise under Louis XIV," *Economic History Review,* 2nd Series, 13 (1960): 19–38; Guy Richard, "Un aspect particulier de la politique économique et sociale de la monarchie au XVIIe siècle," *XVIIe siècle* 49 (1960): 11–41. For a general discussion of derogation, see Roland Mousnier, *Institutions of France,* pp. 131–34.

[2]Du Pont is referring to Anselme de Sainte-Marie (originally Pierre de Guibours, 1625–1694), *Histoire généalogique et chronologique de la maison royale de France, des pairs, grand officiers de la Couronne & de la Maison du Roy & des anciens barons du royaume* (Paris: par la Compagnie des Libraires, 1726–33).

[3]The Damas, from the Forez, constituted one of the most ancient and considerable families of the region from the eleventh to the nineteenth centuries. Among the principal historians of the family, some attach its origins to the period of the Crusades; others assign its origins to Languedoc or the Beaujolais. It is discussed by Father Anselme, vol. VII, pp. 316–42, and by La Chesnaye-des-Bois in his *Dictionnaire de la noblesse,* vol. IV, pp. 463–84. The Amanzé family held a barony that was raised to a viscounty in 1617 and subsequently to a county; they ranked among the most illustrious families of Burgundy. See *Généalogie des alliances de la maison d'Amanzé au comte de Mâçonnais dressée par d'Hozier, les preuves par Paillot* (Dijon, 1659). The Condé family (1530–1830), a branch of the house of

Bourbon, ranked at the very summit of the social hierarchy of the *ancien régime*. Princes of the blood and peers of the realm, the various Condés descended from Louis I de Bourbon, Prince de Condé (1530–1569), Pair de France, Marquis de Conti, Comte de Soissons, d'Anisy, de Valéry, de Roussy, Vicomte de Meaux et de Breteuil, Baron de La Ferté, Seigneur de Beaumont, Pierrepont, Ailly, Bellot en Brie, etc. The most illustrious of their galaxy had been Louis II de Bourbon, Prince de Condé (1621–1686), called the *Grand Condé*, who led the party of the princes during the Fronde. In claiming alliance to the Condés, however indirectly, Du Pont was claiming kinship with the most distinguished family in France, which his self-mockery acknowledges.

[4]H. A. du Pont, *The Early Generations of the Du Pont and Allied Families*, 2 vols. (New York, 1923) identifies the family Bible of which Du Pont speaks as having belonged to the Du Roussets, the family of his mother's mother, but indicates that it did not pass into possession of the Du Pont family; see pp. 458–59.

[5]H. A. du Pont, *Early Generations*, p. 459, identifies Le Grain as Jehan Baptiste Le Grain, Seigneur de Guyencourt and La Laye, councillor and master of requests of the house of Marie de Medicis, queen of France, and as the author of "several important contributions to the history of his time."

[6]Built between 1671 and 1676, the Invalides was designed to provide a hospital for soldiers wounded in the service of the king. Louis XIV outlined its purpose in the Edict of 24 May 1670 and a second, more detailed Edict of April 1674. At the time of the second one, work on the construction had proceeded far enough for the king himself to inaugurate the building. Héléodore de Monchanin's brother would have come there for the care and lodging to which he was entitled as a captain in the royal armies.

[7]Abraham-Joseph Bénard, called Fleury (1750–1822), enjoyed a reputation as one of the outstanding actors of his age and as one of the most celebrated of all times. A reversal of fortunes had caused his father to assume direction of a troupe of actors in Nancy and provided his start. Fleury came to Paris in 1778 and was immediately received as a member of the Comédie Française with which he remained, through its eventful history, until his retirement in 1818. J.-B. Laffitte published *Mémoires de Fleury, de la Comédie Française*, 6 vols. (1835–37) which he claimed to have drawn from notes and papers left by Fleury.

[8]By national liquidation, Du Pont means the "vente des biens nationaux," or sale of lands confiscated from the Church and the nobility who had emigrated. See Jacques Godechot, *Les Institutions de la France sous la Révolution et l'Empire*, 2nd ed. (Paris: Presses Universitaires de France, 1968), pp. 174–87.

[9]The Count of Lally-Tollendal served as commissioner-general of

all French troops in India during the Seven Years War. Despite his initial successes in the first months of 1758, he was forced to abandon his siege of Madras because British superiority at sea jeopardized his supplying his troops. In December 1758, he launched a final attempt to reduce Madras and gain a decisive victory over the British. His attempt failed and by February 1759, he was being beaten by the British and the French were being routed from India. See Walter L. Dorn, *Competition for Empire 1740–1763* (New York: Harpers, 1940; rev. 1963), pp. 367–69.

[10]Armide was the female protagonist of an opera, *Armide et Renaud*, by Jean-Baptiste Lully with a libretto by Philippe Quinault (1686). The opera, considered their masterpiece, was rescored by Gluck (1777) who also used Quinault's libretto. The subject derived from Tasso's *Jerusalem Delivered*. Marmontel also evokes Armide in his memoirs; see Jean-François Marmontel, *Mémoires*, 2 vols., ed. John Renwick (Clermont-Ferrand: G. de Bussac, 1972), I, pp. 38, 89, and 117. For a discussion of Lully's version, see Robert M. Isherwood, *Music in the Service of the King: France in the Seventeenth Century* (Ithaca and London: Cornell University Press, 1973), pp. 208–9 and 236–37.

3

My Father and Mother.

My Father, *Samuel Dupont,* born in Rouen in 1710, was a very handsome man of about five and a half feet, with brown hair and brows, blue eyes, admirable skin, and something about the nose and the cast of the face that recalled the late King Louis XV.

He was extremely dignified in all his movements, danced fairly well; bore arms to perfection, and played the flute passably. He had acquired these talents by the fruit of his labor, for his education had been entirely neglected. His penmanship was good, and he kept his account books well, but he had no knowledge of spelling and had not read widely.

I have told you that he was a clockmaker. He was *skillful,* in both meanings of the word: the one that he worked very fast, in a sure, free, and bold manner, such that the hand of the artist manifested itself with distinction; the other, that he knew how to make watches that ran perfectly, and even how to make a mediocre watch run fairly well. He did not give his work the degree of polish that I have seen in the work of some other artists and that I myself attained; but he was as good a clockmaker as they and I. For the point of this art is to make watches or clocks that tell precise time. The surplus is vainglory, which can be found in clockmaking as in all else, and which I ran after there, as in all else.

My Father did not lack intelligence; his mind even manifested accuracy and charm. But he was neither deep nor broad of spirit. He did not know how to master his passions. Good, generous, sensitive, carried away, angry, opinionated, with ardent courage and severe probity, yet a very easy mark for those who knew how to praise him: he loved women, treated them with delicacy and respect, and readily allowed himself to be governed by them. I shall not explain myself, at least not here, for it would be necessary to tell you everything about qualities and faults that his Son might have inherited from him.

My Mother had beauty without being precisely beautiful. She was especially distinguished by grace and goodness which, without in any way diminishing the nobility of her carriage and gesture, to the contrary, endowed them with infinite charm.

She was very well built. Her elegant bearing exceeded five feet and two inches. Her face was the most perfect oval. Her hair included three colors, brown, chestnut, and blond. Her brow was high, her eyebrows brown, her eyelashes black, her eyes blue. Her most agreeably proportioned mouth disclosed beautiful teeth in a smile that was in no way affected. The dimple that decorated her chin has passed to you, and I like to think that you will transmit it to your children. Her very white skin colored easily, too easily perhaps, with a modest blush at the least word of affection and with a brighter tone at anything that could shock the propriety for which her delicate soul had an exquisite feeling.

She demonstrated an extreme facility for learning anything rapidly and for executing well what she had just learned. All of her spoken and written expressions were at once appropriate, nervous, and brilliant. She joined a virtuous and profound reason to a character of the greatest tenderness and susceptibility to emotion. Capable of a heroic and constant friendship, her highly romantic heart did not allow her to consider any enterprise as above the strength of her courage and her spirit; it added much to the one and the other, and in this trait you will recognize your Father.

I so loved this excellent woman that every time I have felt myself in love, I have sought the ties of resemblance between her and the beauty who had become dear to me—in whom I pleased myself to imagine that it was still my mother that I loved. Alas! I am obliged to admit, to my shame, that most of those who led me into that illusion subsequently applied themselves to destroying it and to showing me by a painful experience that women like my mother are extremely rare.

You must not believe that this little marvel who became your grandmother emerged in all her perfection from M. and Mme *de Monchanin*, like Minerva fully armed from the head of Jupiter. From nature, she only received the germ of all that and two very precious gifts: that *of loving*, which ordinarily leads to that *of pleasing*.

M. and Mme *d'Epénilles* came to *Brinon*. Either some alliance really occurred between them and the *Monchanins*, or they only wanted to reward materially some honest servant who was distinguished by his birth, the probity of his zeal, and his exactitude. Whatever the reason, they displayed great kindness for the Steward's children.

This art of rewarding essential services was one of the advantages of the chivalric spirit and the life of the manor—the currency of the soul—that our erstwhile lords, when they were good, minted well and that that of nickel or paper will never equal.[1]

The little *Anne Alexandrine* was singularly touched by the caresses of Mme *d'Epénilles*. She developed a passion for this lady. She herself was so demonstrative, so naive, so pretty, that she readily made agreeable and touching replies. She wept with so much sensibility, she laughed with such good grace, she so pleased Mme *d'Epénilles* and Mlle *de Jaucourt*, her daughter, who was about the same age as *Alexandrine*, that none of them wanted to be separated from her. They put her in the carriage, took her to Paris, and Mme *d'Epénilles*, who was raising her own children herself, also condescended to raise my Mother.

Never was anyone better brought up. From this upbringing emerged the *Marquis de Jaucourt*, the grandfather of those of today, a man of such goodness and loyalty that his memory is still revered; the *Chevalier de Jaucourt* who went to Holland to study medicine under Boerhaave because he preferred science to vanity, and who has since worked on the *Encyclopedia*; Mlle de Jaucourt celebrated for the brilliance of her mind; and my mother to whom I owe the little I am worth.[2]

Mme *d'Epénilles* gave her much instruction as well as the taste, the need, and the talent to acquire still more. She also gave my mother the habit of judging all actions by moral principles—to put honesty above all else, and then glory.

Do not be surprised, my children, if I know some details of the education of my mother; it was by recounting her own that she educated me. She thus simultaneously satisfied her feelings of gratitude and her desire to shape my heart. I remember at the age of four, when I wanted to be especially happy, I pulled my little chair close to that of my mother and said to her: *Maman, this evening let us chat a little about Mme d'Epénilles.* That excellent woman educated two generations, for I was also her pupil.

I know not, if, as my parents said, I have the honor of belonging to the *de Jaucourts* by any other title than that of descendant of their very zealous and virtuous servants, but I shall always retain a memory of their family such that I cannot hear the name of *Jaucourt* without a small tear's welling to the brim of my eye. I cannot tell you with what joy I saw one of the youngest of them display the most assiduous zeal of our most distinguished luminaries in the provincial assembly of the Ile de France and subsequently earn himself attention in the national Legislative Assembly for his courage, his eloquence, his love of the constitution that we had all sworn to uphold and that deprived him and his of so many advantages. Nor can I tell you how I trembled when I learned that his patriotism had endangered his life—how much, in the midst of my personal dangers, my soul was relieved to learn that he had evaded his assassins.

One of the greatest misfortunes that can befall a young girl is to be raised in a family richer and more illustrious than her own, as a child of the house; to develop pride and a taste for opulence; and then to be sent away—as almost always happens in accordance with the destiny that normally would have resulted from the actual station of her parents. I have seen several very vexatious examples. In such a case, rich people believe they have been beneficent: in fact they only procured for themselves, for a number of years, a doll that pleases them. But they gave her a soul. *The soul of the doll* is torn in a hundred ways once she has lost *her little Stipend.* I would invite those who raise pretty, poor children in their houses to think of this. Do they have the desire and the power to make them rich? Then they do well. Do they wish to return them to their poverty, or even to a mediocre station? They prepare them for a moment the bitterness of which cannot be expressed.

That is exactly what my Mother experienced. When she had turned fifteen, it was decided that she could no longer be the companion of Mlle *de Jaucourt.* She had to be taught that Mlle *de Jaucourt* was not her sister; that she would not ever be *a friend.* She had to tear her heart out in seeing that Mme *d'Epénilles* was no longer, could no longer be her mother. She had to undergo all the little signs of growing coolness that accompany the passage from motherhood to friendship, from friendship to goodwill, from goodwill to a cold and sterile protection. My nerves stiffen to think of it.[3]

My Mother was offered the prospect of remaining in the house as a *chamber maid*. Half of her heart would have wished to do so. She would have done it for Mme *d'Epénilles*. On her knees, she asked to be allowed to do so, provided that it be "*to serve my respectable mother! oh! in any way possible,*" she said, "*even at a station inferior to that which is proposed, if I may.*" But to become the chamber maid of her little companion, who never tired of being haughty . . . after having shared a room with her! Revolted pride, outraged friendship, prompted my mother to say: *no no!** She preferred to learn a trade, or at least she sought independence. Leaves were taken very coldly by those who had loved each other tenderly; and my Mother left the hotel de Jaucourt collapsed in tears, suffocating with sighs and sobs.

Her brother *Alexandre* took her in and showed her how to manipulate a graving scissors. A neighboring clockmaker, delighted to be able to teach something to a bright and beautiful young girl, gave her advice on the art of fashioning metals. She learned to make watch hands with such perfection that so long as she made them, she had no equal at the task. I still recognize hands made by my mother on watches from that period.

When she had learned how to work, her Sister-in-Law insisted that she no longer live in the same apartment, which was perhaps too small. They rented her a room in the house; her bed was placed there, along with three chairs . . . and her work table. No tapestry, a mirror worth six sols, no superfluous piece of furniture. So she was installed there on her own on the fourth floor, in Harlay Street near the Palais.[4] Oh! How far was the hotel de Jaucourt!

My mother closed the door, turned the locks, lay down on the floor, and, in her first sorrow, equally irritated with Madame *d'Epénilles*, with Mademoiselle *de Jaucourt*, with her brother *Alexandre*, with her *Sister-in-Law*, she resolved to die of hunger. She was about sixteen.

Having set her course, she reopened her door, came and went from her brother's, so as to arouse no suspicion, worked, sang— and spent five days without eating, drinking only sugared water. For even in despair the soft habits of luxury persisted.

Happily for her, my Father lodged in the house. Twenty-six

---

*Her sister was less difficult. But she had not been raised in Paris; she had perhaps been a bit jealous to see *Anne Alexandrine* taken there, and it is possible that entering the hotel de Jaucourt in any capacity, at the moment at which her sister left in a kind of disgrace, she believed that she was in some way succeeding her.

years old, at the height of his powers, mounting the stairs like a bird, making weapons like the god Mars in a room that the windows of Mlle *de Monchanin* overlooked. Nothing is so salutary for a young woman who wishes to die as the perpetual vision of a young man in perfect health. My Mother ate. Her long fast and her tears had altered her bosom. Perhaps her life had been invaded, but soon no external appearance remained.

My Father had also paid attention to his amiable neighbor.

Between a very handsome young man who made watches well and was also the first worker of *Julien le Roi*, a neighbor who engraved them so-so, not too badly, and the Sister of this neighbor who, with the most beautiful hand in the world, made watch hands perfectly, there developed a liaison as well as a close understanding. But the outcome was somewhat delayed.[5]

A Genevan, M. *Galatin*,[6] who came from one of the families that considered themselves Patrician because they had almost exclusively occupied the governmental positions in Geneva and had moreover, enriched themselves as much through commerce as through the loans they made to France, England, and all borrowing nations, saw Mlle de *Monchanin*, loved her, asked for her, and, being rich, obtained all the suffrages that were not decisive. My uncle promptly wrote to my grandfather, who had the sense to reply: "I shall give no consent if my daughter does not request it herself."

M. *Galatin* had intelligence and education. My Mother was always somewhat impressed by intelligence. But, all things considered, she deemed that my Father had even more intelligence in his eyes and in the pride of his movements than M. *Galatin* had received from nature or had been able to draw from his studies. The letter that M. Galatin requested for Papa was refused. M. *Galatin* was very much in love: he turned away, drew his sword, and passed it through his body. My Mother cried aloud; my uncle came running; M. *Du Pont* came running. They picked up M. *Galatin*. His wound was not dangerous, but my Father was touched to the quick to see that his rivals were treated in this way—and his rivals who were rich and patrician, or pretended to be so in Geneva.

Such great adventures ripen Romances like hot wax. My mother wrote to her Father, but in favor of M. *Du Pont*. M. *de Monchanin* who had a just spirit, a firm character that transcended prejudices and reverses—who had himself placed his sons in trades, who perfectly understood the state to which the family was reduced—sent his consent without difficulty.

And, in truth, Mlle *de Monchanin,* believing herself noble like the King, raised like a Princess, firmly convinced that she was the Relative of protectors who had abandoned her, but in love and possessing nothing in the world, made an excellent match in marrying the man whom she loved: a young artist of distinguished talent, superb figure, respected honesty, graceful mind, descendant, it was said, of a *Maitre des Comptes,*[7] and certainly the younger son of an honest merchant of Cauldrons.

Notes

[1]Here, Du Pont seems to be directly echoing the nostalgic feudalism of Mirabeau's prephysiocratic thought. Cf. Mirabeau's description of the feudal proprietor: "If he is at the head of production, of which he should naturally be the soul, and in which no one has a greater interest than he, he assures and enlivens the whole canton, he protects the isolated agriculturalist. . . ." Or, "The poor, the sick were succored at the castle; the orphans found their subsistence there and became domestics. There was, in a word, a direct rapport from the lord to his subject and, in consequence, more ties and fewer irritants on one side and the other. . . ." Victor de Riqueti, Marquis de Mirabeau, *L'Ami des hommes ou traité de la population,* ed. M. Rouxel (Paris, 1883), p. 81 and p. 62. The original edition of *L'Ami des hommes* carried on its title page Avignon, 1756; in fact, it appeared in mid-1757. Cf. the chapter on Mirabeau in my *The Origins of Physiocracy: Economic Revolution and Social Order in Eighteenth-Century France* (Ithaca and London: Cornell University Press, 1976).

[2]The Chevalier de Jaucourt was born into a noble Protestant family that had decided to remain in France after the revocation of the Edict of Nantes. Under a veneer of conformity and submission and by accepting the formalities of baptism and marriage in the Catholic Church, they were able to pass unobserved and transmit their patrimony. Various relatives of the chevalier also had chosen exile. But his family, while avoiding the society of the court, enjoyed a worldly and agreeable life in the company of intelligent and influential friends such as the Broglie and Lamoignon families. The mother of de Jaucourt, Marie de Monginot, had tried to transmit her solid Protestant convictions to her fourteen children and her protégée, the future mother of Du Pont. Drawing on this background, the chevalier, Louis de Jaucourt (1704–1780), had completed his studies in Geneva. His most recent biographer concludes that he wrote in all 17,395 articles (28 percent of the total) for the *Encyclopédie,* whereas Diderot wrote only 5,842 (10 percent). Some of his many articles were *Généalogie, Noblesse, Respect, Seigneur, Femme (droit nat.), Impôt,* and *Vénalité des Charges.* See Madeleine F. Morris, *Le Chevalier de Jaucourt: un ami de la terre (1704–1780)* (Geneva:

Librairie Droz, 1979). Hermann Boerhaave (1668–1738), with whom de Jaucourt studied medicine, was one of the most famous doctors of his time. Following 1714, he held the chair in Medicine at the University of Leiden. Boerhaave, who taught a kind of medical Newtonianism, also had a strong influence on the medical and metaphysical work of François Quesnay. See Peter Gay, "The Enlightenment as Medicine and as Cure," in *The Age of the Enlightenment: Studies Presented to Theodore Besterman* (Edinburgh and London, 1967), and the chapter on Quesnay as physician and metaphysician in my *Origins of Physiocracy*.

[3]According to B. G. du Pont, *Du Pont de Nemours*, 2 vols. (Newark, DE: 1933), I, pp. 2–3, the Jaucourts were not wealthy and could not afford to keep her in the family unless she undertook some work.

[4]The Palais de Justice on the Ile de la Cité. The rue Harlay runs roughly north-south along the western edge of the Palais de Justice between the Quai des Orfèvres and the Quai de l'Horloge.

[5]This paragraph apparently was added during a subsequent revision of the manuscript. It is squeezed in at the bottom of the page in a smaller hand and written with a finer pen than the paragraphs that precede and follow it.

[6]The Gallatins (Du Pont misspells the name) were a powerful and influential Genevan family that included bankers, members of the city government, a director of the French mails in Geneva, an army officer in France, and Albert Gallatin, who would have a distinguished career in the new United States. Since Du Pont gives no first name, it is not possible to identify Anne Alexandrine's suitor precisely, although he might have been Abraham Gallatin, the director of the French mails in Geneva who died in 1762; André Sarasin Gallatin, a lawyer and syndic in Geneva who died in 1750; or possibly François-Begon Gallatin, an officer in France who died in 1745. See Herbert Lüthy, *La Banque Protestante en France de la révocation de l'Édit de Nantes à la Révolution*, 2 vols. (Paris: SEVPEN, 1961).

[7]The Maitres des Comptes were the top-ranking officials of the Chambre des Comptes which, like the Parlement and the Conseil du Roi, had developed out of the old royal court. The Chambre des Comptes had the special responsibility to oversee the conservation of the royal *demesne*, the administration of finances, the verification of the accounts of all royal agents. It rivaled the Parlement in its claims to being the oldest royal court and retained the right to register various edicts and declarations concerning the royal *demesne*, letters of ennoblement, naturalization, legitimation, and matters concerning fairs, markets, and fiefs held from the crown. There were twelve Chambres des Comptes including that of Paris. Du Pont's father presumbly would have claimed descent from a member of the Chambre des Comptes of Normandy. The officers of the Chambres

des Comptes enjoyed important privileges, including nobility and exemption from a variety of public charges—*tailles, corvées, péages, aides,* and the obligation to lodge soldiers. See Marcel Marion, *Dictionnaire des institutions de la France aux XVII et XVIIIe siècles* (1923, repr. Paris: A. & J. Picard, 1969), and Roland Mousnier, *Institutions of France.*

4

My First Childhood.

I was born in Paris on the 14th of December 1739, and I was not the first fruit of my mother's loves. She had had another son who died at the wet nurse's while she was pregnant with me. I regret this, for a brother is both a friend and a natural support. You are in a position to know, my children, that brotherhood, joined to friendship, is very sweet; the tie is so great that we call our friends *brothers* when nature has refused us brothers in our family.

I have been told that my brother was as beautiful as an angel. I am altogether put out that this did not pass on to your Father, but I leaned toward the features of the Monchanins, which are strong rather than agreeable. Except for the hair, and no one today would know that mine had been beautiful, something about the eyes of my Mother's expression, and the skin that has always been good in our families, no one who looked at me would judge that I was born of a very handsome man and a very beautiful woman.

It was not entirely nature's fault. It had not yet become established practice for mothers in the city to nurse their own children; *Rousseau* had not yet become the benefactor of the early years of human life. My mother, desolate from the loss of her first child, was determined to nurse me. My Father did not wish her to undertake this duty: even before my birth I was the excuse for their first quarrel, and unfortunately I became the subject of many more. My aunt, older than my Mother and almost her half-Mother, supported my Father.[1] Maternal love, not yet developed, surrendered to their combined forces of love and friendship, and what we call reason. My mother worked, and her work was hardly less lucrative than that of my Father. The young household had little additional fortune; the loss of half its income carried weight in the mouth of my Aunt, all the more since my Father refrained from speaking of it. It is so sweet for a generous and sensitive woman to help her lover, her husband, and to enrich him rather than being a drain. It was decided that a nurse would be found in the suburbs of Paris, that she would be very well paid, and that I would be visited [by my parents] every Sunday, for it was necessary to work the other days of the week. It was believed that a good choice had been made: it was so bad that the robust temperament I had received from a thirty-year old man and a twenty-year-old woman, both equally beautiful, strong, and healthy, was crushed by the detestable regimen of the first months of my life. My natural strength barely saved me from death.[2]

I have frequently been told that I was born with extraordinary size and vigor, that my Mother spent three days in labor pains, even though I was her second son, and, what is yet more singular, that at birth I had a mustache that fell off after a few weeks.

My nurse was neither good, nor caring, nor attached to me; she was not even clean, although she pretended to be the day that my parents were supposed to come. She left me consumed in screams, which are very dangerous for irascible dispositions. She had no milk and gave me only pap, a very unhealthy food that my perpetual cries prevented me from digesting. From indigestion to indigestion, from pain and anger to pain and anger, I fell into emaciation; I became atrociously thin; I grew rickety. After six months, my mother carried me back, dying in her arms and bathed in her tears.

The doctor, to spare her the spectacle of my last sighs, advised sending me to the country, and I was placed at *Savigny sur Orge* with a Mother *Quillou.*

I remember her and even her face; I remember having been to the cabaret with her husband; I remember having seen their son in a soldier's uniform, having seen him kill a pig whose cries and blood filled me with fear and horror; but above all I remember having drunk a great deal of milk in their house. It was principally with milk, first cut and then pure and in abundance, that this good woman began my recuperation. I regained some weight and a little strength; but I remained knotted and lame, and continued so until the age of seven.

A second accident harmed my development. The first attentions of the Mother *Quillou* had been so happy that everyone judged that I should be left with her for a long time and, if necessary, and if it were possible, until I became completely unknotted. I was a good little child, very sensitive, very caressing, and I frequently caressed my Father nurse. He loved me tenderly and brandy passionately. To unite his two inclinations, he took me with him when he went to drink and always gave me a small taste, saying that it would make *my beard grow*, that it would make me *strong*, and that it would make a *man* of me. I think that at first brandy must have seemed pretty bad to me.

But I wanted very much to become a *man*, to be *strong*, to have a *beard*; the great laughs and applause of Father *Quillou* when I drank without grimacing flattered my pride (cursed pride that seizes us in the cradle, only to leave us at death!), and I accustomed myself to spirits. The alcohol burned me: the friendship for the husband destroyed all the good effects of the milk the wife lavished on me. I became thin again, I was perishing for a second time; no one could understand why.

The reason was finally discovered, when, during a little trip to Paris, hearing brandy mentioned, I asked for some saying *it was very good and that Papa* Quillou *gave me some every day*. I was quickly withdrawn from *Papa Quillou's*; and began to taste the sweetness of living with my mother.

I was not quite three years old; I limped severely; I was very small and very weak.

You know, my dear children, one of my mottos, namely, that *with respect to the things that happen to us, God alone knows if they are advantageous or harmful to us*.

It is possible that the physical accidents that endangered my early childhood greatly contributed to forming my moral character.

I could only walk with difficulty, and I was very delicate. I was thus constrained to be sedentary, to seek pleasure in my Mother's conversation, in little games that only exercised the head and fingers, or in reading. I do not remember having learned to read; it seems to me that I knew how to read as soon as I was close to my mother. She has told me that she had very little trouble in showing me and that I took no more than three months to move from my abc's to the moment when I began to read with interest. I thus became diligent, studious, capable of reasoning. Always under the hand of a sensitive, cultured, and philosophical woman who loved me to excess, I became loving like her, and like her romantic. In a body that could barely sustain itself, an ardent soul already began to vent itself. Fairy Tales always presented me with a hero who was showered with benefits for having behaved humanely to a small animal; and when I had given sugar to a fly, opened the cage of a bird, set a mouse free, I did not doubt that I should be awakened one morning by a beautiful lady who would transform me into a *great prince*; and as I fell asleep, I dreamed of the good that I would do, of the milk that I would give to all the little girls and little boys who would have been good, as soon as I became *Prince*.

My Mother needed literature. She wanted to shape my Father as well as me; she read to us and made me read Novels, Poetry, travel literature, Plays. She read perfectly and trained me to read better than I did by telling me that I read well. I spent my days at the foot of her work table or that of my Father. Thus I lived only with great men, Kings, ministers, beautiful ladies, and valiant knights.

I dreamed only of the exploits that I should accomplish one day: of the ways in which I would supplement that which I lacked in bodily strength with wit, with presence of mind, with courage, with skill in battle—and with an intrepid devotion to death. I remember having been seriously preoccupied with how I should vanquish the white bear that devoured the companion of Captain *Beerens* on the ice of Spitsberg.[3]

Having no company but my mother, loving her to idolatry, I told her all my little thoughts, all the dreams of my precocious and delirious imagination; she encouraged and praised me; and even when she scolded me, it was always with a seasoning of praise: what I had said or had done that was bad was not worthy of a good child who wanted to be loved, was not worthy of a child destined to become a great man. Such were almost all the formulas of my Mother's remonstrances: she excessively stimulated me with virtue; she intoxicated me with sensibility; she whipped me with vanity, with glory and ambition. She always spoke to me of the Maréchal de *Besons*, the grandson of the draper; of the Maréchal *Fabert*, son of a small bookseller from Provence; of the general *Rose* who began as a simple soldier; of the Maréchal de *Catinat*, who had

A wonder in the heavens, and how we caught a bear.

begun as a lawyer before the Parlement; of the Chevalier de *l'Hôpital*, son of a Jewish doctor; of *Romée de Villeneuve*, a poor pilgrim
who became minister and legislator; of *King Alfred*, who had been
a street musician for a time; of *Gustavus Vasa* in the mines of Dal-
ecarlie; of *Descartes* with Queen *Christina*; of *Leibniz* giving lessons
to princesses; of *Puffendorf* and of *Wolf*, who became barons of the
Empire by virtue of their learning.[4] She made me read *Corneille* and
dwell on these verses:
"*Je ne dois qu'à moi seul toute ma renommée, . . .*
"*A l'exemple des dieux, j'ai fait beaucoup de rien . . .*
"*ma valeur est ma race, et mon bras est mon Père . . .*"[5]
And then she spoke to me of her *race*.

    She did not dip my body in the Styx, for it was not yet strong
enough.[6] She raised my soul to the clouds and watered it with
ambrosia. You will see something of this in the Portrait that you
have and that was done when I was six, in which, although the
resemblance is mediocre, the eyes are not childlike but thoughtful,
proud, tender.

Today I cannot hide from myself that my Mother cultivated glorious and vain passions in me, giving me motivation and defects, sacrificing me to her own regrets and her own weaknesses. She was humiliated, without daring to admit it, by being reduced to work with her hands in order to live, and to be only the wife of a worthy artist, though she always sought, both by love and by pride, to raise and make something of her husband. She always had the prejudices of the nobility, as she had their manners and apparent grandeur. On her son she sowed the last grain of her disappointed hopes and of her chimeras of novels; she prepared him for every kind of enterprise, but also for every kind of ridicule and vanity.

I remember having learned much that amounted to nothing. My Father, not being what the rules of the guilds called *Apprentice of the city*, had not yet been accepted as a *master clockmaker* to open a shop. He had brought a *Privilège* from the *Prévôté de l'Hôtel*, which conferred the title of *clockmaker of the King*, although one was not, and which added to this *title* a right of *commitimus* and the right to *bear the sword*. I practically do not dare tell you how idiotically proud I was of these fine advantages. I considered my Father *an Officer of the Crown*, and, seeing him wear the *sword*, which was not permitted to his fellow master clockmakers, I believed him almost *noble*. My Mother had to speak to me of another kind of nobility to beat back this smoke, but it was only by another more dangerous smoke.

All children are extremely susceptible to vanity; I have noticed in the countryside that the son of the *Bellringer* is always a proud little bloke since his father makes noise in the village, fights off what he believes to be the lightning he attracts, and calls together the citizens at his will.

My Victor, born to be of distinguished merit, an excellent creature, gentle, good—gifted with a just spirit and ready talent— thought he was lost and would have been if our good fortune had not ruined us. He irresponsibly went through *forty thousand francs* because I was noble, a king, lord of a fief, councillor of state, working with ministers. He thought it beneath him to observe order and economy, not to throw money through windows, to be worth something on his own, and not to expect everything from my credit; today I believe that the nonexistence of my credit, the loss of my fortune, the danger that may come from belonging to me, and the progress of his reason entirely corrected him—and I return to my story.

Toward the age of five, I completed the spoiling of my face

by falling and breaking the cartilage of my nose, which made me more snubnosed than I should have been and removed the only trait I had inherited from my Father's family.

A more serious woe and my first moral sorrow happened to me at about the same period. It was a painful sense of jealousy that gripped me when my Sister was brought home from her nurse.

The care and attention, which I had for so long had the exclusive privilege of receiving, not only had to be shared—which I should have found fair enough (for I myself had an inclination to caress my sister and offer her the honors of the household)—but gravitated to her by preference. That was perfectly reasonable, for it was a question of accustoming her to the paternal house, which initially appears as an exile to any honest child who is removed from her benefactress, and who is delivered over to unknowns who appear to usurp the titles of *Papa* and *Maman*. I could not understand this last point, nor this motive of which I had no idea.

I therefore judged, in conformity with my high opinion of the sagacity and equity of my mother, that my sister must be a charming child since she received even more caresses than I. There I was, disposed to imitate the others, to join them in celebrating the little Sister with whom I was told to play, and who was also supposed to play with me.

I did not know how *to play*—or knew only at most to make castles of cards, roll checkers on a checker board, and make little columns of them; I had not even been allowed to throw a ball into the air, nor an Indian chestnut, except on a walk; in the house it was feared that I would break a window or the work of my Father and Mother, whose work room I never left. My greatest joy was an edition of *La Fontaine* with a print for each fable, and the little discussions I made on the Wolf, the Fox, the Lamb, the Ox, the Grasshopper: what I learned of natural history came from the pictures of these animals.[7] I took my *La Fontaine* to my Sister and wanted to explain a picture to her; she tore it up with a single gesture! She was two and I five.

I concluded, but did not understand why, that she did not like the pictures.

I asked her if she knew *Pibrac's* quatrains.[8] She looked at me with large eyes: my own fixed upon her no less large.

Finally I brought her my entire little library—the Fairy Tales, the Etrenne mignonne, etc. and told her to choose, that these were my most beautiful books.[9]

She threw everything on the ground, and I discovered that she did not know how to read.

My manners bored her, she cried, and she then made a mess around the room.

I discovered that there is nothing more hateful in the world than a little girl, that *it* is stupid, impolite, cursed, dirty, and that one had to have lost one's mind, one's sense, and all judgment to caress it from choice when there are little boys who chatter like a Parrot, who draw direct copies of prints, who distinguish between a dromedary, and an elephant, who read very well all the most beautiful stories in the world, who know at the tip of their fingers all of Pibrac's quatrains and fifty of La Fontaine's fables and to whom one cannot mention one without their citing several verses.

I became jealous and unhappy. My mother told me *"that it is evil to be jealous,"* *"that I should love my little sister."* I do not want to do *evil*; I want even less to cause my beloved Mother *unhappiness*. To the best of my ability I master the external signs of jealousy. I make more advances and caresses to my Sister, and I continued to believe that those she receives from me and others were pitifully, detestably misplaced.

My heart was bursting; all my tender and vain passions burned acutely in my soul, which was already afire in my little body, itself deprived of strength and corrupted with bile; they disorder my stomach and set fire to my entrails. I am put to bed having developed a putrid, inflammatory, malignant forty-day fever that put me at the edge of the grave.

My danger rivets my Mother to my bedside, restores me to her sweet caresses and all those penetrating words on which my health depended. They recall me to life. I recovered. Illness forms and matures the soul, especially the souls of children. My sister was also acquiring form and becoming more lovable; I was not jealous of the friendship she received, but of the slight edge of preference that I thought was my due and that my swollen heart paid for dearly. I believed that I had reconquered my due during my convalescence; priding myself on erasing the memory of my wrongs, I showered my sister with the marks of an affection that had become sincere and has persisted for thirty years without change.

To complete my recovery, my Mother felt obliged to take me to spend some time with my grandmother *Du Pont* at *La Robinette*. I was put in pants. I was given a sword eight inches long, as was then the fashion for children, and this weapon turned the head of the Little Prince of the Fairy Tales with joy. We left for Rouen. We lodged with M. *Compigné*, a wealthy dealer in fancy toys, a friend of my Father. I was not quite six years old. M. Compigné had a son a little more than eight who promptly became my intimate companion. *A chick arrived* . . . a little girl of four and a half, very pretty. Ah! that one did not lead me to say that little girls were accursed! She was called Mademoiselle *Colineau*. She preferred me to *Compigné*, whom she had previously called *her husband*. I still limped a little; I was far weaker than my comrade, but I spoke much better and with a bookish language that was altogether dazzling in the provinces. Moreover, every day I gave Mademoiselle *Colineau* bouquets. I brought her all the candies with which my Father's friends and relatives filled my pockets, and I wrote four very bad little verses for her, the first to come from my brain, but which breathed a thought as true as my age and my heart.

Compigné, who at first had been very complacent, became annoyed that the Parisian had taken over the little friend and told me so. I claimed, like M. *Pincé*, that he was wrong for three reasons: first, that he had ceded her to me; second, that she was mistress of her tastes and her will; and above all that I would not suffer anyone to contest me anything with respect to her. *Compigné*, stronger than I, pushed me to the ground under the eyes of Mademoiselle *Colineau* herself. I have since seen something similar in the Ariosto.[10] Oh! fury! I ran to my sword; *Compigné* also seized his; I descended on him more rapidly than anyone could intervene, I wounded him; we were separated; and there I was, as in love, as insane as a little boy can be. There I was, more convinced than ever that all my romanesque thoughts were true and that no one would ever be able to resist *my sword*.

Mademoiselle *Colineau* died in childhood. I am convinced that had she lived I would have loved her all my life, for she was very grateful for my battle, and, independent of all natural inclination, I have been enchained by *being shown gratitude*.

It was during this voyage to Normandy that I saw my grandmother, my uncle *Nicolas*, who was called *Colin*—a name that appeared admirable to me because of its relation to that of *Colineau*—and another group of my relatives. *La Robinette*, with its courtyard planted with trees, its little wood, appeared to me a beautiful château and a considerable estate. Since my grandmother had work horses, and since in Paris I had only seen Lords, or those who appeared such, with horses, I judged that my family was more important than my mother had told me and the *Du Ponts* did not seem as much lower than the *de Monchanins* as she thought. But then I counted on raising them much higher.

My undoing was completed by these daydreams that simultaneously electrified the soul and the body; by the illness; by my serious little battle; by the fake battles I was drawn into by several officers who came to the house and, having been told my story, delighted in teasing me; by the voyage; by the countryside; by the races that I had begun to engage in. Between six and seven I stopped limping, and the strength of my temperament regained the upper hand from my early youth. The only physical effect that remained was a failure to attain the height of my parents, for which I had been born and which my children have recovered and surpassed, and to have knuckles and joints a little larger than they should have been. But my head, my neck, my shoulders, my kidneys once again became those of a robust man, and I know no one who endures better than I the fatigues of work, of many late nights, and of passion.

To satisfy the ambition of my Mother, I had to receive a stronger and more classical education than she could give me. She knew French perfectly; she read and understood English and Italian; she did not know Latin.

She took two precautions: the first to prepare me well ahead of time to leave her to go to school, as I would do to go to war like a Spartan who, the more he loves his Mother, the more he seeks to honor her name and deserve her esteem. In truth, I needed this preparation, for leaving my Mother struck me as the greatest unhappiness; I should have liked to have spent my days at her feet with my head on her knees, listening to her talk and telling her *"Maman, how I love you!"*

The second precaution was more painful and in one way more serious. It entailed convincing my Father to let me study. He made a fuss about his wife's intelligence and learning. Out of affection for her he saw a few literary people, but he had a deep prejudice against any literary profession.

He had seen several of his friends sent to the Bastille; he had seen others living in poverty. He had seen the worthy *Toussaint,* with whom he was closely associated, and who wrote the book *Des*

Moeurs, exposed to the twin dangers of misery and Prison.[11] In his view, a trade could provide the only good guarantee of peace and subsistence. He was not entirely wrong, but I had to spend fifty years and successively put my finger on all the keys of life to return to his opinion, which my Mother never shared.

He feared that with my taste for reading and my already distinct leaning toward Poetry I should not wish to follow his art. He saw nothing higher than his files, than his wheel, than his shop and his appointment—which he counted on leaving to me. *"When your son has studied,"* he said to my Mother, *"he will disdain all this."* Events confirmed his premonition completely.

My Father did not want his children to rise above his station. He had noticed my mother's very profound desire for such promotion and the more acute this desire appeared to him, the more a natural sentiment of dignity opposed to his wife's dreams of nobility inspired in him a repugnance for everything that would lead me to such a result. He had learned two verses that he quoted to my mother, the literary one:
"Et qu'un riche marchand fasse un fils Conseiller
Ce fils en le voyant craint de s'encanailler."[12]

The two verses shocked my ears, for I felt that I should always love and respect my Father, and that I was devoured with the desire to leave, to make him himself leave, his station, so deeply inferior to that of the great men whose stories I had read. Thus I saw in his citation only that it was possible *for a merchant to make, if he so pleased, his son a counsellor* and I found it very hard, very ridiculous, *that it did not so please* my Father.

Finally, to the happiness of myself and my Mother, he had the opportunity to establish relations with a well-known master of a boarding school, like him born in Rouen and whom he had known in his childhood. It was M. *Viard* who brought strong support to my mother's projects, saying *"that it would be terrible not to cultivate my disposition a bit; that I should not be pushed further than my Father should want; that my health was beginning to be restored; that playing with little comrades would be altogether salutary for me, that I should simultaneously shape my mind and my body."*

My Father thus consented to put me to board with M. *Viard,* under the particular condition that I should not be taught to make verses—as if that were something that could be taught! *Nasceintur Poetae.*

Notes

[1]According to B. G. du Pont, *Du Pont de Nemours*, 2 vols. (Newark, DE: 1933), I, p. 2, Anne-Alexandrine's sister Françoise was seventeen years older than she and had been something of a second mother to her.

[2]The second half of the eighteenth century was characterized by a mounting campaign in favor of mothers' nursing their own children. See among many Marie-France Morel, "Ville et campagne dans le discours médical sur la petite enfance au XVIIIe siècle," *Annales E.S.C.* 32, no. 5 (September-October 1977): 1007–24, and especially George Sussman, *Selling Mothers' Milk: The Wetnursing Business in France 1715–1914* (Urbana: University of Illinois Press, 1982).

[3]By Captain Beerens, Du Pont means Captain Willem Barents, a Dutch explorer who made three voyages to the Arctic in 1594, 1595, and 1596, on the last of which he reached and discovered Spitsbergen. On this voyage, his ship was crushed in the ice off the northern tip of the island Novaya Zemlya, and the survivors spent a winter of great misery. In the spring, they set out for Russia in open boats, but Barents himself perished. Gerrit de Veer, *The Three Voyages of William Barents to the Arctic Regions (1594, 1595, and 1596)*, 2nd ed., ed. Lieutenant Koolemans Beynen (London: Hakluyt Society, 1876), includes Charles T. Beke's introduction to the first Hakluyt Society edition (1853), which provides a history of de Veer's account; this was first published in Dutch at Amsterdam in 1598, and Barents himself probably wrote the narrative of the first voyage which de Veer did not go on. An abbreviated version of de Veer's work was published in French by Constantin de Renneville, as *Recueil des voyages qui ont servi à l'établissement et aux progrès de la Compagnie des Indes orientales, formée dans les provinces unies des Pays Bas*, 6 vols. (Amsterdam, 1702, 1710, 1716, 1725, and 1754). Du Pont probably read one of these editions. The nineteenth-century Hakluyt Society edition contains reprints of the illustrations that accompanied the original Dutch edition; the original French edition, first published in folio in 1598, also included them. Two of the prints especially germane to Du Pont's account are entitled: "A wonder in the heavens, and how we caught a bear" and "How a bear came unto our boat and what took place with him." I have not been able to verify that the plates also were included in the abridged French editions, one of which Du Pont likely read, but his text suggests that he might have seen them. They apparently captured the mixed spirit of fantasy and adventure that also informed his imagination at this period.

[4]Du Pont's mother's catalogue of the heroes whose careers he should ponder and emulate included men who had risen from humble origins. Jacques Bazin de Bezons (1646–1733), Marshal of France, served with distinction in all the wars of his time and became a member of the Council of the Regency in 1715, having been made a marshal in 1709. Abraham

de Fabert (1599–1668), Marshal of France, ranked as one of the most illustrious military men of his time; see Chapter 6, note 10. General Rose proved difficult to identify, but I decided that Du Pont probably meant Reinhold von Rosen, General of the Bernardine troops—the soldiers of Bernard, Duke of Saxe-Weimar, who fought under the command of Turenne in the closing years of the Thirty Years War and mutinied against their French commanders in 1647; see C. V. Wedgwood, *The Thirty Years War* (Garden City, NY: Doubleday, 1961), pp. 479–81. My suspicion was confirmed when I noticed that Turenne had written of Rosen as Rose in his memoirs; see Paul Marichal, ed., *Mémoires du Maréchal de Turenne,* 2 vols. (Paris: Renouard, 1809), I, pp. 307, 311, 104–113, 314–317; II, pp. 8, 22–24, 31; and *passim.* Nicolas de Catinat (1637–1712), one of the most remarkable captains of the reign of Louis XIV, was made a Marshal of France and a Knight of St. Louis in 1693. His outstanding accomplishments notwithstanding, he always retained a reputation for simplicity and lack of pretension. Michel de L'Hospital (1507–1573), who attained the distinguished rank of Chancellor of France under Francis II during the period of the religious wars, had begun life as the son of a man proscribed on account of his loyalty to the Connétable de Bourbon. By Romée de Villeneuve, Du Pont probably meant Rometto, Roméo, or Romieu de Villeneuve, Baron of Vence, constable and grand seneschal of Provence, minister of Count Bérenger of Provence. He became regent in 1215, at the death of the count, and succeeded in assuring the submission of the nobility of the province to the Countess Beatrix. He died in retirement around 1250 and his memory long remained legendary. Alfred the Great (849–899) was the legendary king of England who organized the decisive victories against the Danes (896/897). Gustavus Adolphus Vasa (1594–1632), king of Sweden, commanded the Swedish forces during their participation in the Thirty Years War and died on the battlefield of Lützen. Assuming the Swedish crown in 1611 at the age of seventeen, the young Gustavus II immediately confronted war with the Danes. His success in inspiring energy and affection for himself in the peasants of Decarlia on the Danish frontier "made any permanent occupation of Sweden by the Danes a moral impossibility." See C. R. Fletcher, *Gustavus Adolphus and the Thirty Years War* (1890, repr. New York: Capricorn Books, 1963), *passim* and p. 42 for reference to Decarlia. Gustavus Adolphus's daughter, Christina (1626–1689), ruled Sweden from his death until her own abdication in 1654. During her reign, she attracted many foreign scholars and men of letters to her court, notably René Descartes (1596–1650), the French philosopher and author of the seminal *Discours sur la méthode,* who died during his stay at the Swedish court. Samuel de Pufendorf (1632–1694) ranked among the outstanding jurists and legal philosophers of the seventeenth century. Born in Saxony, he died in Berlin, but during his distinguished career held chairs at Heidelberg and in Sweden at the University of Lund. Among his many writings, *De jure naturae et gentium* (Lund, 1672) proved especially influential on eighteenth-century theories of natural law. Christian, Baron von Wolff (1679–1754), pursued a successful academic career in mathematics and philosophy in various German universities. Both he and Pufendorf were influenced by Descartes. Wolff's prolific writing represented the first attempt in the Germanies to make philosophy available in the vernacular; see in particular *Vernünftige Gedanken von den Kräften des menschlichen Verstandes* (Halle, 1712), which was translated into French by Jean Deschamps as *Pensées philosophiques* (1736). Wolff's thought exercised considerable influence on that of Quesnay. On Pufendorf, see Hans Medick, *Naturzustand und Naturgeschichte der bürgerlichen Gesellschaft* (Göttingen: Vandenhoeck & Ruprecht, 1973). On the influence of Pufendorf and Wolff on French political and legal theory, see Jean Derathé, *Rousseau et la science politique de son temps* (Paris: J. Vrin, 1974). Gottfried Wilhelm Freiherr von Leibniz (1646–1716) was a lawyer, scientist, inventor, diplomat, poet, philologist, logician, moralist, theologian, historian, and philosopher who developed a theory of the nature of being based on the notion of the monad, the irreducible unit of being each of which reflected the greatest monad, God. A Protestant, Leibniz opposed the expansionist pretensions of Louis XIV, served the house of Hanover, and sought to implement a model of universal peace similar to the universal papacy. In science, philosophy, ethics, and politics, he sought the principles of universality. In 1675, he discovered the infinitessimal calculus independent of Newton's almost simultaneous discovery. His many works, including *On the Method of Universality* (1674), *Preface to the General Science* (1677), *The Theodicy* (1710), *The Monadology* (1714), and more can be found in the various editions of his works of which Robert Latta, ed., *The Monadology and other Philosophical Writings* (Oxford: Oxford University Press, 1898) is still the best in English; G. W. Leibniz, *Sämtliche Schriften und Briefe*, edition of the German Academy of Sciences at Berlin (Darmstadt, 1923–) will be definitive when completed. See also Patrick Riley, trans. and ed., *The Political Writings of Leibniz* (Cambridge: Cambridge University Press, 1972).

[5]Two of these lines come from Pierre Corneille's play, *Don Sanche d'Aragon*, first staged in 1649 and published in 1650. "Ma valeur est ma race, et mon bras est mon père" (My worth is my race, and my arm is my father) is spoken by Carlos, Act I, Scene 3, line 253. "À l'exemple des dieux, j'ai fait beaucoup de rien" (Following the example of the gods, I have made much of nothing) is probably a misrendering of Carlos's words in Act V, Scene 6, line 1656, "Qu'à l'exemple du ciel j'ai fait beaucoup de rien" (That following the example of the sky I have made much of nothing). The third, "Je ne dois qu'à moi seul toute ma renommée" (I owe only to myself all my renown), comes from the poem, "Excuse à Ariste," which first appeared in 1637 shortly after the staging of, and

in the middle of the quarrel over, *Le Cid*. See Corneille, *Oeuvres complètes*, ed. André Stegmann (Paris: Seuil, 1963), p. 871. It should be noted that among Corneille's many pronouncements on duty toward and indebtedness to the older generation, especially fathers, Du Pont has his mother select for his special attention lines that emphasize the self-creation and individualism of the hero.

[6]Here, with a touch of irony, Du Pont is identifying himself as a hero by evoking Achilles, dipped in the Styx by his mother Thetis to make him invulnerable. A similar flirtation with himself as hero appears in the fourth paragraph of this chapter, in the description of his birth.

[7]Jean de La Fontaine (1621–1695) was the author of the celebrated *Fables*, of which the first six books were published in 1668, books VII to XI in 1678, and book XII in 1694. The *Fables* enjoyed a brilliant success in La Fontaine's lifetime and became a classic book for children.

[8]The Seigneur de Pybrac published his *Quatrains* in 1674 (Paris: Editions Louis Vendosme Père). During the seventeenth century, they became the children's book par excellence and were cited frequently in the writings of Madame de Maintenon. See Marc Soriano, *Les Contes de Perrault: culture savante et traditions populaires* (Paris: Gallimard, 1968), and Guy Henry, *Les Quatrains de Pibrac* (Toulouse: Privat, n.d.), extracted from the *Annales du Midi* 15, 16.

[9]I have been unable to identify *Etrenne mignonne*. The title can best be translated as "cute gift." I assume that it was an early collection of tales for children. The phrase is dropped entirely from the typed transcript of Du Pont's manuscript made by Mrs. Smith and Sophie M. Du Pont, and from the translation made by B. G. du Pont.

[10]Lodovico Ariosto's *Orlando furioso* was translated by Du Pont and published in 1781 as *Essai de traduction en vers du Roland furieux de l'Arioste*. A second edition of Du Pont's version appeared in 1812.

[11]François Vincent Toussaint (1715–1772) published *Les Moeurs* in 1748. In this work, he defended a notion of virtue, to the support of which he brought an "apostolic zeal" that lay midway between popular and worldly values—what one might also call a notion of bourgeois virtue. See Robert Mauzi, *L'Idée du bonheur au XVIIIe siècle* (Paris: Armand Colin, 1969), p. 601.

[12]The verses can be roughly translated:
"And let a rich merchant make his son a Councillor
This son, in seeing him, will fear to degrade himself."

5

My Stay with M. Viard, and What My Studies Were.

At first M. *Viard* treated me with kindness as the son of a friend: then he began to love me for myself. The ambitious little one could hardly fail to be an ardent student. I was accustomed to reading and to preferring it to other amusements; my memory was accomplished; I knew more French than my comrades; I was in a hurry to learn and, although younger than the others, soon left them behind me.

My very good master decided that the ordinary class held me back; he set me working alone in his study while he taught the others. He gave me a task, and too easy a task, but I did not preen myself on its easy accomplishment. I climbed up on the chairs and on his desk, I took down the books of his library. I read them from nine to eleven o'clock, after which I began my work, which he always found ready when he returned at noon. Thus I read all of M. *Viard's* books, and he had many. The experience left me with an uncertain erudition that sometimes obliges me to quote by saying *an author, one of the ancients* for I remember the fact, or the thought, or the passage, but I do not remember in which book I read it.

When M. *Viard* deemed me ready to enter the fourth class, he sent me, together with his other students of the same level, to the Collège du Plessis and I began that class with a burst under M. *Jacquin* or M. *Guérin*, I cannot remember the name, but it certainly ended in *in*. He was an amiable enough man, who incidentally told us little stories about his travels. I loudly blamed my comrades who stole his Spanish liquorice and fought with one or two of them about the matter. If he had known this, independent of my being a good student, he would have loved me madly, but I took care not to tell him; for honor did not permit my being a *tattletale* (which is how students referred to those who denounced their fellow students).

I did not benefit long from the lessons of the good Professor with the tales and the liquorice, although I feared that having participated in a few was about to cost me all further study. My Father became seriously angered with M. *Viard*, and then with my Mother, who tolerated and justified him. He said that they had not lived up *to the spirit of the bargain*; that he had consented to put me in a Boarding School but not send me to a college; that I had no need to do my classes; that I would already have learned too much for my happiness and for his when I should have learned what they could teach me at the boarding school; and that the right thing would be for him to withdraw me immediately.[1] I wept hot tears.

M. *Viard* consoled me by assuring me that I would lose nothing and that he alone would help me surpass all my comrades at the college. He made me try compositions, praised me, caressed me, loved me. I worked in his study all the time he was not there. I worked in a classroom during part of the recreations. My comrades were jealous of the little distinctions that this unusual work earned me; they came to the classroom to interrupt me. I asked for peace; they refused it; I built myself a rampart of dictionaries, I threw them at their heads, and from throwing weapons, we moved very rapidly to hand-to-hand combat. I was frequently struck, but never conquered. I gained two less than flattering nicknames. The first which derived from my talking, *my little gossip*, gave way to a second derived from my quarrels, *my little spitfire*. When I was in the grasp of the enemy, overcome, chained, I told him *"kill me,"* and as soon as my conqueror had let me go, I fell upon him with fury. I was often wounded seriously in this game. Neither M. *Viard* nor my parents ever knew. For nothing in the world should I have chosen to pride myself on my defeats, nor to become a tale-bearer: *to fail in honor!* in two ways! Give in to my comrades, obey them, I could not; complain of them to a master who had already protected me in too obvious a fashion, I could not. Die under their blows, I could very well, and more than once I felt myself close to that outcome. I do not even know what might have happened if God had not sent me from England a small boy of my age named *Osborne*, who stayed in the boarding school for about six weeks and taught me the principles of *Boxing*. All my life, I have wanted to find M. *Osborne* again. The favor he did me is one of the greatest I could have received. He instructed me and gave me advice and an example by sometimes helping me to beat off my adversaries. My big companions, proud of their size and their emerging beards, would have disdained to be introduced to *Pugilism* by two little snot-nosed kids. They lost their superiority. It was no longer in their power to trap me and to transform the fight into an unequal one; their blows *in the French manner,* delivered *on the edge* (if it is permitted to use the expression for one weapon for another) rarely attained their target and fell flabbily from the strength of the muscle alone. Mine, delivered *on the point,* never failed to hit their target and acquired an awesome weight from the entire length of bone that supported them. No longer was I wounded, and students who were six years older than I, who were twice as strong, now had to explain why their nose was crushed or their teeth broken, or why they were spitting blood.

I acquired respect, I was believed to be stronger than I was; my fist served to excuse my brain; and my comrades began, like my master, to take pride for the school in my little successes. M. *Viard* based his hopes for the future on them, and I was lucky enough to be useful. He displayed me to people who wanted to send their children to a boarding school. He introduced me to his friends. He made me reply to questions and declaim before them.

M. *Restaut,* the author of a rather mediocre French grammar that I had learned by heart was among their number. M. *Restaut* demonstrated great benevolence for a child who knew his entire grammar. He was a very good man and a very good citizen. He collected together the students who showed promise, had them compete with each other, and distributed at his own expense prizes that our young heads considered greatly increased in value by the hand of such an illustrious grammarian as M. *Restaut.*

I earned the *Spectacle of Nature*[2] from him for having translated

Cicero's beautiful verses from the *De Devinatione* in the following fashion:

> Even as from the great Jupiter one sees the terrible Bird
> Suddenly wounded by a horrible Serpent,
> Which, from the trunk of an old oak, with thrusting force
> Holds him entwined in his tortuous folds.
> He flies off, he carries to the seat of thunder
> The reptile terrified of abandoning the earth,
> Which twists, struggles, tires itself in vain efforts;
> A steel lock subjects its body
> That the beak of the conqueror tears into a hundred shreds.
> It dodges its poisons, but soon expires.
> And avenged, satisfied, the Eagle drenched in blood,
> Throws it scornfully away and glides on the summit of the
>   air.[3]

This translation, the masterpiece of a child of eleven or twelve, can in no way be compared with the admirable verses with which *Voltaire* rendered the same piece.[4] But it was faithful enough and did not lack the proper number or harmony. They were found to betray the germ of a poet, and my competitors' having only done translations in prose, M. *Restaut* was not wrong to award me the prize.

My Father had done well in forbidding me to learn to write poetry. I never wrote good Latin verses; but in French I wrote them every day, sometimes passable, more often mediocre or bad. I was the *Poet of the bouquets* that we offered to M. *Viard*. If my preceptor gave me a *Punishment* of copying a hundred verses of *Virgil* or *Horace*; I evaded the punishment by an improvisation of eight or ten French verses, and M. *Viard* was at the height of his hopes.

He set us to writing letters on subjects that were sometimes assigned and sometimes left to the will of our imagination; the prize for the conqueror was an extra apple at dessert. Of one hundred apples that he distributed thus, I had *eighty-seven*.

Finally he deemed me capable of undertaking a public exercise. He had had me take courses in Rhetoric with the *Abbé le Batteux*, who also came to instruct and encourage me. He charged me, as he said, for the instruction of my comrades, to prepare an abstract from the logic of *Port Royal*.[5] He made me learn the *Institutes of Justinian* by heart and joining that to my everlasting *Restaut's* grammar, he had the pleasure of announcing that one of his students, of about twelve years, was capable of responding to questions on French and Latin grammar; of translating pieces from the best Latin authors; of sustaining an exercise in Logic, Rhetoric, the Apologue, the Ecologue, the Epistolary Style, and Roman Law.

I had an audience of four hundred, and this assembly, as I passed through it, inspired in me a certain timidity. Happily I said to myself, "If these people did not have a favorable disposition toward the child who is going to speak, they would not have come to hear him." This little reflection restored my courage.

I did very well. I had some arguments prearranged, for I had several confederates in the group: M. *Restaut,* M. *Le Batteux,* the Abbé *Mahaut,* the Abbé *Asselin,* and some other friends of M. *Viard.* I nonetheless had some unforeseen questions, and had, what made me tremble, to explain a passage of *Tacitus* for which I was not prepared. I had the good fortune to understand it. I say *good fortune,* for I have always been *fortunate* in translation; when I understand half the author's words, I guess the rest. In truth, I gave the impression of knowing many things; and I had some idea of many things that children of my age did not know; but I was very weak in *Latin.* I have been obliged to learn it again since then, and even today I am not able to speak or to write it with facility. My mother, who had learned it by herself at the same time as I, was able to follow my work and advise me, for she learned it incomparably better than I ever did.

It is a beautiful day for the child nourished on the cookies of self-love, as I had been to that point, when he honorably completes a public exercise. There are no words to convey the pleasure that I experienced as I was carried from arm to arm from my chair to the place where my Father and my Mother melted in tears of joy. My Father also wept despite his repugnance for literary glory and work. Oh! How happy he made me! I believed that he loved me more than he had up till then; I believed that I had vanquished him. I held them, my mother and him, in my little arms, in the middle of clapping hands, the three of us bathed in each other's tears. I have only had one other moment of comparable happiness in my life and, my friends, I shall not tell you which.

During the evening I had a second sweet pleasure. I must tell you that, although I had learned to fight from *Osborne,* I was very awkward at all other exercises, for I had always used my mind, but my body very little. I ran well enough in a straight line because that is accomplished partly through will, effort, and courage. In

Prisoner's Base, I was only useful to deliver prisoners; I did not know how to dodge, for that required practice. We had a game that amused us very much; it consisted of throwing a javelin toward a target. It was established practice to wager the apples we got for our dessert, and I had lost all my ordinary apples, my *eighty-seven* extraordinary apples, and *one hundred and fifty* more on my word—ten with one of my comrades, six with another. There was not one who did not have a few apples to claim from me, and we had been obliged to keep a Register to regulate the order of the payments. My fellow students assembled in the evening and, having deliberated, unanimously concluded that the honor that *Du Pont* had brought the school merited that his comrades remit the apples for which he was indebted.

They came to me in a procession, with torches in their hands. *Faure de Beaufort*, who has since become a well-known doctor and who was the best student after me, took the floor and made a beautiful speech to me; he presented me with a written deliberation, signed by all my comrades, and then they all embraced me ceremoniously. That was much sweeter than fighting them. I accepted with gratitude. I told *Faure* that I deeply regretted that he did not owe me any apples so that I could remit them to him the day he would make me forget. He was perfectly capable of doing so if only he had been able to declaim without monotony. In addition to kisses, I had received *an écu* from my Father which showed me as much as his tears that he had been deeply touched. I had received *another* from my Mother, and the day after, no longer speaking of *apples*, I had the small satisfaction of ordering one hundred and fifty little cakes and as much cider as they could drink, and to render to my comrades courtesy for courtesy; I was a very happy little boy.

M. *Viard* was preparing me and preparing himself for yet more brilliant laurels. He and the *Abbé le Batteux* arranged a much more difficult exercise than the first. I was supposed to treat the same subjects, and, in addition, the epic, Roman history, and the history of France. He spent several months, and I all my strength, to prepare me to sustain this second public act of nascent glory. The day was arranged; it was to be the twelfth of August 1752. I was a little more than twelve and a half. Programs were printed. All the professors of the University and the Royal College were invited by circulars. Tickets were distributed. I believed ahead of time, like Horace, that I should *"strike the stars with my illustrious forehead."* I did not have that honor.

Monseigneur, the Rector of the University, accompanied by his counsel and abusing the Privilege of teaching with a jealousy far beneath the respectable body over which he presided and of which he was the mouthpiece, judged that M. *Viard's* school could become too famous and it could not be suffered that a simple private *educator* present the spectacle of a child who had not followed classes in any college. As a result he prohibited, *by Mandate* of his *rectorial authority,* the exercise from taking place.[6]

M. *Viard* was very much affected. My Mother and I were in despair. My Father accepted the occurrence with patience. The dazzle of my first exercise having passed, he had thought that his wife, his friend *Viard,* and his little boy were dragging him beyond his plans and his means; and after we had fully lamented the *tyranny of Monsieur le Rector,* he said to my mother, *"I have done what you have wanted: your son has studied more than I believed necessary; he has succeeded fairly well, I am pleased; it is time for all that to end and for him to think of working, for one can only live by working. I am withdrawing him from* M. Viard's *without fanfare, without haste; let him finish the month, but let him be here by the first of September."*

Once my Father had taken it upon himself to express his will so clearly, the eternal Father could not have moved him.

On precisely the first of September, I was back in the paternal house, and there was talk of building me a work table, of buying me a vise, a lathe, some files.

Files, and a work table! For a child of such great promise! My Mother wept quietly, for she was losing the fruit of twelve years of projects and of more than six years of sustained efforts to influence and direct her husband. Me, I wept openly as soon as I was alone, for in front of the imposing figure of my Father there was no way to whisper, to breathe.

Notes

[1]On the history of education in France in the early modern period, see R. Chartier, et al., *L'Éducation en France du XVIe au XVIIIe siècle* (Paris: SEDES, 1976). The "college" as a distinct institution, devoted to secondary in contrast to primary education, had taken shape by the end of the sixteenth century. The Brothers of the Common Life had provided the initial inspiration as early as the fifteenth century. They established the system of "classes" that associated each one with a specific subject: the eighth, seventh, and sixth classes were devoted to grammar; the fifth to

grammar and logic; the fourth and third to logic and rhetoric; the second and first to ethics, philosophy, and some material from the *Quadrivium*. During the sixteenth century, the University of Paris assumed the form it would retain until the expulsion of the Jesuits. University reformers, Jesuits, and Protestants all contributed to shaping the characteristic pedagogy, program, and order of the college. By 1789, one boy in fifty-two benefited from that education. The *pension* (boarding school) that Du Pont attended was a much more informal affair that was intended mainly to provide primary education and perhaps a bit more for boys who were not to go on to a college.

Both Morellet and Marmontel discuss their years at a college in their respective memoirs. In not having this experience, Du Pont not only missed the standard training in Latin and rhetoric, but also the companionship of the young men who would become the administrators and intellectuals of his generation. See Jean-François Marmontel, *Mémoires*, 2 vols., ed. John Renwick (Clermont-Ferrand: G. de Bussac, 1972); *Mémoires inédites de l'Abbé Morellet, sur le dix-huitième siècle et sur la Révolution*, 2nd ed., 2 vols. (Geneva: Slatkine Reprints, 1967).

[2]*Spectacle de la nature ou entretiens sur l'histoire naturelle et les sciences*, 9 vols. (Paris, 1732) was written by Noel-Antoine Pluche (1688–1761), a Jansenist who had been director of the College of Laon until he was forced to resign for refusing to adhere to the Bull Unigenitus.

[3]Compare the edition of Cicero's *De Divinatione* in the Loeb Classical Library, *Cicero in Twenty-Eight Volumes*, vol. XX, *De Senectute, De Amicitia, De Divinatione*, with an English translation by William Armistead Falconer (Cambridge, MA: Harvard University Press, 1971), p. 338, and the English translation, p. 339.

> Hic Iovis altisoni subito pinnata satelles
> arboris e trunco serpentis saucia morsu
> subigit ipsa feris transfigens unguibus anguem
> semianimum et varia graviter cervice micantem;
> quem se intorquentem lanians rostroque cruentans,
> iam satiata animos, iam duros ulta dolores,
> abicit ecflantem et laceratum adfligit in unda,
> seque obitu a solis nitidos convertit ad ortus.

> Behold, from out the tree, on rapid wing,
> The eagle that attends high-thundering Jove
> A serpent bore, whose fangs had wounded her;
> And as she flew her cruel talons pierced
> Quite through its flesh. The snake, tho' nearly dead,
> Kept darting here and there its spotted head;
> And, as it writhed she tore with bloody beak
> Its twisted folds. At last, with sated wrath

And grievous wounds avenged, she dropped her prey,
Which, dead and mangled, fell into the sea;
And from the West she sought the shining East.

Du Pont's French translation reads as follows:

Tel du grand Jupiter on voit l'Oiseau terrible
Subitement blessé par un Serpent horrible,
Qui, du tronc d'un vieux chêne avec force élancé
Dans des plis tortueux le retient enlacé.
Il s'envole, il emporte au séjour du tonnerre
Le Reptile effrayé d'abandonner la terre,
Qui se tort, se débat, s'épuise en vains efforts;
Une serre d'acier assujettit son corps
Que le bec du vainqueur en cent lambeaux déchire.
Il darde ses poisons; mais bientôt il expire.
Et vengé, satisfait, l'Aigle de sang couvert,
Le jette avec mépris et plâne au haut de l'aire.

Du Pont transcribed the original Latin thus:

Sic Jovis altisoni subito pennata satelles
Arboris a trunco, serpentis saucia morsu,
Ipsa feris subijit trans fignes unguibis anguem
Semi animum, et varia gravitas cervise micantem
Quem se intorquentem lanians rostroque cruentans
Jam satiata animos, jam duros ultra dolores
Abjuit efflantam, et laceratum affligit in undas
Seque obitu a Solis nitridos convertit ad ortus.

[4]Voltaire's translation of these verses can be found in the Preface to his *Rome sauvée ou Catilina*, a tragedy in five acts first presented in Paris on 24 February 1752; see *Oeuvres complètes de Voltaire*, nouvelle edition . . . (Paris: Garnier Freres, 1877), vol. IV, p. 207. He translated them as follows:

Tel on voit cet oiseau qui porte le tonnerre,
Blessé par un serpent élancé de la terre;
Il s'envole; il entraine au séjour azuré
L'ennemi tortueux dont il est entouré.
Le sang tombe des airs. Il déchire, il dévore
Le reptile acharné qui le combat encore;
Il le perce, il le tient sous ses ongles vainqueurs;
Par cent coups redoublés il venge ses douleurs.
Le monstre en expirant se débat, se replie;
Il exhale en poisons les restes de sa vie;

Et l'aigle tout sanglant, fier, et victorieux,
Le rejette en fureur, et plane au haut des cieux.

[5]Du Pont probably meant *La Logique de l'art de penser* (1662) by Antoine Arnauld, Pierre Nicole, et al., called the "Port Royal Logic." On the Jansenist influence on education, see Howard Clive Barnard, *The Port-Royalists on Education* (Cambridge: Cambridge University Press, 1913), and his *The French Tradition in Education: Ramus to Mme Necker de Saussure* (Cambridge: Cambridge University Press, 1922, repr. 1970).

[6]The Rector of the University of Paris was elected by the proctors, or highest officials, of the four nations into which the faculty and students were organized. The highest ranking figure in the university, he was elected for a term of three months in principle, but in the eighteenth century the term was frequently extended to a full year. See Barnard, *French Tradition in Education*, p. 3, and Chartier, et al., *L'Education en France*, pp. 250–51.

6

My Second Studies in Metaphysics, Mathematics and Military Art in the Paternal House. Support and Counsels that my Mother gave Me. I lose Her at Sixteen.

My Mother knew from experience that it was impossible to change my Father's resolutions; but that it was not impossible to move him with caresses and good tactics, to gain time and to lead him far from the goal he intended.

It is my profoundly painful opinion that I owed two little sisters, and that my poor Mother owes the death that they gave her, to the negotiations she was obliged to enter into to defer my *work table* and to preserve my freedom to reach where my spirit could carry me. It had been ten years since she had had a child; she feared them because her labors were very painful; then she had two, one on top of the other, in the midst of her efforts on my behalf. Excellent woman! But more excellent Mother![1]

I have told you that they were very zealous Huguenots in my family; that was the starting point of my Protectress. She claimed that a child had never been placed in *apprenticeship* before making his *first communion*.

The first communion brooked no reply.

A preparation was necessary; I had only pursued worldly studies at M. *Viard's*. With some ostentation they found M. *l'Honoré*, chaplain of the Dutch Ambassador and a fairly good Preacher. He was asked to recommend a capable man to complete my education and put me in a position to be interrogated by a Pastor, such as himself. He was told of my little literary successes; he was given the Programs of my exercises; he was told that the plans of my family were to have me follow clockmaking, but that I missed my studies; and that above all that since I had heard him I had conceived a great desire to become one day like him a minister of the *Holy Gospel*. At the time I really cherished this desire. Minister or Doctor were the only literate professions within the reach of a young Huguenot. My Mother had sounded out my Father with respect to Medicine by speaking of a famous and wealthy protestant Doctor, Dr. *Du Moulin*. She was outwitted and rebuffed by the idea of the expense required for this kind of study; and the madness, when one does not want to support one's children for ever, of giving them a situation that does not become lucrative until an advanced age. There remained the Pastorate; and effectively M. *l'Honoré's* sermons had seemed touching to me; I recited those of *Saurin* fairly well, and I found that the advantage of speaking, sometimes in giving way to affection, sometimes in deploying authority over the faithful who were obliged to listen to you with attention, submission, and fervor constituted a very beautiful ministry.[2]

My Mother, by thus haranguing her Pastor drew him into a common cause and made of the holy man a support against my Father, as she had previously done with M. *Viard*.

Throughout the congregation she enjoyed a fine reputation for intelligence and benevolence. She assisted the Poor with her efforts and her purse beyond anything that could be expected. I have an account for close to *twenty thousand écus* of that period which, given the difference in the price of goods, are worth more than *one hundred thousand francs* today, which she used to raise children, relieve the elderly, furnish advances to young households for their commerce. It is true that many of them returned the advances. When she was told that she gave too much she replied, *"It is like the widow's pitcher; the more she pours, the more God permits it to be refilled."* She was entitled to be generous; I also have the account of what she earned after her marriage with the work of her hands in making watch hands in the midst of her literary occupations, the care of her household, that for my education, those which she took for all the unfortunates who had recourse to her; it exceeds *eighty thousand francs* of that time—which would now be worth close to *fifty thousand écus*. One can imagine the esteem she inspired by this generosity, joined to the most obliging discourses pronounced in the tones of her most agreeable voice. By her conversations with other influential women she had made for myself a little reputation for intelligence, talent, and wit.

M. *l'Honoré* was flattered and did not flatter us. He set forth for us all the inconveniences and mortifications of the position of the Priest in general and of the Calvinist Priest in particular; he spoke almost philosophically and finished by promising to help us to the extent that he could.

For instructor, he gave me M. *Bosc d'Antic,* who had been received a minister at Lausanne, who subsequently became *Doctor of the Protestant Hospital* in Paris, then chemist and director of the manufactory of mirrors at *St. Gobain,* then entrepreneur of that of Rouelle in Burgundy, then Doctor a second time, with a somewhat usurped reputation.[3] He really had great intelligence and a fairly broad knowledge.

He was *publicly* charged, for two louis per month, to prepare me for my first communion; and, *confidentially* by my Mother, to supplement any imperfections in my preceding studies. On this count, he was admitted among the most intimate friends of the house; he had a place at the table, he found advances of money for his projects and his studies in chemistry.

On his side, he had me continue to translate Tacitus and Horace and Cicero; he introduced me to metaphysics, Theology, Controversy and a little physics; he was another Pangloss.[4] My Father found all these studies rather protracted for a *first communion*; but he was told that a distinguished child such as I had been at my school could not be reduced to common instruction. M. *D'Antic,* M. L'Honoré praised my progress and assured him that I needed only a few more months of studies to become an accomplished child, who would bring great honor to my Parents. Time passed.

From this fine work a great difficulty for my plans for the Priesthood emerged at least for the heart of an honest man. For in studying Metaphysics and Theology, I had ceased to be a Christian.

I had noticed that Christianity was entirely based on *original Sin,* for which reason it is supposed that god has damned all men for four thousand years, and this opinion that god could *damn one man for the faults of another, thousands of men for the faults of only one,* appeared to me as it is, the most impious and the most atrocious calumny that one could imagine against the Divinity.—I then saw that to appease god, it had required that an inconceivable mixture of *god-man* be put to death. Absurd doctrine of expiatory victims, shamefully beneath a just and good god who should weigh works, not sacrifices, and who should hold human sacrifices in horror. Extreme insanity to think that God should have been appeased because men should have committed toward their own kind—if *Jesus* is man—toward God himself—If Jesus is god—a much greater crime than those for which he had been angered in the first place.— I finally saw that by this *immolation* of God, who offered, it is said, himself to himself, by means of a horrible forfeit of men, to *redeem* the human species, he nonetheless *redeemed* almost no one; that nine tenths of the inhabitants of the Globe who were not of his Religion remained just as damned as if there had been no *Redeemer*; that nine tenths of the surplus being great rascals also continued to be damned. So that after having, with the utmost injustice, punished *the entire human race* for the fault of *a single man*, the door of salvation was only opened to at the most *a hundredth of this race* by the juridical murder of a god, calumnied as a man and publicly condemned, on the pretext of sedition, at the request of a troop of Priests of this same god and of other, very nasty fanatics. Perversity, immorality, lunacy always insult the Creator and the Benefactor of the world in such a Theology. *I also find the Protestants very silly, for people who had* invoked reason, for having reformed *Purgatory*, which allowed the idea of a god of mercy to persist, while retaining the application of eternal sufferings to passing faults with the cruelty of *a devil*, while I sought in the Supreme Being that which should be found there—infinite goodness, infinite clemency.[5]

I concluded that a pious man of good sense could be neither Catholic nor Protestant; that one had to respect the uniform and the divine morality in all Religions, scorn the dogma in all, and as to worship, to ceremonies, that one had to submit to the custom, the laws of the Country just as one would wear a dolman in Constantinople and a juste-à-corps in Paris.

My religious Fatherland in France was my Family. I made my *first communion* in its fashion and six months thereafter, a second; that was plenty; that is all. I nonetheless found in this Protestant communion, in this bread broken *in common*, in this wine drunk by all the participants from the same chalice, something paternal and ancient that touched the heart and that the Catholic communion does not have.

I did not hide my difficulties from M. *d'Antic* nor from M. L'Honoré, but they judged that my result being to follow the practice of my Parents, it was pointless to engage me in a controversy in which I should have overcome them; and they admitted me. At the bottom of their hearts, they thought as I did; and what is more, I was the son of a woman highly regarded in the Church.

I have found among the papers of my Father some of the essays I had written in this period and given to my Mother. They are very methodical, well-divided and subdivided, reasonable and even strongly so, of a clear and irresistible logic, written quite clearly but with a glacial coldness; and I had difficulty understanding how a very sensitive child who loved his Mother with passion, who even younger had loved Mlle *Colineau*, who had been nourished on the Poets, who had written many bad verses and a few adequate ones, could at thirteen years old write with this coldness that he had never demonstrated heretofore and would never recover. There must be a refrigerant in metaphysics and a kind of shiver in the physics of man that precedes the fever of puberty and of the Passions. The phenomenon is strangely marked in my first essays in metaphysics, in Theology and Countertheology.

Even as I wrote these cold and wise thoughts, the *first communion* was upon us in spite of ourselves, and the *work table* in its wake. How could we again delay this object of my terrors and the disgust of my mother who nonetheless spent eight or ten hours a day at her own and perhaps hated it more.

She imagined having me learn *mathematics*. Ah! that was a step toward clockmaking, my Father had nothing to say.

He said that he did not know it. He was answered that M. *Julien Le Roi*, his first master, knew it, and that the two sons of M. Julien Le Roi knew it so well that one of them was a member of the *Academy of Sciences*. I had never let a word go by that might stir my ambition and the *Academy of Sciences* was another of these words.

My mother went to see M. *d'Alembert,* accompanied by her little boy as always, and asked the learned geometrician to recommend a *Mathematics master* who could lead a young man, born with some predispositions and a great desire to learn, to the point at which he could one day profit from the works and the advice of the Philosopher to whom she dared address herself.[6]

M. *d'Alembert* received us with kindness, induced me to chat and happily for me, dropped me a few words that provided me with an opportunity to use *d'Antic's* metaphysics, which appeared rather strange in the mouth of a child. He caressed me and never ceased wishing me well. He sent me to M. *Roussain* for a master, from whom I learned the elements of geometry and of Algebra and the Science of Machines.

M. *Roussain's* lessons opened my eyes to another career much closer to my character, my ambition, to that in which my Mother had cradled my childhood. But before speaking to you of it I must tell you of a service that my Mother rendered to my entire life and that stopped me shortly thereafter from losing my reason and my honor in the most dangerous trap to which a young man could be exposed, exalted as I had been by the type of culture that had been offered to my mind and heart.

My Mother wanted me to have a reputation, but not gratuitously. Her elevated character required that I deserve it in all respects, that I be a man of the elite and above all a good man; you have found some weaknesses in her that were due to her birth and to the education that she herself received, but her soul was full of grandeur and virtue.

She gave me the same day *Robinson Crusoe, Montaigne,* and *Sir Charles Grandisson.*[7]

"My dear child," she said to me, *"it is no longer a question of reading for your pleasure and of learning for trivial exercises of appearance; you must have no faculty of either body or soul that you cannot execute with distinction. You see what pains it has cost me and what it has cost me every day to have led you where you are now. You are not far. You must nonetheless become a great man or be nothing and lose all the fruits of the worries and tears of your poor Mother.*

"Your Father demands that you know his craft; you must learn it. A craft is always useful, and it is not enough, one must know ten. One should, if it were possible, know all the arts and all the sciences; but one must primarily be master of oneself and not permit oneself a single action of which one cannot say it is estimable. For in deserving esteem and friendship everywhere, first one is happy with oneself and then one is carried forward by the support of all those who love and esteem us.

"I am giving you three excellent books; meditate on them, learn to guide yourself.

"I am turning you over to yourself; God bless you, my child."

This speech has never left my memory or my heart.

But if such warnings should and could direct me toward the good path and form my head, I also encountered seductions capable of deranging it forever.

My mother had become acquainted with the Marquise *d'Urfé,* a woman of much intelligence, some knowledge and a brilliant imagination, but totally misguided.[8] She was in some ways the President, and I think even more the dupe, of an association of cabalists in which the Baron de *Beauvais,* her friend, was taken to be the most astute man under her.

Mme *d'Urfé* was dazzled by my Mother's intelligence and dazzled her with praise; and my Mother who could not do without her son made the serious mistake of introducing me into that strange society where I was soon overwhelmed with exaggerated praises myself.

Madame *d'Urfé* scorned the *Gnomes,* believed herself to be in touch with the *Sylphs* and the *Undines,* and sought to be in touch with the *Salamanders.* For her operations, she needed a grown child of completely pure body and soul; she determined that I was that child and showered me with presents and goodness. I thought that I had found a second Mme *d'Epénilles.*

She told me that my Mother was a *Sylph* disguised in the body of a woman: Oh! I believed it! My mother seemed celestial to me. She told me that I myself was a *privileged Being*—my self-love was not indisposed to believe her.

She offered me very logical and poetic rationalizations on the chain of beings from the stone to God, in the middle of which man is placed just under the Genies, with whom, she told me, he can communicate if he purifies his soul, raises his heart and his mind. In this conversation and various instructions of the same kind, frequently repeated, sometimes in the presence of my Mother, sometimes to me alone, she interrogated me on my morals in such a manner that I understood nothing, and my stupidity provided her with a better answer than my protestations could have.

She then tells me that I had become worthy of seeing the *Undines,* calls for a glass of water, places it on a table covered with a white cloth, places a cross beneath the base of the glass, makes some conjurations, makes me repeat others, orders me to look carefully, assures me that I shall see *Uriel.* Far from daring to disprove her, I did not dare doubt a word that she put forth. I look and I see different reflected colors. She tells me to look yet more carefully, to notice that they are assuming a form, and to recognize *Uriel.* My imagination, troubled by the certainty of her assertions, assists my sight and I think I see Uriel. I was then thirteen and a half years old; here I was showered with praise by the entire company, treated with respect that could drive crazy a child disposed to illusions, to vanity, and to all their nefarious effects.

The experiment was tried again in front of my Mother, and

in her absence. She thinks she sees one time, then is not able to see and does not think that she has ever seen, but that she has lost the ability. I am consulted like an oracle; I reply as I think reasonable. My replies are admired and I believed in good faith for the first minutes that they had been inspired. I was embarked on the route of the fanatics and the prophets. The seduction was extreme and my peril was imminent in a company in which everything conspired to enervate me: the luxury, the rank, the titles, all the way up to that of an hereditary *Prince* who today reigns in Germany and who also took lessons from Mme *d'Urfé*.

The flattery of all those people was a veritable poison for a young man who considered following the profession of his Father as the greatest possible misfortune, who had hoped for everything from the protection of the Greats whom he thought his friends because they caressed him and flattered him, for a poor idiot lad of less than fourteen who imagined himself attached at all to these important personages by his merit and by the quality of *privileged Being* that they bestowed on him.

Nonetheless, I escaped, as I had recovered from the rickets that had made me lame in childhood. My good fortune had determined the depth of my spirit was robust like my physique, that my qualities as a man of sense outweighed my failings; it also determined that Mme *d'Epénilles* endlessly repeat to my mother, and my mother to me, to put *Probity before everything*.

Finally, I had the good sense to perceive, and the courage to say first to my mother, then to Mme *d'Urfé*, that I had surely been mistaken and that all I had seen in the glass were the reflections of the adjacent objects and especially at Mme *d'Urfé's*, of the crimson curtains with gold trimmings.

Satan did not fall more rapidly from the heavens than I fell in her esteem and her favor by my frankness. She treated me very harshly and told me that *I had assuredly lost my innocence* (of which I did not yet have very clear ideas); that if *I had behaved myself well, I would have touched glory and good fortune;* that *so far I had only seen the Undines;* that *in a few days she would have shown me the Sylphs in a mirror;* that *the Prince would have taken charge of me;* that *I had been destined for the most brilliant fortune, the most distinguished employments, the friendship of sovereigns and of the greatest men of Europe;* that *I was losing everything and deserved to lose everything;* that *she abandoned me to my ungrateful feelings, to my evil mind, to my already corrupt heart, to my reprobate inclinations.*

I felt struck by lightning! I nonetheless had the courage to reply to her: *"Madame, I am not an ingrate and I shall prove it to you: you despair of me, but I was obliged to tell you what appeared true, and to warn you of the illusion as soon as I perceived it. Above all, I regret your kindnesses, which I so fully appreciated. What I lose shows you how deeply I feel myself obliged to be sincere; for, in beginning to speak to you, I did not fail to recognize that I risked losing everything you mentioned."*

She replied to me half with pride, half with goodness, by these four words: *"Adieu, my poor Du Pont."* And I never saw her again. The spilling of my Jug of Milk caused me some grief, but I was proud of having had the resolution to throw it to the ground.

My Mother, Sylphide that she was, was banished like me from the Hôtel *d'Urfé* and took it in a virtuous spirit; *"My Dear,"* she said to me, *"you followed your conscience, I can only and should only embrace you."*

That kiss completed the payment of my good deed. After having savored it, I walked up and down in the room for half an hour; I exercised that faculty, which I have had all my life and which you have sometimes seen me use, of forming a great plan in a few minutes.

I returned to my Mother and kissed her again. "Rest assured, Maman, I have given serious thought to what mathematics can lead to; believe that I shall make a more distinguished fortune for myself than that which Madame d'Urfé, her Prince and his friends could procure for me, and I shall owe it only to my courage and my talents—to the goodness with which you support my zeal and my work. Only give me a little money to get some books."

I had *le Blond*, I bought *Bélidor, Vauban, Puységur,* several other works of geometry and of Tactics.[9] I furiously studied the art of raising a siege, military architecture, construction, the attack and the defense of positions, the fortification of the countryside, and the location of camps. I dreamed, I imagined, I took no walk that was not a *reconnoitering expedition* and from which I did not bring back the sketch of a plan; I saw camps and outposts everywhere. I persuaded my Father to give me some lessons in fencing, and he willingly agreed since it was something that he did perfectly. At the same time, I abandoned my bed. I began to lie on the ground, learned to sleep on the floor, I prepared myself to become engineer, aide-de-camp, colonel, general, Marshal of France like *Fabert*, but above all to be a hero.[10]

From my heroism of this period, I won smallpox, and to my

shame, I contracted it from my cousin *Marianne Oulson,* whom I could not stand and whom I affected to nurse through her illness by sheer bravado and to demonstrate that a man such as myself was afraid of nothing, not even an atrocious illness. Mlle *Oulson* had a benign case; I had an extremely runny and cruel case, at that period of puberty at which it is always most dangerous. At that time it was not known how to treat it; and my case was aggravated by a treatment that emphasized keeping the patient as warm as possible.[11] I had become so disgusting and hideous that looking at myself in the mirror, I could not understand how my Mother could care for me so tenderly. That adorable woman had a million ways in which to inspire and suffuse my heart with love for her. The illness was as horrible inside as out; it covered my tongue and deprived me of speech for several days. Finally, I died of it and I understood for the first time that to suffer is something, but to die is nothing, that when danger takes over, stupor follows and deadens all pain for the sufferer. My poor Mother had the misery of shrouding me. Several hours later, I came to and uttered a feeble cry that upset with fear the guard, her table and her light, and restored my Mother to life and to intoxication. I remembered the great noise that this caused in the house; I remember the maternal tears and caresses. How I lost consciousness and the external signs of life, I no longer have the least idea. My right eye had been especially heavily covered with pocks; it remained closed for almost six weeks, and when it reopened its range was infinitely shortened. It became truly nearsighted; it sees the smallest objects as if under a microscope, but does not reach more than two feet beyond itself. The sight of the left eye remained in its natural state, and is no shorter than a good ordinary sight. I call the left eye that sees at a distance *my eye of war* and the right, which is suited to the finest observations, *my eye of science and peace.* I have, therefore, nature and accidents to thank for having given me two eyes in the full sense of the term, while other men have only one eye in two volumes.

After my convalescence I wrote some verses for my Mother, for my Aunt; I resumed my warrior studies, and I began to know the sweetness of friendship. M. d'*Antic* had introduced into the house a young man of *twenty-five* or *twenty-six years,* of the noblest and happiest physiognomy. He was called M. *Volpelière,* he was at the time a clerk with M. *Sellont,* the banker, and believing himself to be beginning a vast career by becoming an exchange broker, he only needed to subsist economically until his negotiations yielded him the ease that should result from them. He came to the house as a boarder. Here, he lodged in a little room on the Palais Royal that I have since occupied and that, as you will see, does not play an insignificant part in my story. Every night I went to chat with him. He liked me very much; I loved him like a first friend. He is the oldest of my remaining friends; he is the one who is currently working on the accountancy of the *assignats*.

I also felt a flurry of love for a very beautiful lady, daughter of a M. *du Carroy*, from whom I had learned to write; she prided herself on her nobility and claimed to be related through her Mother to M. *Villeneuve de Vence,* descendants of that notorious *Romée* of whom my mother had spoken so much. Mlle *du Carroy* had married an American named *de Lesgallery d'Apinat*. This American was receiving no income from his residence in Grenada. My generous Mother, who had advanced some money for the Marriage, took the young couple as lodgers (which was never paid and still figures among the bad debts in the succession of my Father). Madame *de Lesgallery* was not yet eighteen; she succeeded in dissipating the coldness of my style, and I felt for her a passion that I could only express to her with extreme timidity and with which I regularly bothered *Volpelière*, who, as I have thought since, was much better instructed than I in the charms, the beauties, and the faults of that woman.

My Mother saw the agitations of my heart and, seeing in them but one more way for me to gain elasticity and vigor, which was the great goal to which she sacrificed everything, she only smiled. I have never been able to master the art of concealing from anyone, much less her, my inclinations or emotions; they are too vital; I am too free, too proud, too frank, too assured in my conscience for any evil principle to sway me. *"My son,"* she said, *"will be transparent like a lantern throughout his life."* I have never disproved her prediction.

While my days passed in this fashion—between military heroism, a tender friendship, a nascent and little favored love—my Father finally decided that I was overextending the study of mathematics and that it was possible to pursue it in conjunction with the study of clockmaking. He decided that the mornings would be for *this pursuit* and the afternoons for my geometry, which was said to be so necessary. The moment of recreation after dinner would be for fencing. My *work bench* was set up. My Father took me by the hand; he sat me beside him to file and turn the lathe. My Mother ordered me particularly, and with tears, to obey. I resolved to do so provisionally; I worked little and poorly; I had a book under the work bench; I stole time from the mornings to study, and my Father treated me roughly for doing so. Ten times I found the poor woman torn between her imperious husband and her impetuous son; ten times I told her that it was all over, that I would never touch a file in my life, that I would leave, that I would become a soldier.

> "*Par ce métier l'honneur n'est point blessé*
> "*Fabert, Rose et Chevert ont ainsi commencé.*"[12]

I reminded her of her examples and her maxims.

She spoke to me so sweetly, penetrated my soul with such art and shaped it so well, approved of me, blamed me, asked me with such engaging charm to do what my Father wanted, that I always ended by collapsing in tears at her feet and by telling her, "*everything you want, Maman; nothing for coercion, but for the love of you anything, anything in the world.*"

The sorrows that I brought upon my Mother were not the only ones she experienced. She had undergone cruel ones, occasioned by the bad character of her brother *Etienne Auguste*, which it would be futile for me to detail here. She had undergone other fairly acute ones on account of my Father's niece, *Marianne Oulson*, whom she had taken in and raised in the house after the shipwreck and death of Captain *Oulson* had left his children without resources. In telling me of her grief, she rendered all the more sacred for me the duty not to increase it by a resistance to my father that he would have attributed solely to her.

Through all these storms, my Mother had a child and after this child a hemorrhage of milk from which she was long ill and which altered her breast. Barely back on her feet, still suffering, still drinking donkey's milk she had a second child.

Her illnesses aggravated my chains on the one hand by depriving me of her aid and on the other by depriving me of all desire to provoke any quarrel between my Father and me that might afflict her.

Never was there a sweeter bond of zeal and friendship between a Mother and a son than that which made my happiness while the heavens preserved my Mother. I shall tell you one feature of the efforts that it inspired me to make; it is impossible for me to paint for you the penetrating impression made on my soul by her sensitivity to it.

One day during her last pregnancy we had dined at the house of M. *Doré*, whom you have met and who then lived on Montmartre. He brought my Mother back in a one-horse chaise with an excellent horse; we came back on foot and they already had a long lead on us. Suddenly, it struck me that my mother, ready to give birth, needed a chair to help her to descend from the carriage, that she would neglect to ask for one or would find no one to bring it to her. I took off like a flash and ran as I have never run in my life. I caught sight of the chaise in the rue de Richelieu, but I was exhausted, ready to die from this strain on my respiratory organs called a *swollen spleen*. It was not a question of living or dying: the only point was to get there. I doubled my efforts, and I arrived at the same time as the carriage, begging my Mother to await her chair before setting foot to the ground. What did her delicate tenderness say? *"I well knew, my child, that you had the heart of an angel, but you also have its wings."* One could not reply; one kissed her hand, one cried. One is refreshed; one tastes a celestial beatitude.

The child with which she was pregnant brought her, after a fairly easy delivery, another hemorrhage of milk, which, affecting the same organ that was already affected, carried her off in six weeks, July 21, 1756, at the age of thirty-six years. She took my Father's hands and my own and said to me, practically as she expired, *"Try to make each other reciprocally happy."*

Permit me to stop, my dear children allow me to weep for my Mother.

Notes

[1]This paragraph was excluded from the transcript of the manuscript of the memoirs made by Mrs. Smith and Sophie M. Du Pont, and from the translation made by B. G. du Pont.

[2]I have been unable to identify Dr. Du Moulin, although it is possible that he descended from the important Protestant family that included Pierre Du Moulin (1568–1658), the author of *Les Éléments de la philosophie morale, traduits du Latin* (Sedan, 1624), and Pierre *fils* who was the author of *Traité de la paix de l'âme et du contentement de l'esprit* (Sedan, 1660). The Saurins were another distinguished Protestant family with members in Holland, France, and England. Du Pont probably means Jacques Saurin, a reformed pastor who was born in Nimes in 1677 and died at The Hague

in 1730. His career included emigration to Geneva following the revocation of the Edict of Nantes, a stint in the army of Victor Amadeus of Savoy, and a pastorate at the French Church of London before being called to the Walloon Church in The Hague. He published *Sermons sur divers textes de l'Écriture sainte* (1708–25); *Abrégé de la théologie et de la morale chrétienne, en forme de catéchisme* (1722); *État du christianisme en France* (1725–27); and other writings.

[3]Paul Bosc d'Antic (1726–1784), a physician for Louis XV, was interested in physics, natural history, and the fabrication of mirrors and glass. He published a number of respected treatises on glassmaking.

[4]Du Pont's reference is to Pangloss, the preceptor of Candide in Voltaire's tale of that name, who taught "métaphysico-théologo-cosmolo-nigologie."

[5]The two preceding paragraphs and the sentence that introduces them—"I had ceased to be a Christian"—were not included in the type-script or the translation made by Du Pont's descendants. The family also dropped his analogy between religious observance and fashion: "just as one would wear a dolman in Constantinople and a juste-à-corps in Paris."

[6]Jean le Rond d'Alembert (1717–1783), the illegitimate son of Madame de Tencin and an artillery officer, Louis-Camus Destouches, became a distinguished mathematician and scientist, effective co-editor with Diderot of the *Encyclopédie*, and permanent secretary of the Académie Française. Never married, he was a leading figure at the Duchesse de Maine's court at Sceaux and in the salons of Madame du Deffand and Julie de Lespinasse. Above all, he was one of the leaders of the *parti philosophique*. See Ronald Grimsley, *Jean d'Alembert 1717–83* (Oxford: Oxford University Press, 1963).

On Julien Le Roi (Le Roy), in particular, and clockmaking in general to which Du Pont refers throughout the text, but especially in Chapter 3 *supra* and Chapter 9 *infra*, see David S. Landes, *Revolution in Time. Clocks and the Making of the Modern World* (Cambridge, MA: Harvard University Press, 1983).

[7]Du Pont is referring to Daniel Defoe's *Robinson Crusoe* (1719) and Michel de Montaigne's *Essais*, of which various editions appeared beginning in 1580. The definitive edition was published in 1635, and in 1724 there was a new revised edition that served as the base for the editions of the eighteenth century; see Montaigne, *Essais*, 3 vols., ed. Maurice Rat (Paris: Garnier, 1958), which includes a chronology of publication. Samuel Richardson, *Sir Charles Grandison*, 7 vols. (London, 1753–54), presents something of a problem. Du Pont, throughout his memoirs, places considerable emphasis on *Grandison* (whose name he misspells as Grandisson) as his model of the perfect gentleman. Here he ties his admiration for *Grandison* to his love for his mother, who he says had given him the book. But it is not clear that *Grandison* even had been published at the time he

claims to have received it; it assuredly had not been translated into French. A little later in this chapter, Du Pont refers to himself as a little boy who was not yet fourteen years old; he would have been fourteen in 1753, the year in which Richardson began to publish *Grandison.* Two French translations appeared in 1755–56, one by J. G. Monod at Göttingen and Leiden, the other by the Abbé Prévost at Amsterdam. On the publishing history of *Grandison,* see Samuel Richardson, *Sir Charles Grandison,* 3 vols., ed. Jocelyn Harris (London: Oxford University Press, 1972), vol. I, pp. vii–xliii.

    Du Pont does not establish the chronology of his own life with great precision. This chapter ends with the date of his mother's death, 21 July 1756, and opens with the assertion that his mother had not borne a child for ten years. Du Pont's sister, Anne Alexandrine, was born in 1742, which would place the opening of the chapter in 1752 and suggest that the events it discusses occurred during four years and included his mother's two pregnancies, the second of which killed her. Du Pont could easily be treating the chronology of his own life loosely, but the dates of his sister's birth, his fourteenth birthday, and his mother's death are certain. This evidence strongly suggests that he is attributing to his mother the gift of a book that she could not have given him at the time he claims and is unlikely to have given him in a French translation prior to her death. In short, it appears likely that *Sir Charles Grandison* constitutes his image of the model she set for him, but not a model that she transmitted directly. This possibility inescapably raises questions about the accuracy of his attribution to his mother of the gifts of Defoe and Montaigne. I have addressed the general question in the Introduction, but it is worth noting that familiarity with both Defoe and Montaigne was common among Du Pont's contemporaries, and both fit with the other evidence he offers of his mother's culture.

    [8]I have been unable to identify the Marquise d'Urfé, but so was Ambrose Saricks, *Pierre Samuel Du Pont de Nemours,* who suggests that she might possibly have been "the notorious Madame d'Urfé to be celebrated in Casanova's *Memoirs.*" Saricks also suggests that the Marquise d'Urfé was a rather well-known Parisian figure whom Du Pont may have added to his memoirs for effect (p. 362, note 23).

    [9]Guillaume Le Blond (1704–1781), a French mathematician, wrote the following work that Du Pont might have consulted: *Essai sur la castramétation* (1748). Le Blond subsequently wrote *Éléments de tactique* (1758), *Artillerie raisonnée* . . . (1761), *L'Arithmétique et la géométrie de l'officier* (1768), *Traité de l'attaque des places* (1780), and *Éléments de fortification* (1786). He also produced editions of Saint-Rémy's *Mémoires d'artillerie* and of Sauveur's *Géométrie,* and wrote the article "Art militaire" in the *Encyclopédie.* He was, in short, an important authority on military and tactical questions during Du Pont's lifetime, but he had not published the works for which

he would become widely known at the time Du Pont claims to have read him. Bernard Forest de Bélidor (1697 or 1698–1761) was a French engineer and general who did publish most of his influential writings prior to the time Du Pont is discussing: *Sommaire d'un cours d'architecture militaire, civile et hydraulique* (1720), *Cours de mathématiques à l'usage de l'artillerie et du génie* (1725, rev. 1759), *La Science des ingénieurs dans la conduite des travaux de fortification et d'architecture civile* (1729), *Le Bombardier français* (1731), *Traité des fortifications* (1735), and the highly reputed *Architecture hydraulique*, 4 vols. (1737–54). Jacques-François de Chastenet, Marquis du Puységur (1656–1743), served on active duty in Flanders, Spain, and the army of the Rhine in the wars of the League of Augsburg and the Spanish Succession. In recognition of his services, he was named a member of the Counsel of War (1715), commander of the army in Flanders (1734), and Marshal of France (1734). He wrote a highly esteemed treatise, *L'Art de la guerre par principes et par règles* (Paris, 1748), published by his eldest son. Sébastien Le Prestre de Vauban (1633–1707) enjoyed a reputation as one of the greatest strategists and experts in fortification of the *ancien régime* and has been called the "most accomplished and skillful engineer" in French history. In 1678, he became general commissioner of fortifications and, in 1703, a Marshal of France. His military writings included *Mémoire pour servir à l'instruction dans la conduite des sièges* (drafted 1669, published 1740), *Le Directeur-Général des fortifications* (The Hague, 1683–85), and, after his promotion to marshal and the end of his active military career, *Traité de l'attaque des places*, *De la défense des places*, and *Traité des fortifications de campagne*. Late in his life, Vauban also turned his attention to political economy and the welfare of the subjects of the French king. In 1698, he wrote *Projet d'une dixme royale*, which was published in 1707 and immediately suppressed on the king's order; this work, although probably not what Du Pont had in mind at this stage in his life, was much admired by the physiocrats. See Vauban, *Projet d'une dixme royale*, ed. E. Coornaert (Paris: Felix Alcan, 1933).

[10]Abraham de Fabert (1599–1668) had a distinguished military career, avoiding participation in any of the conspiracies against Richelieu and Mazarin, and became governor of Sedan in 1642. In that office, he made the first attempt at a responsible survey of lands to be used as a basis for the assessment of taxes; he also encouraged the textile industry in the city. He was made a Marshal of France in 1666 in recognition of his record as one of the most illustrious generals of his day. *Vie de Fabert*, a "life," as it was called, by the Father Bane, appeared in 1752 and may well have been known to Du Pont.

[11]The treatment of smallpox was controversial in the mid-eighteenth century. See Antoinette S. Emch-Deriaz, "L'Inoculation Justifiée—or Was it," *Eighteenth-Century Life* 7, n.s. 2 (January 1982): 65–72, and her discussion of Samuel-Auguste Tissot's attitude toward appropriate

treatment, "Towards a Social Conception of Health in the Second Half of the 18th Century: Tissot (1728–1797)" (Ph.D. diss., University of Rochester, 1983). Tissot himself had smallpox as an adolescent and discovered that the "hot" treatments administered by his doctor only made him worse. He developed a "cold" treatment for himself and promoted it for others as well as inoculation. Du Pont's account suggests that he had become aware of the new treatment later in his life and was judging his earlier treatment by those standards.

[12]The verses can be translated as follows:
"By this occupation, honor is not wounded.
Fabert, Rose and Chevert began thus."

François de Chevert (1695–1769) was a lieutenant-general in the French army who served in the Bohemian and Italian campaigns of the War of the Austrian Succession. By Rose, Du Pont apparently means General Reinhold von Rosen; see Chapter 4, note 4. On Fabert, see note 10, *supra*.

7

Situation in which I Remain in My Father's House.
Kindnesses of M. d'Argenson, the Philosopher, to Me.
Break Between My Father and Me. Our Separation.

The loss of my Mother threw my Father and me into a mortal sorrow, but it left my cousin, *Marianne Oulson,* mistress of the house and of the mind of my Father—which proved almost equally deleterious for him and for me.

My Sister, who was only thirteen or fourteen, was in Geneva, where she had been sent because of fears of persecution of Protestant girls that had been propagated in Paris by some worrisome incidents in Languedoc, although this close to the center of enlightenment, greater tolerance had always prevailed.[1]

My Father found himself caught between his *twenty-four year old* niece, who had long since applied herself to studying and pleasing him, and his *sixteen-year old son,* who had always lived somewhat distant from him in the special company of his mother, or in studies, and who was not in perfect understanding with his cousin.

This cousin tried in the first days to establish herself as my second Mother, and I received her advances poorly. She had little trouble in persuading my Father that I should be *very difficult to handle.* I certainly was so for her, and I dare not say that I was not so for him; we shared several similar faults and we had only a few analogous good qualities. Nonetheless, the last words of my Mother had inspired me with the most perfect devotion to everything that my Father would require.

I promptly gave rather striking—perhaps even rather misplaced—proof of this devotion the first time that my cousin, trying out her adeptness and her power, led my Father into an action totally in contradiction with his principles, his views, his invariable probity. She persuaded him that on the one hand to diminish the costs of justice and on the other to hold more firmly in his dependence the young, and, as she said *difficult to handle,* children, it was not appropriate to include in the inventory made after my Mother's death all of the goods of the community: that he should set aside the possessions that could be excluded without scandal; that this action would not injure my sister or me since we would recover them at the death of my Father, who did not want to dissipate his fortune; and that would, on the contrary, do us good by rendering us more reasonable and tractable to his will, which would never have anything but our advantage for object.

I have said that my Father had a straight heart, a severe virtue, and a mind of little breadth. He was duped by the sophistry; he believed that he was accomplishing an action of virtue and morality and being a good Father of the family; he believed it so firmly that he discussed the problem in front of me and asked *if I approved the principle that determined it, if I would regret that my fortune depend in part on him.* I saw the trap, and that my cousin was working for herself. I could have enlightened my Father with one word that he would have understood as well as I in an instant; but in blushing for the error he could have involuntarily resented me for having noticed it, and my cousin would not have refrained from pointing out to him that I was already defending my interests against his, which had been heartily blamed in the family in the case of my uncle *Jacques* against my Grandmother. I replied to him that *I knew the purity of his intentions, the rectitude of his heart, and his friendship for us; that I need no reason of special interest to submit to him; but that I should never refuse in this respect to make my interests conform to my desire.* And I allowed myself the affectation of helping to transport the most important article of our clockmaking stock and some other precious effects to my cousin's room.

As a result, our furniture, including the merchandise, did not amount to *fifteen thousand francs* on the inventory; and since we were then three children, the inheritance of our Mother was only valued at *one hundred louis* for each of us in a house in which the income exceeded *twelve thousand francs* in an average year. My Mother, it is true, had been extremely generous; but she more than subsidized it by her work and, all in all, she had never cost her husband anything.

My Father found no advantage in this operation other than that which was only justified by the aberration of a worthy principle. Since the death of my Mother, although the charitable expenditures were much restrained and the average home income remained from *nine* to *ten thousand francs* per year, as I saw in our commercial books, his fortune progressively declined, his shop collapsed. He died in straightened circumstances, needing assistance from me; and his niece, who apparently should have been rich, economized so poorly for herself that she is now destitute.

I did not cede a part of my fortune to my Father without resistance only to contravene him in matters much closer to his heart and with respect to which he only sought my dependence. I forgot my ambition; I resigned myself in good faith to becoming a clockmaker. The last wish of my Mother, pronounced by her faltering lips, seemed to take precedence over that of my entire life; and, in the reciprocal efforts that she asked of my Father and me to make each other mutually happy, I found it just that I should take all the first steps. I took a tender pleasure in my efforts, which seemed to me an homage to the adored shade of the Mother whom I so missed. I thus set myself to working at clockmaking more assiduously than I had done so far and to relieving my Father in his writing and his errands. With respect to the former, he only permitted me to aid him in his correspondence, and always reserved to himself the keeping of the books, which he did not want me to see. But he took me with him to all his customers, asking them on my behalf for their goodwill and their confidence, and charged me to go to wind up some of the pendulum clocks that he maintained on a yearly basis. That is a very reasonable speculation in which most clockmakers engage: for a very modest sum, which becomes considerable as a whole when one has many subscribers, they undertake to wind and to regulate all the pendulum clocks in a house. As a result they are sought out for all repairs and all purchases of watches and clocks, and that is what constitutes the basic stock of a clock shop.

Among our Regular Customers was the Marquis *d'Argenson,*

the author of a number of excellent works of political economy, of the admirable maxim *do not govern too much,* and that which could have saved the Kings of France, *the Monarchy is the friend of democracy, it is the Aristocracy that is the enemy of both.*[2]

While winding and regulating Clocks and watches, there is always some occasion to talk, and I spoke with more instruction and more facility than clockmakers do ordinarily, particularly clockmakers of sixteen or seventeen years. M. *d'Argenson* noticed me, made me chat, became friendly toward me, gave me his book, was impressed by the reasoned way in which I praised it, and penetrated my soul by telling me *that I could follow a more distinguished career than that of clockmaking.* His words made my heart beat and burn, they erased all my good resolutions.

I replied with tears in my eyes that I had always hoped to do so, that I had prepared myself to be an *army engineer* and that I dared believe that I had the requisite capacity and value. I requested his good offices with his brother the Minister of war, and we were then at war.[3]

"But it is necessary to know," he told me, *"if you really have some skill; could you make a blueprint?"*

I rose before the day; I worked after I left the table, during the hour that Father allotted me for recreation, I worked every time he was obliged to go out and throughout the time that he was out, I wrote every night, and at the end of the week I took M. *d'Argenson* two plans quite clearly drawn: one containing a sketch and sections of a heavily mined fortress; the other that for an attack on the same fortress. To them I joined the defensive memoir supposedly drawn up by the governor, and the offensive memoir supposedly drawn up by the attacking general.

M. *d'Argenson* was struck by the scant amount of time I had taken and by the knowledge of the trade that was manifest in the two memoirs. He caressed me more than ever, assured me that I could count on him, promised to speak of me with great interest to his brother.

I do not believe at all that I was in a state to join the corps of engineers, for I was too weak a geometrician; as to the practical and philosophical views of this part of the military art, I certainly had them. Today I think that the only thing M. *d'Argenson* intended to request for me from the Minister was to admit me to the school or to the entrance exams to the school. But at the time I thought I should immediately become a *second lieutenant* of foot. At that time, no corps rigorously insisted that young officers be noble, and in the corps of engineers, above all, intelligence was the only title of admission. The reverse stupidity dates from the reign of *Louis XVI.*

I returned from M. *d'Argenson's* drunk with joy. I told my Father that he had seen my deference to his will, which had no object other than ensuring me a situation, but that he surely would not oppose my taking one that was equally sure and better in all respects; that he would place no obstacle in the way of my advancement and my fortune; that M. *d'Argenson* is protecting me and is going to ask to have his brother to have me received as an *engineer.*

My Father replied very dryly; *"you are a young man who should not have opened his mouth to M.* d'Argenson *without having warned me."*

He goes to see him the next day, thanks him; tells him that he is very grateful for his kindnesses to me, but that Engineers are, of all military men, the most exposed; that he has no son other than me; that he intends me for his own trade, his establishment, his charge; that he does not in the least desire to send me off to war.

M. *d'Argenson* said to him, *"Monsieur, I shall do neither more nor less for your son than you wish; I thought that he had your consent."* And there was another of my *Jugs-of-Milk* spilled; there was my Marshal of France's baton burned down before the tree that was to produce it had even been planted!

This adventure resulted in much coldness between my Father and me. He felt that I had *betrayed his confidence* in taking steps toward Protectors to whom I had access because of his position, and in order to leave it, without his knowing anything. I found that he *betrayed Fatherhood* in opposing the goodwill shown to me, the elevation that would result from it, and what I considered my good fortune and my glory.

Captain *Thurot* had completed his armament and I brazenly asked my father to leave me with him, advancing the example of *du Gué Trouin.*[4] My Father replied marvelously and shamed me for thinking—when it was possible for me to earn legitimately by the upright and honest means of work and commerce—of taking the goods of others as a pirate. *"The authorization of the King,"* he said to me, *"has nothing to do with it; stealing is an evil act, it does not become good simply by virtue of a patent."* Marcus Aurelius could not have spoken better. Reason dressed in morality has always carried weight with me; I did not insist for a minute.

Nonetheless our mutual misunderstanding persisted, it was carefully cultivated by my cousin *Marianne Oulson.*

We lived in the Rue de Richelieu. Our house faced on the

Palais Royal. There a young lady *Van Laan* frequently walked—a pretty brunette with great sparkle who lived with her mother, a widow of a chaplain of the ambassador of Holland. This young girl sparkled with wit, but was very light and thoughtless; my Cousin and my Father said much ill of her. I fell in love through a spirit of contradiction or of chivalry, as the Righter of the wrong they did her. She had a cousin of my age; I became friends with him; he took me to visit his Aunt, and there I spun around Mademoiselle *Van Laan* a passion in the manner of books, the most ridiculous possible. I had a large number of rivals, and Mlle Van Laan was accustomed to treating us all well when we were there, to giving hope to each of us, and to mocking us with the others when we were absent. I had my fair share of these treatments, especially of the last, and I believed myself loved to distraction.

I wrote letters, verses, impromptus, acrostics, all the platitudes that the mind can fabricate. I spent part of my nights in the *Palais Royal* where Mlle *Van Laan* remained very late. My father noticed, locked me in my room, and forbade me to see Mlle *Van Laan*.

I deem that he exceeds his powers, that there is no evil in seeing Mlle *Van Laan*, who does me the honor of receiving me and whose station and fortune were much superior to mine; that locking me in my room is a tyranny. I disobeyed decisively on two points. My room was on the floor on the garden; I went out of the window as soon as I had been locked in; I returned in the same way; I no longer remembered having been lame. But I lost my time, I rose late; I lathed and filed very little; my Father was very much displeased with me, and he was correct.

Although I was no longer Christian, and although I no longer made my *communion*, I went regularly to the chapel of Holland because Mlle *Van Laan*, daughter of a Minister never missed, and on the return I took her hand. A very mediocre Pastor had succeeded M. *L'Honoré*; he was called M. *de la Broue*, and we considered it good taste to make fun of his manner and his oratorical flourishes. I told of my previous desire to become a *Pastor of the Holy Gospel*, and I pretended that I should have preached sermons at least as good as those of M. *de la Broue*. Mlle *Van Laan* said that my kind of sermon would be a curious piece. I composed one on the text of St. John, *"Whomsoever loves is born of God and knows God, but whomsoever does not love has not known God, for God is love."*

In my sermon I parodied M. *de la Broue*—his divisions, his subdivision, his formulas; I quoted from Scripture, the Fathers, the

Poets. I proved, I no longer recall in how many points, that when one has made love well, one has accomplished the essential duties of Religion. I preached this beautiful production on a large table between three armchairs at Mlle *Van Laan's* house, and this time to her sincere applause and that of her very crazy assembly.

My friend Volpelière, a much more substantial boy than myself, also belonged to the court of my Sovereign and was not amused, like me, by vain discourse and vainer writings. Having not been at the presentation, he requested my Manuscript, I lent it to him. He brought it back to me at my Father's; I thought I put it back in my pocket; I set it aside; my Father picked it up and found the demonstration of three points: 1) that *against his prohibition*, I continued to see Mlle *Van Laan*; 2) that if I was making hardly any wheels and pinions, it was because I was making, and again *in spite of his prohibition*, much more prose and verse; 3) that I applied them to *parodying holy things*.

It was a question of Sermons, so he sent to find M. *de la Broue*: the latter was even more scandalized in recognizing himself. He concluded that I would never be anything but a bad egg; commiserated with my Father; advised him to treat me rigorously, to force me to work hard, and firmly to disengage me from all these insanities. My Father had seen M. *de la Broue* one evening; he came home with a severe and preoccupied air and supped without saying a word. After supper he indicated to me that I no longer had a room, that he had set up a bed for me in a loft from which one could not see clearly, between his shop and his bedroom *"which would put him in a better position to observe what I did during the night and to make me get to work early in the morning. Go up there, Monsieur."*

My room that gave me the allure and the liberties of a big young man, my room where I had my small library and all my military and literary jumble, my room where I wrote all night if I pleased, my room where I had arranged a sample natural history exhibition—including some shells that a merchant, a friend of *Volpelière*, had sent me from the Orient, of some scraps that I had bought, and of castoffs from the beautiful collection of M. *d'Avila*, who lived in our house, received me with kindness, and always gave me some lesson, some madrepore, some stone, some mineral of small value—my room, in short, from which I went to visit my Mistress in three paces even after I had been shut in by a double lock, was for me a property of an inestimable price; on another side, to pull back, to descend, to be disparaged, treated as a child was a torment that was impossible for my pride to bear. To my shame and misfortune, I have always had a temper, but since I have become a man, I master myself; at seventeen, I did not master myself. I was the most uncontrolled brat I have known. (I am mistaken *Irénée*.) I mounted to the loft following the order I had received; the Cook lighted my way and my Cousin accompanied me, delighting in my grief, pretending to console me, advising me to be patient, redoubling my furor.

In this sad loft I find an old hunting knife; I pull it and would have killed or dangerously wounded myself if the two women had not snatched it from me. They took it to my Father who was not far; he calls me. I regain that kind of courage that is only concentrated anger in hardy souls; I come with slow steps. My Father had no less of a temper than I; it was one of our common qualities. He takes me by the collar and gives me a hundred blows with the flat side of the blade of the hunting knife, then throws it aside and slaps me with his hands. My cousin screamed at me to go. That was not my opinion. I wanted my Father to beat me to the point of collapse and establish the wrong on his side. I remain silent under the blows, with an imperturbable gravity; he takes me by the collar, turns me over and rolls me around the room with kicks. Finally he tires and tells me: *"Get up."*

I lift myself to one knee on the ground and say to him in a very moderate tone, *"My Father, I have surely done you many wrongs and I beg your pardon. I have expiated them under your anger. Such scenes become neither of us. I can only be beaten by you, and should not be beaten twice. I shall never expose you to anything similar again. I promise you to remain in your house only for such a time as will be necessary to find another lodging.*

"I beg you not to concern yourself with my condition or my needs; you have liberated me from your solicitude."

My Father had my bed carried into his room; I spent the night there; it was the night of Thursday or Friday after Easter of the year 1757. The two following nights I slept in the loft where he had placed me. We spent Friday and Saturday without looking at one another, without speaking.

I went to see *Volpelière*, who then lived in an apartment on the rue Beaurepaire, which had an adjacent room that was rather a bright kind of kitchen he did not use. I told him of my adventure and said to him: *"My friend, you owe me an asylum, for if you had not borrowed the Sermon, none of this would have happened to me!"* He exhorted me to remain at my Father's; I assured him that I should do no such thing and that if he did not want to rent me his empty room I would seek another; that no human power could ever make me remain with a man, even my Father, who had outrageously beaten me. *Volpelière,* who knew my equally impetuous and opinionated character, thought he owed it to my Father and me not to reject me. He consented to lease me his room and left me master of establishing the price, which I evaluated at ten écus a year.

I had a little silver sword; I sold it for *seventy pounds.* I sold my Collection of natural history, which I thought was worth an immense amount and for which I had trouble in getting *eighteen écus* from a man who engaged in this trade on the quai du Louvre, and who had sold me the tenth part for three times what he gave me for the whole.

With the five louis I bought a small bed, three chairs, a glass, a water pot, a large stoneware pot to serve as my cistern, a candle-stick, and iron candle snuffers.

The Sunday of Quasimodo, at seventeen years and three months, after having rewound the Clocks of my Father's regular customers and passably endured a sober dinner during which he said a few words to me that showed that his anger had passed, I let him go alone to the Café where we normally went together. I wrote him a respectful and tender letter of adieu, a copy of which I long kept but which finally went astray. I gave my letter to my cousin with the watch that my father lent me to get the exact time on the clocks I was in charge of regulating; and I left, taking nothing with me that belonged to him, leaving nothing that belonged to me.

I arrived at *Volpelière's* with the small amount of furniture that I had bought, my clothes, my linens, my tools, a place setting in silver that my Aunt *Françoise de Monchanin* had given me. *Volpelière* lent me sheets, which my finances had not sufficed to acquire and which I had resolved to do without if he had not offered them, although I was accustomed to using no covering other than a sheet and that which came with my bed was nothing other than an old canvas counterpane.

The next day I had my work bench set up, for I intended to rely on my trade to live until I found something better to do than watch movements. Once the Carpenter had been paid, I had *fifteen francs* left—liberty, independence, and the consolation of friendship.

These did not last long.

Volpelière played the role of gallant man. He recounted to my father what had occurred, took his orders and his instructions.

My Father gave him two, including one of which I knew nothing, which was to pay my Baker when my depleted resources would have obliged me to ask for credit. This paternal solicitude would not be good for anything. It is very doubtful that I should have profited from it even if I had known—I was too proud; but having no knowledge of it, I should have died of hunger rather than ask credit of the baker from whom I could only expect a refusal, for I was in no way known to him and neither my room nor my furnishings could inspire great confidence in me.

I was, on the contrary, very well informed of the second instruction that my father had given my friend. Madame *Van Laan* told me about it; it consisted in requesting that this woman no longer receive me in her house. Imagine my sorrow! It was in large measure to preserve the freedom to see Mlle *Van Laan* that I had left the paternal roof! I had counted on the sweetness of love, I had even counted on many resources that flowed from it. I had flattered myself that Madame and Mlle *Van Laan*, who had many acquaintances, would arrange for students to whom I would teach mathematics, and calculated that only four students at *thirty-six francs* a month would assure me a sum of nearly *eighteen hundred pounds* a year, which would grow as the number of students multiplied. I had once again made myself a Jug-of-Milk that I had not even time to set on my head.

I asked Madame *Van Laan* how my Father, who had no relations with her, had been able to make the request of which she spoke. She made the mistake of telling me that a common friend, M. *Volpelière*, had performed the commission.

There I was in an extreme rage. I found that *Volpelière* had betrayed friendship; and since Mlle *Van Laan* testified to only a very slight regret at my withdrawal, I concluded that he had supplanted me and that he had stolen my Mistress. I returned to the house shaking with anger and wanted to force *Volpelière* to take up his sword. He was wise enough to refuse, saying *that he would never fight with his friend, nor with the son of his friend.* We ceased to see each other, although I lived on the same landing and was his tenant.

He had a housekeeper, fairly ugly, named *La Gorce,* whom he treated very harshly. She complained to me and did little favors for me. I imagined that I could console her, and was not encumbered by great scruples. I had not yet reached consolation, and I was addicted to writing little notes. *Volpelière* discovered one and sent away *La Gorce*, who became a laundress of silk stockings.

I was deeply affected and tormented to have contributed to this girl's losing the bread that *Volpelière* gave her. In the poverty in which I found myself, I forced her to accept a jewel that I had gotten from my cousin *Fouquet*, the Dutchman—it was what is called a *Case of English coins* in silver—and I stopped seeing her, voluntarily renouncing an initiative in which I found myself in the wrong and to which I had never attached much interest.

So here I was alone, without a friend, without neighbors, without an acquaintance in the world, without money, almost without the capacity to earn any and almost without possessions; given over to my thoughts, abandoned to a cruel misery, at about seventeen years old, and led to this end by my pretensions, my intelligence, my vanity, my confidence in the happy auguries that my Mother and M. *Viard* had conceived for my talent, and my disdain for the more solid and less noble advice of my Father.

Notes

[1]The Edict of Nantes of April 1598 had established the rights of "ceux de la religion prétendue réformée" as the rights of an order of the kingdom with a distinct civil personality. Those rights and especially their territorial foundations had been eroded by the policies of Louis XIII and XIV. By 1685, when Louis XIV promulgated the edict of the revocation of the Edict of Nantes, the Protestants had lost their separate political, military, and judicial organizations. The revocation was intended to destroy Protestantism completely and to ensure the religious—i.e., the ideological—uniformity of the realm. Implementation of that uniformity included *dragonnades*—armed attacks on Protestants—and a series of measures that prohibited any practice of the Protestant faith, Protestant marriage, the exercise of many professions to Protestants, and a sustained policy of turning Protestant children over to Catholic relatives or institutions. Many Protestants fled the realm; many others converted to Catholicism, at least nominally. Throughout the first half of the eighteenth century, there were waves of repression against the remaining Protestants and a regular policy of attempting to separate Protestant children from their obstinate parents, sending boys to the army and girls to religious orders. The Protestants had organized their first synod "in the desert" in 1715. Thereafter, the Church of the Desert persisted underground, with its strongest center in Languedoc, but was subject to recurring attacks. For Norman families

like the Du Ponts, Protestant worship had been reduced to a largely domestic affair. But even they had to worry when there occurred a renewed outbreak of open attacks against the Protestants of Languedoc. Here, Du Pont is probably referring to the assault upon the Protestant churches at Nimes and in the Cevennes in 1751 and 1752, and the accompanying abduction of Protestant girls. These abductions were so numerous that the convents could not handle the massive influx. See H. Carré, *Le Regne de Louis XV (1715–1774)*; part ii of vol. vii of Ernest Lavisse, *Histoire de France depuis les origines jusqu'à la Révolution* (Paris: Hachette, 1900–11), 9 vols., pp. 332–37; Emile G. Leonard, *A History of Protestantism*, 2 vols., ed. H. H. Rowley and trans. R. M. Bethell (London: Nelson, 1967), vol. 2, *The Establishment*, pp. 359–436, *passim*; Roland Mousnier, *The Institutions of France under the Absolute Monarchy 1598–1789: Society and the State*, trans. Brian Pierce (Chicago: University of Chicago Press, 1979), pp. 383–410; Warren Scoville, *Persecution of the Huguenots and French Economic Development 1680–1715* (Berkeley and Los Angeles: University of California Press, 1960).

[2]René-Louis de Voyer de Paulmy, Marquis d'Argenson (1694–1757), was successively intendant of Hainault, councillor of state, and minister of foreign affairs. He retired from public life in 1747 to devote himself to letters and philosophy. The phrase Du Pont cites comes from his *Considérations sur le gouvernement ancien et présent de la France . . .* (Amsterdam, 1784). The work was published posthumously by his son, but Du Pont would certainly have read it by the time he was writing his *Mémoires,* and it contains many points of similarity with physiocracy.

[3]Marc-Pierre de Voyer de Paulmy, Comte d'Argenson (1696–1764), brother of the marquis, served in turn as lieutenant of police, intendant of Touraine, councillor of state, and minister of war. He was responsible for the establishment of the Ecole Militaire in 1751. Like his brother, he was a friend of Voltaire and the *philosophes*; Diderot dedicated the *Encyclopédie* to him; he belonged to the Académie Française. On both d'Argenson brothers, see H. Carré, *Le Règne de Louis XV (1715–1774)*; part ii of vol. vii of Ernest Lavisse, *Histoire de France depuis les origines jusqu'à la Révolution* (Paris: Hachette, 1900–11), 9 vols.; *Journal et mémoires du marquis d'Argenson*, ed. E. J. B. Rathery (Paris, 1859–67), 9 vols.; Rohan Butler, *Choiseul*, vol. 1, *Father and Son 1719–1754* (Oxford: Clarendon Press, 1980).

[4]François Thurot (1727–1760) was a surgeon and privateer who inflicted considerable damage on English shipping during the War of the Austrian Succession and the Seven Years War. René Duguay-Trouin (1673–1736) was a celebrated French privateer and lieutenant-general of the naval armies who came from an old merchant family. He played an active and important role in the wars of the end of the reign of Louis XIV; he withdrew from action with the Peace of Utrecht in 1713 and wrote his memoirs. In 1723 he was called to Paris to become a member

of the Counsel of the Indies and, in 1728, was successively named commander of the Order of Saint-Louis and lieutenant-general. The privateers were extremely important auxiliaries to the regular French naval forces which never matched those of the English; in addition, privateering provided a marvelous opportunity to recoup, defend, or augment personal fortunes. See for example J. Auzanet, *Le corsaire Duguay-Trouin* (Paris: Editions de France, 1936); F. Tuloup, *Corsaires oubliés* (Paris: Editions du Seuil, 1970); Paul Butel, "L'Armement en course à Bordeaux sous la Révolution et l'Empire," *Revue historique de Bordeaux* (1966).

8

My Poverty. My Vexations. My Disgusts; My Projects to Get Out From Under Them.

In the midst of my misfortunes I was in no way beaten down. The coldness of Mlle *Van Laan* upon our separation had cured me of my love for her. I tasted the price of Liberty, I savored with delight the sweetness of walking for a part of the night without the worry of being scolded by whomever at my return. I found an inexpressable charm in taking up the thread of all the dreams that had preoccupied me, and that I never doubted would be easily realized by a *man such as myself* who was no longer enchained by his relatives. Each day I would add a new chapter as romantic as the preceding ones.

Meantime, it was necessary to live, and it was necessary to renounce promptly the hope of founding my affluence and my success on the teaching of mathematics.

I went to see M. *du Voisin*, M. *de la Broue's* colleague at the chapel of Holland. I wanted to have at least one of my Pastors on my side. I presented him with a little manifesto and submitted to him a copy of the letter to my Father; I then begged him to help procure students for me to whom I would demonstrate Mathematics. He presented me with very praiseworthy exhortations on the appropriateness, the utility, the obligation to reconcile myself with my Father, and offered me his good offices to facilitate our reunion. As for students, he did not think of procuring me a single one; and doubtless judged that at my age I should be a very bad Master.

I went to see my cousin *Du Bucq*, M. *Doré*, a dame *Poly* who was a friend of the household—everyone thought that I was seeking negotiators to intervene with my Father, whereas I wanted nothing less than I wanted that, and none of them entered into my project to get me students. I went to the different cafés where I was known; I said I was a Geometrician; everywhere I requested students, and no one showed any inclination to take, nor to hire as a master for his children, a Geometrician of seventeen.

The only man from whom I could have hoped efficacious assistance in this matter was M. *d'Alembert*; and he is the only one to whom I did not have recourse. Had I addressed myself to him it is practically without doubt that I should effectively have become a geometrician, that I should have taught mathematics, and that, bringing to this science my opinionatedness, my career would have been completely different. But I believed that M. *d'Alembert* was cross with me because I had neglected him and I did not dare present myself to him. I had courted him assiduously so long as I flattered myself that I was a man of letters or a military man, in short, in a state that I believed worthy of his counsels and his company. As soon as I was obliged to pursue clockmaking seriously, I considered myself as having fallen beneath any interchange with one of the most illustrious Scholars of Europe. I should have feared telling him that the man who entertained the ambition of becoming his student was lowering himself—and voluntarily at that—to turn pivots. I did not accord clockmaking the esteem it merited, nor the esteem that learned men accord it, as much for the intelligence it demands as for its relations to astronomy, to navigation, and its usefulness in all the general and particular observations of physics. I saw it only as a trade in one of the most scientific and ingenious arts, and this was the fault of my Father who had never presented it to me as anything but a trade, only a *way of making a living*. Thus more than a year had passed without my having seen M. *d'Alembert*; I imagined that he would have noticed my absence, that he would receive me badly, and although I perfectly understood how advantageous it would be for me to invoke his favor, I could not make the effort to present myself to him. Several times, I got as far as his door—never did I have the courage to enter; and once, as I came back to it with a prepared speech, I thought I saw him come out, and took off at full speed. I only saw him again when I had begun to be known as a man of letters and administration, and having met him at M. *Quesnay's* and M. *Turgot's,* I was able to remind him of the goodwill he had manifested toward me when I was still a child. He had not forgotten me. For myself, by my stupidity, by a misguided and ridiculous timidity related to my pride, I lost the only avenue I had to arrive at the goal that I had set myself.

Meanwhile, my pittance of money was running out even though I had set myself to live on bread, water, and an allowance of *eight coppers* for better food. It was time to think of really earning something from my trade. I began a watch mechanism. I was a very bad watchmaker and as slow as could be with my work; it took me three months to make this mechanism that an ordinary worker could have made in two weeks, some in one. It was necessary to pay, above and beyond my very slight nourishment, for laundry, shoes, darning, and the wigmaker, for I did not know how to arrange my hair, and having very beautiful hair at the time, I placed a silly importance on having it well-dressed.

I sold my silver place setting, which was very light; I sold my silver buckles and my collar box, which were equally light. I sold my books volume by volume, and always for a pittance.

There my great sufferings began. The Bible and Robinson made no impression on me, nor Daniel's history of France. The Geometry Books caused me some regret, but I was angry at them for having failed to provide me with students. Rollin's ancient history affected me; I sighed for M. d'Argenson; I wept for Montaigne.[1]

But when it became necessary to choose between *The Spectacle of Nature,* which I had earned from M. *Restaut* for my most beautiful verses, and Grandisson, my friend, my Protector, whom I resolved to take as my model, who protected me against a thousand questions by the internal question what would Sir Charles Grandisson do in this case? the struggle between my past and future glory became extremely painful. *The Spectacle of Nature* went first. A few days later, Grandisson had to follow. All that remained was the *Discourse on the inequality of conditions,* the *Spirit of the laws* and *Caesar's Commentaries.* When I had finished one I read the other, and then I began over. Later, I added *d'Alembert's Letter on the Theaters,* the *Social Contract* and *Emile,* and until I was twenty-two years old I had no other library.[2] It was good; it left me time to think, to judge for myself. I do not know if you know the Dutch Proverb: Beware of a man who has only one book, only such people can think profoundly.

At the beginning what did I not have to think of? My books, although very good, sold for less than the value of the binding and had not been able to take me far. It was necessary to give up all food other than bread; even the bread had to be rationed, and in the age of the largest appetite, only four pounds a week could be eaten.

An unhappy little cat who had adopted me was almost the only being who deigned to love me. He shared my fortunes and my bread. As soon as I pulled him from the wardrobe in which he was drying himself, the poor cat, no less famished than his master, climbed on my shoulders; I let a little crumb run off my lips; we ate beak to beak; he thanked me with his gestures and in his language, and I said there was still someone who was interested in my fate—and I added with pride *there is me*.

It was no longer necessary to preach to me to get me to rise in the morning. From the break of day I hastened to try to complete my watch mechanism, but I broke first one piece then another, and the moment of completing it and putting it up for sale always fled before me.

Three weeks of this Regime taught me how hunger weighs in the miseries of life. When, at the corners of the streets, I saw a Soapmaker or a Mender of old clothes in their casks, eating an old tag end of beans, I said: *I bet those people complain of their fate and perhaps envy mine because I am dressed a little better than they; nonetheless they have their fill of beans and bread.*

When the three weeks ran out, the cousin of *Mlle Van Laan*, M. *Des Rivières*, who had abandoned me, but to whom I had only spoken of my hopes and not of my misery, came to see me and found me in the affliction of having broken the shaft of a pendulum and not knowing when my eternal mechanism would be completed. This time I did not dissemble that I needed to sell it. *Des Rivières* loaned me an écu and—consider my madness—I put twenty cents of it on the Lottery to open a door to fortune and to gain for myself, until the moment of the drawing, the sweetness of castles in Spain. I have been accustomed to building them since childhood; I had not yet lost the habit, they really contributed a lot to that succession of agreeable sensations that is called *happiness*.

They began the instant that my comrade left me, it was the

evening and I had to wait until the next day to enjoy my great and unexpected wealth of *sixty* cents. I passed a very sweet night.

The lottery satisfied, I permitted myself the magnificence of restoring—but for this one day only—my old ration of *eight* cents, in order to revivify myself by eating soup, which seemed delicious to me. The remainder furnished me bread and water for two weeks; my work could not last that long, and, assuming that the big prize failed me, I had made a plan worthy of myself.[3]

It was becoming evident that no one wanted me to teach him mathematics and that I could not live from my work as a clock-maker. It was therefore necessary to chart another course, but this other course required advances and I had to make these advances from the sale of my mechanism.

I wanted to return to my Marshal's baton, to raise myself by my compass and my sword; I had to begin by becoming a soldier. But I did not want to enlist in a regiment that was employed in Europe: two reasons dissuaded me. The first—the prudence of my Father, of all my Relatives having established like a maxim in the family *that any young man who enlisted was a libertine*—was that I did not want to be taken for a *libertine*: I did not want my Father, of whom I intended to keep the right to complain, to be able to allege any solid reproach against me.

The second is that I had understood very well that if I were to find myself in the middle of an army of one hundred thousand men, whatever merit I might have, I should be lost in the crowd; lucky to become, perhaps, a sergeant. I therefore needed a more restricted theater in which the competition would not be so great, and I had chosen Canada.

There, in an army of 800 men, where engineers and artillery men would be rare, and detachments in little troops would be frequent, I judged that a soldier who would know how to indicate a maneuver, seize a position, direct and defend a campaign forti-fication, place a cannon or a shell at its greatest advantage, and who could appropriately cite Polybus, Puységur, Foland, Santa Cruz, the great Duke of Rohan, Montecuculli, and Turenne would make his mark, would distinguish himself, would necessarily become an officer.[4]

The combination was very good; I have frequently regretted having abandoned it, and I am still led to believe that, had I not renounced it, I would die—not a Marshal of France, but certainly a Field Marshal.

To execute this plan, it was still necessary not to enlist in Paris, for on the one hand I should have had, with respect to my family, the discomfort that I wished to avoid; and on the other I should not have lacked people who after having enrolled me for Canada would have sent me marching off to Westphalia. I had to go to Brest; embark as a volunteer, on whatever count, on a vessel of the king, and only become a soldier in Quebec. It was to this end that I intended to devote the product of the sale of my mechanism and that of my furniture.

The circumstances and, especially, the goodness of my uncle *Pierre de Monchanin* decided otherwise.

He was my guardian, but he had broken with my Father as a result of the vexations that had multiplied in the family of my uncle *Etienne Auguste*. This incident had led me to receive coldly the goodwill that he had shown me and the offers of service he had made to me, having come to see me first and to talk with me about my situation shortly after my departure from my Father's house. I did not want the latter to be able to say that in leaving him I had been reunited with people whom he did not like and whom he regarded, altogether wrongfully, as his enemies. I had limited myself to thanking my uncle and assuring him that I needed nothing. But his advances did not end, and the exhaustion of my finances being easily presumed, I could not refuse the repeated visits of my uncle and refuse, under his pressing questions, to tell him how and on what I lived. He began by inviting me to supper; this offer was very attractive, and I replied in an equivocal manner and did not go. I preferred to eat my bread in the company of my cat.

My uncle returned two days later and reproached me in a most friendly manner. I then told him frankly that not having had the honor of dining at his house before my separation from my Father I did not think that following it I could take the liberty which would give my Father the opportunity to complain of me.

I thought of that, my uncle said to me, *and I have taken care of it. I took it upon myself to go see your Father. I did not find him as furious with you as I would have thought. He told me to sound out your heart; he retains a personal sentiment for you of which I will give you proof as soon as your pride will permit you to do your duty which is to recognize your wrongs and to ask his pardon.*

Although I did not then believe that my Father was correct to hold himself as offended, the idea that he still loved me was sweet and dear to me. It touched me.

I confided to my Uncle my plans for America to show him

that my Father's help was perfectly useless to me. I added that I would, on that account, only be more appreciative of his affection and that I wished before leaving to make complete peace with him and to receive his *Benediction*. The filial spirit with which my mother had infused me rendered this word of *benediction*, the movement of the soul that inspires it, the gestures that accompany it, the prejudice and happy augury that result from it, infinitely more precious, truly necessary to my heart.

My Uncle cultivated this good disposition in me with more artfulness and tenderness than his grave character and external coldness seemed to comprise; he proceeded very slowly, but with a sure pace. For the moment, he limited himself to telling me not to despair and to renewing the invitation to come in the evening to discuss all of this with him. It was a great relief for me to know myself authorized by my Father himself, and to find, after the complete desertion in which I had seen myself, a friend, a wise protector, a good man, the brother of my Mother.

My uncle's supper seemed excellent to me, and I could not refuse to see that his advice was full of reason and morality.

By degrees, he led me to agree that if my Father had, once in his life, beaten me, it was a liberty that almost all Fathers had taken twenty times with their children without anyone's making so much fuss about it; it was evident that I had disobeyed several of his orders, laid down with a view to my own best interest; that I should be grateful to him for being disposed to restore me to his goodness; and that if it was dear to me I had only one noble and fitting way to merit it—that was not to pretend to cavil about one item or another, and to put myself at his mercy.

It is my opinion that once one determines to do a thing one should not do it by halves, and when my uncle had convinced me that I should prefer paternal affection to everything, I begged him to tell my Father that to obtain its restoration I would do *whatever he was pleased to prescribe*.

In the interval I had my mechanism, and it was so bad that instead of selling it for two louis as I had hoped, I sold it for only *eighteen francs*, so that in three months I had only earned six francs a month by my own hands. It is true that the eighteen francs joined to those that I could have drawn from my tools and my furniture would have sufficed to take me to Brest and beyond. But I had lost the freedom to embark on the voyage by the *Carte blanche* that I had believed myself obliged to give to my uncle and my Father.

The latter seemed to me to use it very harshly. First he exacted my consent to be reinstated in apprenticeship with a M. *Guizot*, a Genevan, who lived in my uncle's house. He rejected my proposition to be allowed to leave for Canada and my other—if he wished that I remain in Paris—to devote the same sum that the apprenticeship would cost him to having me enroll in the Ecole des Ponts et Chaussées or the Architecture courses of *Blondel*. It was perversely to destroy all my plans.

Then he ordered that as a punishment for having proposed to M. *Volpelière* to draw swords, that I renounce the sword, have my hair cut and wear it in a bowl cut, and change my dress only when he would permit it. This pain, which only appeared a trifle to anyone, was cruel for a chivalrous young man who put an infinite price on his sword. My Father knew as much; he knew all the pain that this rigorous law caused me, but he intended to puncture my self-respect, to turn me, in all respects, into a little garret apprentice. I do not think that he saw any further. The plan could nonetheless serve him in another way by breaking entirely the network of my previous acquaintances. For I should never have dared appear dressed in this slovenly manner at a lady's, nor propose to any of the young men I had known to go out for a walk together—in this period in which no young man went out without a sword. He allowed six cents for my small pleasures each Sunday instead of the *écu* that he had been giving me before I left his house.

I consented to all, and believed that he would at least come to install me at M. *Guizot*'s, but he chose not to and let everything be done by my uncle, who assured me that my submission would restore my Father to me entirely. I believed him; my uncle, in order to obtain my absolute renunciation of myself, had treated me to a pious fraud by depicting my Father as much more softened than he was. It was possible that he also painted me to him as more docile than he found me. He deceived both of us, but as a good Relative and a clever Negotiator. I soon had bitter proof.

I had been at M. *Guizot*'s for about three weeks, resigned to my lot, not betraying my word, forgetting the dreams of my childhood and of my adolescence, or considering their accomplishment as a happiness that was not in my destiny; remembering the last exhortations of my Mother and—in their spirit and in the calm of my passions—judging my own conduct severely, putting myself in my Father's place, seeing that he could only have judged me from his own perspective and following intentions that were fundamentally very good. I told myself: he attaches a great importance to his condition because he likes it and because he owes to it all the fortune and the happiness that he has enjoyed; he opposed my seeking another position because he believed it hazardous; it is just that a Father decide on the surest path for his children; it is a mark of friendship to which they should be sensitive even when it thwarts them; he treated me with great gentleness right up until I had spoken to M. *d'Argenson*; he feels offended that, without consulting him, I have taken that initiative; he is correct; he does not know that M. d'*Argenson* as much as led me on, and in truth, I should not have made my plans in secret without his knowledge; the familiarity that he permitted me deserved more confidence; he wisely and nobly disdained the project of joining the troop of Captain *Thurot*; he wanted me to work; but nothing was more reasonable— is one a worker in order to do nothing? He expected me to rise in the morning; can I blame him for hating in his son what he considered to be laziness? He was not obliged to know that I had spent my nights at other work; when he knew, he became angry, did I have the right to pretend that he should prefer that which he was bound to consider at the least as useless games to a work that he saw as essential? He was unjust toward Mlle *Van Laan,* that is a question; it seemed very clear to me that this beautiful young lady was mocking me. He was scandalized by my sermon, there were grounds; could I find it bad that he had remained such a good Christian—he who had not studied at all—while I should have been one as well if I had not been put in a position to evaluate properly the bases and dogmas of that religion?

This soliloquy, after having occupied me for several days and several nights, having proved to me that I was completely in the wrong with respect to my Father, determined me to perform a brilliant action that would prove to him that if I had returned to him, to the duties that it pleased him to impose on me, to the desire to render him complete satisfaction, it was neither from the disgust of poverty alone—which could have no effect on such an intrepid and firm heart as mine—nor as a result of the advice and instigations of my uncle, but of my simple, free, and own will—of the development of my reason, of the good reason that penetrated my soul.

Full of this praiseworthy resolution, I also believed that I should not mention my new design to the good Uncle who served as my mentor. If I speak to him of it, I said to myself, he will alert my Father; will want to accompany me, and it will be believed that he is leading me. Thus to erase all memory of my having lacked confidence in my father, and principally by timidity, I stoutly lacked confidence in my uncle by a very formal plan.

I left one Sunday morning, judging the hour at which lunch was finished, when my Cousin had gone back up to her room, when my Father was alone, preparing to go out; I wanted only him and me at our interview and on this point I succeeded very well.

I arrived at the door of his room, he had his back turned and was looking for something in his bureau; I waited for him to turn around. He did so and I had not finished uttering *my Father* . . . when, in an imperious tone that he alone possessed to that extent, he said to me: *What are you doing here, Monsieur? Leave.*

I reply without rebuff, and with a tear in my eye, "my Father, I have come to bear witness to you of my sincere regret for my wrongs against you and to ask your pardon."

"*Leave.*"

I weep harder, "Permit me not to leave without your rendering justice to the feeling that has brought me here and without your having had the goodness to let me kiss your hand."

"*Leave.*"

I get down on my knees, "My Papa. . . ."

"*Leave. Must I take a riding-crop to get you outside?*"

Then I got up, my tears dried in an instant, anger and indignation took possession of me. I repent only having repented.

My Father missed a beautiful occasion to submit me entirely to his will; had he welcomed me well it is probable that my entire life would have been different and—given that it did take a course closer to my own inclinations—I should perhaps consider the cruel grief that I experienced that day as one of those events that desolate us and that are happy for us. I have since convinced myself that if my Father demonstrated as much harshness as imprudence in that decisive moment, it was principally for lack of presence of mind. He was accustomed to consult my Mother or my Cousin or myself in all his affairs and when he had consulted himself he did so very slowly. I took him by surprise—he followed his most recent errors. Having dropped an imperious word, he did not know how to come back on it, and felt no other need than to cut short a tiring interview in which he feared to give me or to allow me to take some advantage, while I only wanted to put myself morally and physically at his feet.

Upon leaving him, I went to see his friend Mme Poly. I needed to calm my head and my heart by talking with a woman; it is one of their great uses in life that, when they are good, they have minds and spirits as soft as skin; and I dared not go directly to subject myself to the remonstrances of my very good but very grave uncle. My Father entered Mme *Poly*'s at the moment at which I left; he doubtless felt the same need as I. We greeted each other, but it was he who put some warmth in his glance: his was beginning to show some emotion, mine had passed.

I had to return to find my Uncle, tell him of my initiative and my disappointment, and as I had foreseen, my Uncle blamed me sharply. He would have praised me had I succeeded; one always judges by the event. Nonetheless, on the hypothesis of success, he would always have wanted to have had a part, and the cares he had taken for the last two months gave him the right. Moreover, the two nicknames by which he was designated, *the man of good sense,* and *the man of substance* indicate well enough that he would have found my resolution frivolous and precipitous. I was wrong to speak the private language that I had shared with my mother to very estimable men who did not know it, and who had another.

For the rest, my Uncle drew from his measured character a very good formula whenever he had to preach to me or to scold me. It was to invite me to dinner or to supper; the small attentions that were manifest in the meal confirmed his affection and thus softened the reprimand that never came until after the dessert.

He was my only friend—a very serious and very impassive friend for one of my age and of my poetic and romantic imagination. The only amusement he offered me was that of playing three games of chess, neither more nor less, with him on Sunday. My only distractions during the week were those of giving some Latin lessons to his oldest son during the evening and of making kites for the younger. The rest of the time, I was alone with my work and my thoughts, reproaching myself bitterly for having tied myself by my word, for having promised to follow the Law that my Father would dictate and that would take no account of my submission or of his motives. I was more irritated with him than on the day that I had left his house; the reception he had granted me remained imprinted on my haughty soul. To withdraw and to recant was impossible for my heart; not to detest clockmaking, which had caused me so much pain, was equally impossible for it.

I have never been able to await my destiny from events:
"At the altars, the Bulls fall in sacrifice,

The trembling criminals are dragged to their torment,
The generous mortals dispose of their fate.[5]
I have always needed to have a plan of action drawn up in my mind. So long as it is not formed, my soul is in pain; when it is formed, however long or difficult its execution may be, I no longer think of it and am restored to serenity. Here is what I fixed upon.

To learn clockmaking since I had engaged myself to do so, and to leave the others, even my Father, far behind me in this art; to earn enough money from it to furnish the advances for another station. When I should have that money in my possession, to make a watch of the most beautiful execution, give it to my Father and say to him: *I have fulfilled my promise. You see that I am leaving clockmaking neither from impotence nor to be a burden to you. I repossess my liberty.*

I had the good fortune to realize my resolution point by point.

Notes

[1]In addition to books already identified, Du Pont presumably is referring to *L'Histoire de France* by Père Gabriel Daniel (1649–1728) which first appeared in three volumes in 1713, and was in the process of being reissued in seventeen volumes during the period of which Du Pont is writing (1755–60); and either *Histoire ancienne* (1730–38) or *Histoire romaine* (1738) by Charles Rollin (1661–1741). Whereas Rollin's work was much appreciated by Voltaire and Montesquieu and belonged to the current of eighteenth-century enlightened thought, Daniel was sharply criticized by Voltaire and Mably. His history of France concentrated primarily on military affairs. He had inaugurated an abridged edition of his work in 1724, and it was continued by Père Dorival in 1751; the abridgement, which Du Pont might have read, ran to twelve volumes. Daniel also wrote a two-volume *Histoire de la milice française* (1721), which probably fell within Du Pont's interests at this time.

[2]Here, Du Pont is clearly establishing his relation to enlightened thought, with a bow to Caesar and the classics. His copy of *Le Contrat social*, which can be found at the Eleutherian Mills Historical Library, contains marginal annotations that appear to derive from two separate periods of his life. His respect for Rousseau was always mingled with serious criticism, but it is likely that Rousseau was especially present in his thoughts when he set himself to writing his own memoirs. On his copy of *Le Contrat social*, see Jean Perkins, "Rousseau jugé par Du Pont de Nemours," *Annales Jean-Jacques Rousseau*, 39 (1972–77): 171–95.

[3]This entire paragraph was omitted from the typescript and the translation of the *Mémoires* made by Du Pont's descendants. It is a little

difficult to understand why they dropped it, if they did so intentionally. The only possible reason for censorship could be the reference to gambling.

⁴Du Pont is establishing his own knowledge of military history and science. Polybius (c. 200-after 118 B. C.) was the Greek historian of Rome's rise to world power; Du Pont must be referring to the first five books of his *Histories* which stress the political and military history of the Punic Wars. For Puységur, see Chapter 6, note 9. The Chevalier Jean-Charles de Folard (1669–1752) was a French tactician and soldier. Although his difficult personality impeded his personal advancement and the direct realization of his tactical ideas, his writings influenced the development of modern tactics. His *Nouvelles découvertes sur la guerre* was published in 1724; he also wrote a *Commentaire sur Polybe* first published in an edition of Polybius's works (1727–30), and then separately (1757). Either version could have served as Du Pont's introduction to Polybius as well as to Folard. Alvaro de Bazan, the first Marquis of Santa Cruz (1526–1588), was a distinguished Spanish admiral, the victor of the battle of Lepanto, and the likely instigator of the idea of the Armada, although he did not live to participate in the great battle in the English Channel. Henri, Duc de Rohan (1579–1638), was a Protestant captain and leader of the Huguenot forces under Louis XIII, a position he attained following the death of Henri IV. After the war with Richelieu (1625–29) had broken the Huguenot forces, de Rohan retired to Venice where he wrote his *Mémoires,* and then to Padua where he wrote his most famous work, *Parfait capitaine.* Although temporarily recalled to French service, he spent most of the years 1732–38 in exile in Protestant countries. His other writings include *Traité du gouvernement des treize cantons* (c. 1633), which he wrote in Baden; *Mémoires sur les choses qui se sont passées en France depuis la mort de Henri le Grand jusqu'à la paix faite avec les réformés au mois de juin 1629; De l'intérêt des princes et états de la chrétienté* (1638); *De la conception de la milice; Mémoires et lettres sur les guerres de la Valteline,* 3 vols. (1758). Du Pont could have been familiar with any of his works, especially the last which was published at precisely this time. Assuredly Du Pont's mother, identifying so strongly with the Protestant nobility, would have taught him to revere the career of the great Protestant leader. See M. Petitot, ed., *Collection des mémoires relatifs à l'histoire de France, depuis l'avènement de Henri IV jusqu'à la Paix de Paris conclue en 1763,* vols. 18 and 19, *Mémoires du Duc de Rohan* . . . (Paris: Foucault, 1822); on Rohan, see Auguste Laugel, *Henri de Rohan son rôle politique et militaire sous Louis XIII 1579–1638* (Paris: Firmin-Didot, 1889), and Jack Alden Clarke, *Huguenot Warrior: The Life and Times of Henri de Rohan 1579–1638* (The Hague: Martinus Nijhoff, 1966). Raymond, Count of Montecuccoli (1608–1681), became the generalissimo of the Austrian armies. During Louis XIV's Dutch wars in the 1670s, he fought in defense of the Dutch against the great French general Turenne. At his death, he left a work, *Mémoires militaires, Commentarii belici* (Vienna, 1718). Henri de la Tour d'Auvergne,

Vicomte de Turenne (1611–1675), was one of the greatest French generals of the seventeenth century. He played an important role in the last years of the Thirty Years War and was made Marshal of France in 1643 in recognition of his services. After dabbling with the party of the princes during the Fronde, he returned to the service of the crown and enjoyed his finest hours in opposing Montecuccoli during the Dutch wars. He left his *Mémoires,* but knowledge of his career would have been readily available to Du Pont from a variety of sources.

[5]In French the verse reads:
"Les taureaux aux autels tombent en sacrifice,
Les criminels tremblans sont trainés au supplice,
Les mortels généreux disposent de leur sort."

9

I finally learn clockmaking to acquire the means of forsaking it. How I also study Medicine. Obligations that I incur to M. Barbeu du Bourg. Why I abandoned these studies, which I enjoyed.

I remained with M. *Guizot* hardly more than two months; he lost his wife and sent his apprentices away. This was fortunate for the intention that I had just formulated, for M. *Guizot* was a mediocre clockmaker and had no connections with those who were first-rate.

My Father found me another Master. He was an Englishman named *Prignan*, who lacked neither skill as a clockmaker, nor intelligence as a man of letters, nor talent for acting, nor pretensions, nor passions; he had everything except the love of work.

He taught me very little about clockmaking; in return I perfected myself, while with him, in fencing. He took lessons from M. *Ravet*, whose game, without being brilliant, was based on good and sound principles. M. *Prignan* alone paid the master; he took pleasure in having us repeat the lesson, and there were three of us who profited from watching him learn and then practicing among ourselves and with him, wagering *two coppers* and then up to *six coppers* on the first thrust. I had received a good introduction from my

Father, but from *Ravet* I learned not to get overheated, to make little movement, not to cry, to play from the wrist, never to lose contact with the blade of the adversary, not to lunge at him or move to disarm him except when the blow was certain. Although my hair was cut in a bowl and I had been prohibited from having a sword, I wanted to reassume it one day and to be able to handle it. *Sir Charles Grandisson* had forcefully incited me to this end, as he had to assure myself of the advantage and to inflict neither more nor less damage than I intended on my adversary.

My Father who perhaps regretted, albeit too late, the welcome he had granted my repentance, handled the arrangement with M. *Prignan* practically alone, consented to see me on that occasion, and even permitted me to come to dine with him on Sunday; but the occasion was without freedom, without familiarity. I remained no less alone.

This solitude, my dress, which afflicted me and distanced me from women and from young men, made me sober, silent, embarrassed at the least company. My Father teased me about this gauche manner on the part of a man who had been so much in love and had made so many romantic projects, and thereby he greatly increased my awkwardness. I fled from his house as soon as I could; I went to walk wherever I could in the countryside, bereft of friends, of books, of a mistress, forced to mine my soul, to link my ideas the one to the other, to shape human opinions on all subjects into a philosophy of my own, and to forge my character in such a way that it could pull me out of this abyss and create a happier time for me.

Although M. *Prignan* did not teach me clockmaking, I learned it to a high degree of perfection in less than a year during my stay with him. This I owe to M. *Fol* the son, a friend of M. and Mme *Prignan,* and who was then the foremost clockmaker, especially for the execution of what are called *white mechanisms.* I had seen nothing like his work. He had taught himself practically alone and gave me his secret, which consisted in exercising the greatest efforts of attention and will: those two things were within my power. I deployed them entirely. No one told me: *Do it this way.* But I looked at what came out of M. *Fol's* hands; I resolved to equal him, and I sought or invented the means. I saw that he made part of his tools, even his files. I took the trouble to do the same and no clockmaker who does not will ever make anything beautiful; for the tool merchants only have tools appropriate to the most common work.

My Father, M. *Prignan, Fol* himself were surprised by my progress. I have never been a mediocre clockmaker. I had been a detestable one, then excellent, and this rapid transition restored paternal goodwill to me. With it I reacquired the faculty of speaking at my Father's house and at that of his friend, M. *Doré,* where he went to dine on two Sundays, once with his family of which I was once again becoming a member and to which my sister had also been reunited.

Elsewhere I could not put two words together: I blushed; I became uncomfortable; my accursed dress rendered me stupid, for I imagined that I had the appearance of stupidity, and indeed, I had it so decidedly that I have known people who at that time had inquired with a feeling of pity whether the poor young man reduced to that sad condition *were not an imbecile.* I had been too much flattered in my childhood, and in my adolescence I saw myself scorned.

The effect of my reawakening credit with my Father was to make him commit a blunder. I was supposed to remain with M. *Prignan* for two years during which time he was obliged to nourish me and to teach me in return for the profit that he could draw from my work and for *six hundred francs* payable in two installments. I had only been there for six months when his business was much upset by his taste for all forms of pleasure; I engaged my Father to advance the second payment, which did not save *Prignan* from seeing his furniture sold by the authorities. He had two children and a wife who, like all Englishwomen, allowed herself to be ruined with angelic sweetness. We all withdrew to Passy and with them I experienced a second assault of poverty almost as rigorous as the first. I was beginning to work very well, but since it was a result of great care, it was also very slow; although my work commanded a high price, I did not earn in proportion to its price and its quality, and there was hardly anyone but me in the house who worked. When we did not have anything for dinner, *Prignan* made himself a turban with a napkin and declaimed the role of *Orosmane* and made me leave my wheel to play *Nerestan.* His wife, whom the children asked for bread, cried; and he said in a tragicomic tone: *Zaire, you are crying.*[1]

Finally I left them, although not without regret, over I no longer know which quarrel that he picked with me and that I did not want to endure.

It was during my stay with him that I met my good, wise,

brave, and faithful friend *Berneron de Pradt*. His Mother, who is still living, was reason, sweetness, and gaiety themselves; she wanted to love me like one of her children. She had three boys and two girls; the oldest girl recited verses with M. and Mme *Prignan* and had at first somewhat touched my heart, which subsequently turned toward the younger, whose sweeter and more tender character was better suited to my own. I wrote her letters, and I received marvelously executed answers. But I did not always write, and since the missives were animated by the success of the dialogue, Maman said to me one evening: *Let's call an end to the correspondence Du Pont, for I do not know where you will lead me.* And I learned that it was she who had, up until then, dictated the letters to her daughter. This cooled my ardor for the daughter: at first I was cross; then I determined to laugh, and we remained the best of friends—the Maman, the brother, and I. We even remained very good friends with the Beauty herself, but that was all, for one does not fall in love twice. Of the three brothers, the oldest, today a Field Marshal, was a noncommissioned officer in the constabulary; the last, today a Colonel in the Army of the North, was leaving for India. One could write an *Odyssey* of the adventures of the second, who is my friend; I shall return to them later, when they will be connected to my own. Here, I have somewhat gotten ahead of myself concerning the events that concern his Mother and his sisters; but, having to speak for the first time of an intimate and frequently tested friend, I thought I should say a word about my relations with his family.

In order to make watches, I no longer needed a Master but, having myself become a distinguished artist, I had acquired the need to live in this regard in good company, and I rented a little room in the house of *Coupson*, emulator and friend of M. *Fol*. Both were students of the celebrated *Jodin* and introduced me to him and his large, strong, singular, and crazy daughter, who has since become a leading French actress who plays in foreign countries and who even at that time had determined to imitate Mlle *Clarion* in everything, beginning, as was appropriate, with the beginning.[2]

M. and Mlle *Jodin* had ties to *Diderot*, whose varied works all have an original and real merit, and who was, in conversation, the most dazzling man one can imagine—especially when, in his study, before his desk, in a dressing gown, he suddenly got up, removed his nightcap and, surrendering to his poetic or philosophic enthusiasm, deployed the faculty, which I have encountered only in him, of moving his ears and raising his hair.[3] *Diderot* impressed me at

M. *Jodin's* house, and intoxicated me entirely when he permitted me to steal a few minutes at his own house. I fell in love with him and judged that the supreme good fortune would be to please his daughter. But I did not have this good fortune and, for having aspired to it, I lost almost all of the society of the Philosophe. The *Gyneceum* in the house was extremely different from the *Lyceum*. Mme *Diderot* was so abrupt and so lacking in taste, Mlle *Diderot*, although possessing spirit and beauty and playing the clavichord perfectly, appeared so icy to me—at least where I was concerned—that after insistently having asked to see them and never having doubted in taking leave of her Father that I should love Mlle *Diderot* to distraction, my certainty that I displeased the mother and the daughter first led me to keep away and then to stop all my visits out of fear of meeting them. Since then, I have again seen *Diderot* with delight, but several years later, when, with my heart otherwise occupied, I could enjoy in peace his poetry, his metaphysics, his enlightened taste for the sciences and the arts. In this first period I withdrew into my own.

M. *Fol*, M. *Coupson*, M. *Jodin* and M. *Romilly*, from whom I also took some advice, placed me in the first rank and above all my rivals for that part of clockmaking which is called *the White*, which consists in making all the pieces of a watch except the finish of the escapement, that of the Pivots, and that of the teeth of the wheels; for normally the Pinions and the other finished pieces are only added when *the white* has been properly completed. This process is called the *finishing* and today, being done with machines—of which I invented one—is extremely easy. When *the white* is badly made, the most accomplished *finisher* cannot make a good watch.

There were in Paris only three of us clockmakers with this kind of approximately equal skill—M. Beauvarlet, the brother of the famous engraver; M. Boulanger; and myself; and I had a somewhat higher degree of refinement, care, precision, and style in my work than the others. We were paid three times more than the price established by those who were the best workers after us, and who nonetheless upheld the honor of French clockmaking. We had agreed, my two rivals and I, never to work for a lower price than each other, and the small number of masters who coveted a great reputation never let us lack for work. At this trade, M. *Beauvarlet*, who was the least skilled of the three, but very diligent, earned *a louis* a day; *Boulanger* and I ordinarily earned only *one hundred coppers*, rarely *six francs*; and since I soon permitted myself, as you shall see, a considerable number of literary distractions, my average profit did not exceed *three to four louis* a month. But I had learned to be poor and consequently economical, so that on the basis of this mediocre earning I lived for three years. I dressed myself neatly enough; I bought back some books; I went to the Comédie every Saturday; and every month I was able to make those little expenditures which come from the pleasure of playing a little.[4] I paid the advance on my last watch, and I collected twenty-five gold louis.

My uncle had asked me, as much with a view to economy as to prevent me from letting myself go entirely to my predilections, to share my little room, and to do my little bit of cooking with a young man named *Paillard*—devout, of little spirit, with a difficult character, a slightly better than mediocre, if efficient, clockmaker. This netted me a rather considerable saving; we took turns cooking and did so very cheaply; but *Paillard* annoyed me excessively. He did not have this misfortune long. He became the victim of a much more serious one and opened to me, entirely in himself, the door to a new kind of instruction, which I followed with great ardor, which again seemed to change the plan of my life, and from which I at least drew a real benefit for myself and others. The poor boy, devout as he was, had a venereal disease of small consequence that a charlatan latched onto and made very dangerous. A second charlatan, M. *Dibon*, the surgeon-major of the Cent-Suisses, treated the disease, which had taken a bad turn, with a remedy that he kept secret and that was only the *corrosive sublimate*.[5] Either because he did not know how to control it or because the patient, although apparently robust, had a delicate chest, pulmonary consumption set it.

M. *Barbeu du Bourg*, a very estimable physician, was called.[6] First he treated the illness of the chest and considerably reduced its symptoms, but those of the Syphilis thereupon appeared more virulent. To combat them, a surgical operation and some light frictions were necessary, and reduced them, but increased in the same measure the progress of the Phthisis.[7] Between these two enemies, one of which could not be attacked without increasing the other, the poor wretch was bedridden on Ash Wednesday and buried on Good Friday in the year 1759.

I did not like him, and when he fell sick I was on the verge of begging him to find another residence; but his condition evoked my pity. He had a brother in Paris who was even more stupid than he, and married to a woman no less silly, who would have felt himself compromised by offering the least assistance to a man inflicted with venereal disease. This brother knew how to do nothing but come twice a week to leave money for the Doctor or some bouillon for the young man, who did not lack it, and who thus had only me to give him really useful care. I did so with great zeal, with the attentions that a good heart inspires, with the exactitude and the accurate observation that derive from a literate education and the habit of reflection. M. *du Bourg* found clarity in the detailed report that I gave him of everything that occurred between visits. He called me his *aide-de-camp*; he taught me to recognize the different variations of the pulse and the diagnosis that could be drawn from them; I listened to him with the greatest attention; from one day to the next I tried to show him that his instruction was not wasted. He was gratified and frequently repeated that I would have been a good Doctor: *that I was born for medicine.*

I have been thought to have been *born* for many disparate things, because to a sustained will, I joined a fairly easy talent. But do you want to know why I was really born? To want to *do well* whatever it might be and above all what is useful to others independent of all praise and at the risk of blame; to desire, nonetheless, glory; to be affected by praise but even more by the pleasure of deserving it; to adore a wife, cherish my children, love more than my life one or two friends. Give those qualities to a courageous man who is not stupid and you will make him do anything that pleases you.

It is clear that in telling me that I had another vocation than clockmaking, M. *du Bourg* spoke to me according to my heart, since I only made watches temporarily in order to acquire the money and the liberty that my Father denied me, and that were necessary for me to do anything else. Medicine, which consecrates the life of he who cultivates it to the service of humanity in the greatest interest that it has in this world, effectively appeared to me to be the noblest career to which a good mind and a sensitive heart could commit themselves. If it were the *art of healing*, it would be the function of a God; as the *art of relieving and consoling*, it is the worthy task of a good man. I became taken with that beautiful Science, and I resolved to pursue it in conjunction with the work of clockmaking that was indispensable for me to live and to underwrite the cost of my new studies.

The first anatomical operation at which I assisted was the autopsy of my poor companion, for M. *du Bourg* thought it useful to examine the phenomena caused by the complications of the two illnesses. M. *Louis* and my cousin *Du Pont*, the Dutchman, conducted the autopsy on which M. *du Bourg* gave me several lessons.

The study of anatomy inspires a mixture of horror that one cannot overcome and an interest that one cannot repress. It incessantly attracts and repels; it holds the soul and the mind in perpetual combat. It caused me much pain; it would cause me much more if I undertook it again; and if I found the occasion to do so I should find it very difficult to resist. I should die in it, as I had thought to die, in admiring the cogs of sensibility and of life, and in vainly tiring my head in trying to understand by what celestial mainspring the great Benefactor who disposed them so ingeniously could animate them.

I divided my time between the courses at St. Cosme, combined with individual lessons from M. *Louis* at la Charité and those of M. *du Bourg,* and the work I needed as much to live as to avoid a break with my Father.[8] Instead of chumming around with the clockmakers, I began to associate with the students in surgery; they still form a society of spirited people who eat cats—in stews, chopped, and in pâté; a good woman prepared all that for us for a slim remuneration. M. *du Bourg* lent me the books of the most learned Doctors and sacrificed all the moments he could spare to teach me *Physiology* and to enlighten me on my readings, of which I submitted my notes to him.

But the fatigue caused by a double work load on top of that which I had undertaken as nurse, the multiple late nights, the bad air of the hospitals where I went to see surgical operations performed, and above all the nervous contraction, the feeling of horror that these operations gave me—the cries, the effusion of blood that accompanied them, the sight and the dissection of the corpses— disturbed my health. I was attacked by small eruptions of the skin and a chest illness that lasted eleven months with a persistent spitting of blood that sometimes became vomiting and that, in this case, M. *du Bourg* attributed to the effects of excessive work.

Witnessing the suffering that studying from nature caused me, he told me to abandon it and to instruct myself only with books. *I did not claim,* he told me, *that you were born for surgery but that is all you are studying; study the Medicine that will cure you.* To which I replied: *Yes, if it can.*

It almost failed not to be able to: youth was stronger. My good Maman *Berneron de Pradt* wore herself out making me whey, bouillons of beef marrow, turnip, and onion juice. Her son and another comrade advised me to amuse and rest myself. Once they took me to eat green walnuts and drink wine to excess, and that certainly was not what cured me, but thereafter I spent more than two weeks doing nothing at all except walking quietly in the sun while warbling verses. Temperament, left to itself, saved the invalid.[9]

My finances had fallen behind. It was necessary to devote two months entirely to clockmaking to regain a bit of money; then I recommenced dividing my time with less frenzy. M. *du Bourg* enjoyed a worthy reputation without being a famous doctor, but he was an excellent teacher and very philosophical in his attitude toward Medicine. At the time he was editing a health journal and let me place a few articles in it. I still remember having inserted some curious Observations on an *imbecile* dog.

I was not rich enough to be admitted to the faculty of Paris: but I was counting on being received as a *Doctor* in one of the provincial faculties as soon as I could practice without danger for my patients; then I hoped to find someone who would lend me enough to buy a small office as a Doctor at the court, the property and wages of which would remain with him and which would give me the right to practice medicine in Paris.[10]

Happily or unhappily, the habit of observation led me to make a too correct one on myself and upset all my plans. I noticed that I never thought of the thing I should have said, and that I only thought of it after having left people, when I was replaying in my memory their words and mine: so that every day I was beaten in discussion by men more ignorant and stupid than I. This defect was at the time much augmented by the silly feeling of humiliation, the timidity, the awkwardness that my dress gave me; but there was also something natural, for I have still not lost it entirely. *How now, unfortunate one,* I said to myself, *you want to be a Doctor and your thought almost never arrives until after the fact! You will remember in the Faubourg St. Germain what should have been ordered in the Faubourg St. Antoine; your patient will die; his image, and remorse, will follow you without end. When one's head is made in this fashion, whatever the too good* du Bourg *may say, one is not born to be a Doctor, or at least a practicing Doctor such as your poverty would oblige you to be.* I thus abandoned, on account of delicacy of conscience, that study which I had embraced and pursued with such enthusiasm—and largely on account of a moral scruple.

I have involuntarily resumed it since then, in my eleven-year association with M. *Quesnay,* and having thereafter had to live in the country and seeing the intrepidity with which the village surgeons killed the peasants, I resumed my books for a third time, and since then I have practiced medicine successfully for almost six years. But I am still very far from those two epochs in my life.

Notes

[1]Prignan was assigning to himself and the members of his household roles from Voltaire's play, *Zaire*: Orosmane, sultan of Jerusalem; Nerestan, a French knight; Zaire, a slave of the sultan. The play was first performed in 1732.

[2]Claire Joseph Lerys (1723–1803) (or Legris de la Tude, according to Joseph-Marie Quérard, *La littérature française contemporaine*, 6 vols., Paris, 1842) became one of the most successful and celebrated actresses of the Comédie Française during the mid-eighteenth century. The illegitimate daughter of a seamstress and a sergeant in the French army, she began life in straightened circumstances. Her mother opened a lodging house in Rouen when Claire was about fifteen. The house rapidly became known as one of the most successful "maisons de passe" in the city, and it was rumored that Mme Lerys's most valuable commodity was the virtue of her young daughter. Tales of her unofficial career—she was officially only a third-rate provincial actress—circulated and, from The Hague, generated a brochure, *Histoire de Mademoiselle Cronel* [an anagram for Clairon] *dite Frétillon* [wriggler]. In her own *Mémoires et réflexions sur la déclaration théâtrale* (Paris: Buisson, 1799), Mlle Clairon vigorously denied this slander, but the tale is surely what Du Pont had in mind. See Edmond Goncourt, ed., *Mademoiselle Clairon, d'après ses correspondances et les rapports de police du temps* (Paris, 1890); and Barbara Mittman, "Women and the Theatre Arts," in Spencer, ed., *French Women in the Age of Enlightenment.*

Marie-Madeleine Jodin (b. 1741) was the daughter of a neighbor of the Diderots, the widow of a Swiss watchmaker. Diderot developed an interest in the young actress, with whom he corresponded and to whom he tried to give advice. An extremely hot-tempered and undisciplined young woman, she, together with her mother, had been imprisoned in La Salpêtrière for prostitution, shortly after her father's death in June 1761. This episode accounts for Du Pont's likening her beginnings to those of Mlle Clairon. In May 1765, the Comédie Française allowed her to make her début. See Arthur Wilson, *Diderot* (New York: Oxford University Press, 1972), p. 497 and p. 810, note 25; and Paul Vernière, "Marie Madeleine Jodin, amie de Diderot et témoin des Lumières," *Studies on Voltaire and the Eighteenth Century* 58 (1967): 1765–75.

[3]For Denis Diderot (1713–1784), standard-bearer of the Enlightenment, writer, editor of the *Encyclopédie,* aesthetic critic, and more, see Wilson, *Diderot.*

[4]Du Pont means the Comédie Française, the official existence of which began in 1680 when Louis XIV ordered the merging of the three most important troupes of actors in Paris. At the time at which Du Pont attended its performances, the Comédie was located in the Rue des Fossés-Saint-Germain-des-Près.

[5]The Cent-Suisses was an elite company of infantry attached to the person of the king. Swiss had begun to fight in the French army as early as 1464, but the company of the Cent-Suisses, as it persisted until 1792, was organized under Charles VIII in 1496. The Cent-Suisses indeed comprised one hundred men, not counting the officers and junior officers.

[6]Jacques Barbeu-Dubourg, a respected Paris physician, wrote on a number of subjects other than medicine, notably botany and matters of social policy. His principal scientific works included an elegant treatise on elementary botany, *Botaniste français* (1767). He served as editor of the *Oeuvres de Franklin,* translated by L'Ecuy (1777). He entered the controversy over inoculation with a defense of the inoculationists, *Opinion d'un médecin de la Faculté de Paris sur l'inoculation de la petite vérole* (Paris, 1769). In *Calendrier de Philadelphie, ou constitutions de Sancho-Pança et du bonhomme Richard en Pensylvanie* (Philadelphia and Paris, 1778), he had Sancho and his imaginary interlocutors condemn luxury, intolerance, slavery, and usury, and praise work, saving, companionate marriage, and maternal nursing. And in *Petit code de la raison humaine, ou exposition succincte de ce que la raison dicte à tous les hommes pour éclaircir leur conduite et assurer leur bonheur* (Passy, 1782, 1st ed. London, 1774), he praised the family, marriage, work, and tolerance and defended the right of property and a tax on land—in short, ideas that would have been extremely congenial to Du Pont.

[7]The disease was consumption; i.e., tuberculosis.

[8]The Collège de Saint-Côme offered instruction in surgery; Saint-Côme itself was the corporation of surgeons who, throughout the early eighteenth century, had been waging a battle to sever their profession from that of the barbers with which it traditionally had been linked and to gain equal status with physicians. See my *Origins of Physiocracy,* "Quesnay Physician and Metaphysician," and Hecht, "Vie de François Quesnay," as cited in Chapter 12, note 10. The Hôpital-Général de la Charité had been founded in 1656 under government sponsorship by the Compagnie du Saint-Sacrement as an assault against beggary; it combined the functions of confinement and minimal medical care. See Emmanuel Chill, "Religion and Mendicity in Seventeenth-Century France," *International Review of Social History* 7 (1962): 400–26. Medical education and public health became subjects of growing concern during the second half of the eighteenth century and would claim the attention of Du Pont and

many of his friends and associates. See Georges Gusdorf, *Les Sciences humaines et la pensée occidentale,* vol. V, *Dieu, la nature, l'homme au siècle des Lumières* (Paris: Payot, 1972), pp. 424–525, *passim,* 436–37, on surgeons; and George Rosen, "Mercantilism and Health Policy in Eighteenth-Century French Thought," in his *From Medical Police to Social Medicine: Essays on the History of Health Care* (New York: Science History Publications, 1974), pp. 201–19.

[9]Du Pont has a note in the margin of the manuscript: "1760?" Probably he was trying to sort out the chronology of his life for himself.

[10]Here Du Pont is describing precisely the way in which François Quesnay became a doctor in Paris when he did not have the means to attend and be accredited by the Paris Faculty of Medicine. See my *Origins of Physiocracy,* "Quesnay Physician and Metaphysician," and Hecht, "Vie de François Quesnay."

10

At what I spent my time after I left medicine until the beginning of my political career. My friend de Pradt; our projects; Mademoiselle Le Dée. How she contributed to settling my destiny.

Clockmaking and the small resources that it netted me always profited from the pauses that occurred in my other projects; and at those times I advanced considerably in the affections of my father. He liked tales; I had collected some very pleasant ones in the company of all the Gascons who were my comrades in surgery; and when my store was depleted I invented some. He took so much pleasure in them that when he was in a bad mood or he had had a quarrel at the house, my sister, and even my cousin, sent for me to come to supper and cheer up Papa with stories.

Nonetheless, my stories would have continued a long time without earning me the liberty to let my hair grow, and to reassume the blade to which I was silly enough to attach so much importance, if I had not had the sense to associate myself with some young people who acted in bourgeois comedies and whom I had known at M. *Prignan's* house. This association rather pleased my Father, for I gave him tickets for himself, his daughter, and his niece, and when once I had put on my sword to play *Valère*, or *Lélie*, or the

Marquis du Lauret, there would have been no reason to take it off the next day, which was perhaps a day of rehearsal. Thus this weighty matter that had tormented me for four years was settled by itself, and without any granting of the formal permission that had been stipulated.

Theater societies have their advantages and their inconveniences. Here were the advantages.

I lost some of my awkwardness. I learned how to dance indifferently or, to put it better, badly, but enough to enjoy it for an entire winter, and to fill in at the little dances attended by the young ladies to whom M. *Vincent* (a very distinguished miniaturist and the Father of the only history painter who today rivals *David*) taught printing and drawing.[1] My sister was a member of this school and had introduced me. These young ladies made me pose and did my Portrait in a hundred ways; I found the game very sweet. Among them was Madame *Boucher,* who did the only portrait of your mother we have—and had to do it by instruction since your mother was dead; Madame *Guyard,* who already displayed great talent; and the little *Lançon,* who has since become Madame *Du Barry.*[2] But I am not among the predecessors of *Louis XV.* I behaved very well in this company of which the pleasures were drawing and dancing and for which the only expense was a bouquet of roses.

The inconveniences were . . . first, to produce bungling scripts for two tragedies, one of which was *The Sons of Samuel,* in which I rendered a rather brilliant characterization of *Phineas* and in which I intended to demonstrate that man can have no merit great enough to excuse a bad government. The goal was good—the play detestable.

My second tragedy, entitled *Clytemnestra,* was only a reworking of *Orestes.* It had three good acts and above all two very beautiful and entirely new scenes. I do not know what has become of the manuscript, but if I look I shall find the two scenes and perhaps the entire Tragedy in my memory. Other inconveniences were quarrels and a fight the occasion and singularity of which justify that I speak to you of it. In our troupe there was a young man who had himself called *St. Yriex* although he had another name that I have forgotten. A handsome, strapping fellow, he fenced like a demigod and regularly won twelve coppers off me in our pretty game of six coppers for the first lunge, while I was delighted to rewin six from him from time to time. He spoke very lightly both of the favors that had been shown him, he said, and the wrongs that had subsequently been done him by a lady whom I barely knew by sight, whose manners were interesting and noble, who did not act in our plays, but who received tickets, came to applaud us, and danced at the little balls that concluded our performances. Courageous and gallant Du Pont has never been able to suffer that evil be spoken of the absent, much less of ladies; he put *St. Yriex* to shame and told him that should the deed be true, he was behaving as a dishonest man, but that this last point should convince anyone that the deed itself had not occurred, and that what he said was a falsehood. *St. Yriex* replied by railleries and haughty airs, which drew upon him threats to which he replied with insulting jokes; in short, it was decided to take a walk together and without witnesses in the Bois de Boulogne. They were on their way when, near the walls of Chaillot, *St. Yriex* said to *Du Pont: But you are crazy, you know that you do not have the strength to draw against me; what mania possesses you to get yourself killed for that woman?* You know how much I have the misfortune to be proud in anger; I have never been able to suffer that anyone in the world assume an air of superiority with me. I seized him by the arm, dragged him behind the village, pushed him in front of me, remained behind to close off his return, and placed the sword in his hand. He defended himself serenely, with confidence in his talent. I no longer engaged in parry, in which I was not sure enough to match him, but exchanged blow for blow, which equalizes the danger. He did not wait; in less than two minutes, I had three inches of steel in my breast. Happily, I was very adept; the blow, which fell almost parallel to my short ribs, had neither depth nor [caused] pain in the first moment, nor danger. Since my adversary had started perhaps a tenth of a second quicker than I, his head turned [as if] to seek the blow that I was delivering and received it between the right eyebrow and the nose with such violence that my sword bent as if against a wall, and two inches of the breaking point remained buried in his skull. His pain was atrocious; he let out a cry, staggered, gave me an instant to parry and to dislodge his sword—a blow of *Grandisson* that I had studied carefully and that has always been dear to me. *St. Yriex's* sight was disturbed, he was fainting. I received him in my arms, returned his sword, which he neither would nor should use since mine had its point broken off and which I think he would have made poor use of at that time. I took him to the surgeon of Chaillot, who could only withdraw the point of the sword buried in the bone with pincers and by causing him a great deal of pain. Then he bandaged me; I had lost a lot of blood while I was helping *St. Yriex*, and in spite of the care that I had taken on the road thereafter to hold my handkerchief on the opening of the wound, I was beginning to feel dizzy. They sent for a cab for us; I brought back my comrade; he had his lesson—I needed mine, and here is how I received it.

The Lady who had occasioned the duel was informed of it by a friend who was nursing *St. Yriex*. She was grateful to me, wanted to know me, wrote me a note, very regularly sent to have news of me, begged me to visit her as soon as I had regained my strength, which was only diminished by the loss of blood—as much by that which my wound had caused as by that which Louis implacably and more than abundantly drew from my arm to prevent the effects of internal hemorrhage. An acquaintance thus begun progresses rapidly. When confidence had been established, the lady invited me into her room and addressed these very words to me: *It is impossible to be more touched than I am, my dear Du Pont, by what—without knowing me—you have done for me; that comes from a very honest heart and a very noble soul. I thank you although I am cross about it and although, independent of the interest that I take in you today, the spectacle of such a public quarrel can only be disagreeable for a woman. But I beg you, another time do not put your life at risk so cheaply, for with the frankness of my character—which I may owe to your behavior—I shall not hide from you that it was he who was right.*

I do not know what excess of exertion again attacked my breast. The irregularities were so severe that my master *Barbeu du Bourg*, student of *Bordeu*, and *Bouvard*, whom I had not wanted to see because he was his mortal enemy, but to whom my Father took me, agreed that there was imminent peril.[3] I believed I really was dying; I even composed, in honor of this hasty end, some fairly beautiful verses, harmonious, sentimental, philosophical—and you will find them in some corner.

My Father brought me back to his house to nurse me and despite the announcements of the doctors and the Poet, rest, ewe's milk, and my natural strength restored me a second time after a short delay.

As my convalescence passed almost into good health, my Father left me the administration of his shop and of all his trade during a month that he used to make a trip to England. I have reason to believe that he went to consult my Uncle *Pierre* concerning his intention of wedding their niece *Marianne Oulson* and that my uncle advised him not to do anything of the kind, but, to marry her off and to assure her all the pecuniary advantages he could without wronging his children. I even partially attribute to this project, which he wanted me to accept patiently—which I always could be led to do by good behavior—the marks of affection that he bestowed on me during my illness and the unaccustomed confidence that he showed in me during his trip. Perhaps also, they were simply the effect of that agitation of the soul which, when one wants to do something that is bound to afflict those one loves, involuntarily and by a kind of compensation, redoubles the goodwill we bear them.

What is certain is that before his trip my Father had made a Will to give his niece a child's share in his succession; that on his return he made a second to name her his universal legatee, reserving for my Sister and myself only our strict legal share; and that very shortly afterwards he married her to one of his workers named *Vaudry*, lodged them both in his house, and let them conduct all his affairs.

What further confirms my opinion is that instead of keeping me in his home to follow his trade as his old plans would have urged and as seemed to be indicated by the path he had taken in entrusting it to me entirely during his absence, he did not make the least proposal to me on the subject and allowed me to rent a new lodging in the Quinze Vingts together with my friend *de Pradt*.

I had trembled lest he lure me with his caresses and his favors to slight my resolutions again and enchain me, in spite of myself, for the rest of my life to his profession, my antipathy for which might have been overcome by the praises that it earned me from my rivals and my peers. Thus I have always considered as one of those occurrences that I cannot explain and that I call *good fortune*, of which no man has had a greater number than I, the facts, which I half ignore, that led my father, who held me in his hand, to let me go in the face of all probability, and to let me try my wings.

It was one of the fortunate periods of my life that I spent lodging with *Pradt*; supping with his mother, when not with my Father; putting on with him to amuse this good Mama, impromptu comic operas, which contained scenes that made all three of us collapse in laughter; and enjoying in expectation the high destinies for which I hoped, and which finally were ceasing to be so far removed from me.

The treasure of my primitive advances already amounted to more than twenty Louis. My last watch was begun on the principles of my Father, but, following a new plan that I had made, I devoted to it those moments in which I felt my hand the surest, my glance the most exact, my execution the most brilliant.

I was going to be free; I would be able to live more than six weeks without manual labor and without assistance; I soared above the world. I reviewed with *Pradt* the different enterprises that might suit two men like him and me; and, all things considered, we determined that we needed a *Kingdom*.

There was one to our liking; it was that of *Corsica*. *Theodore de Neuhoff* had had it and had no friend.[4] We were two friends in whom we found in particular and reciprocally an incredible multitude of resources of intelligence and a great variety of understanding, courageous as our swords, ambitious as Caesar, virtuous as Cato, patient and opinionated as Fabius, united like Orestes and Pylades; nothing seemed impossible to us.

Pradt was willing to cede me the honors of the diadem. I piled on him the offices of Captain of the Bodyguards and of first Secretary of State; and while awaiting our departure in a very extraordinary adventure in which without his natural wisdom he could have committed a great blunder, I limited myself to serving as his escort and charged myself, on all points, with the subalternate role. For do you wish to have friends? Pay them—above all with your person.

Here is how our plan was conceived: the Corsicans were at war with the Genoans, and Paoli, who did not lack ability or genius, lacked bravery.[5] We would go to Corsica as volunteers animated by the love of liberty, by hatred of oppressors, but with the esteem inspired by a nation that resists them. We would become frankly Corsican, real wolves of the woods, and in small matters we would rivet the attention of our comrades by our valor. But I knew warfare as an Engineer, an Artillery man, a General of an army; Pradt who had served in the first Regiment of the Dragoons of the King of Naples, knew it as a particular officer and a soldier. It was by our exploits that we wished to deserve and win confidence.

Military successes can only be lasting if they are supported by a good civil and political constitution and by wise Laws. I had in my head the Social Contract, Montesquieu, and several of my own ideas that have since merged in the doctrine of the economists.[6] I would propose institutions so wise, so perfectly linked the one to the other that, especially coming from the most qualified and bravest of the army, they were bound to receive universal suffrage. Thus we founded a Republic for which agriculture would have been the foundation and freedom of trade the support, in which the citizens would have had the greatest extent of political rights, in which the King would only have been the first Magistrate, and we were content with this limited authority joined to the magnanimous right of its favors.

We had not forgotten that *Paoli* could be taken with the desire to have us assassinated, but we flattered ourselves that at first he would only see us as useful warriors, and that, by the time he would deem it appropriate to rid himself of us, he would find us warriors who had become such great personages that his fruitless attempt would be the true means to assure us the remaining credit that would elude him.

So reasoned two heads of which the more sensible was twenty-five years old and the more enterprising about twenty-two. It might be said that they were crazy, and it is true that they had little understanding of the world as it is, but they had greatness, exhaltation, and even some logic and some sense.

It was not for the adventurers who dreamed these dreams to examine what could have happened thereafter if the Corsicans had been able to confront France with leaders of greater valor and superior military capacity to those of *Pascal Paoli*. It is probable that both would have been shot by the friends of this General as soon as they had earned some attention. Love, the true master of the world, had prepared them for a different fate. It retained one of the two in France; it sent the other to Russia.

My father's friend, M. *Doré*, married a young lady called *Le Brun*, a former beauty of sprightly wits, a coquette who married him to end up respectable. Each had an insufficient fortune in life annuities and decided that in combining them and living in the provinces they would enjoy the ease to which both were accustomed. Madame Doré, who had lived among what was called good company, found her husband's circles terribly bourgeois in their manners, ideas, and education; in the midst of one of these circles she met a young man who had pursued five or six educations and who nurtured a thousand projects. He stood out from the rest; she was susceptible to infatuation; she became infatuated. On condition that he do as much for her, she praised outrageously the verses and the prose that he wrote, and all the more or less fortunate words he might say, for she also produced verses, prose, and above all, clever sayings.

This elegant lady was the cousin of Mademoiselle *Le Dée*,

served in part as her mother and had an infatuation with her, the object of which was, by boasting of her, to marry her off, richly if possible. Mademoiselle *Le Dée*, a tall brunette, built like a nymph, and with soft although black eyes, deserved the praise for her beauty, for her noble and simple grace, for her modesty, and above all for her intelligence, which made a striking contrast with the pretensions and airs of the protecting relative. The latter called me her son, she named Mlle *Le Dée* her daughter; we had the prudence, she and I, never to treat each other as Brother and Sister.

It is impossible to praise perpetually to each other a man of twenty-two years and a girl of eighteen without reciprocally convincing them that one is right and without inspiring in each of them the desire to cast eyes on the other marvel. The charm worked. It was not the intention of Madame Doré; it was the inevitable effect of her rather light conduct.

She bought a very pretty house in Nemours and took her Relative there. It was of course necessary that I take some trips there to see a *Maman* who treated me so kindly. They multiplied. The continuous praises, the freedom, the garden, the meadow, the neighboring woods distinctly furthered my progress with the good, amiable, and naive young lady. A great piece of news afflicted both of us. It was a question of marrying her to M. *des Naudières*, the tax collector of Nemours, who had in addition to the prerequisites of his office an income of roughly *fifteen thousand livres* from his patrimony, but who was already a widower, who in his first marriage had proved himself to have a difficult and hard temperament, and who moreover was fifty years old.[7] Mlle *Le Dée* would have cried but obeyed. She thought that I would have more credit than she with Madame *Doré*, and I spoke to that Lady.

"*You want,*" I told her "*to perpetrate an abominable act. To marry your young Relative to a man who is three times her age and who is not good; to render her unhappy for her entire life, or to endanger her morals while she was born to be virtue itself. There is nothing as atrocious as sacrificing or corrupting honest youth. What I say to you is against my interest, for if this marriage were to take place and if ever your beautiful cousin needed consolation, your kindnesses have linked us sufficiently that the choice could only fall on me. But I should prefer never to pretend to anything than to contribute to spoiling such a pure heart.*" I thus presented my remonstrances in the tone of the Lady who received them. When I began, I did not harbor the design of marrying Mlle *Le Dée*; marriage could not be reconciled with my Corsican plans, with the resolution to spend several years on the rocks and in the woods in the midst of rifle shots. I was animated somewhat by heartfelt emotion, but mainly by a feeling of probity that I wished to inspire in our common friend. If the marriage proposed had been appropriate with respect to age and moral qualities, I loved the young person with too tender friendship and too little passion to have opposed it.

Madame Doré replied: *"You speak very well, but this beautiful child possesses nothing in the world. She must have a husband, a situation, a fortune.* M. des Naudières *offers her all that. If I found another who would give her only an honest comfort and who was twenty years younger, I am so convinced that you are right, that he would indisputably receive preference."*

I hesitated to reply. My attachment, my zeal for the Young Lady, the role that I had just espoused of counsel for and preserver of innocence pushed me forward. My prospective Kingdom, which, even if I should perish in seeking it, would give me at least, as it had to *Neuhoff* and to *Paoli*, a place in history—the chimera that has always been my self-indulgent desire—and the glory that either success or misfortune also appeared to assure, held me with considerable force. One does not sacrifice, without weighing, a heroic and brilliant dream in which one has cradled one's soul for six months.

I left Mme *Doré*. Four or five times I walked slowly around the very large garden, prey to a violent agitation of thoughts. Finally, I concluded that after the step that I had just taken, and that Mlle *Le Dée* had wanted me to take, and the obliging and even affectionate things that we had said to each other, behavior toward her, honor with respect to Mme *Doré*, the obligation not to allow my young friend to be immolated, when I saw her certain peril and when this path of advice was inadequate to save her, demanded that I not allow myself to be only a halfway *Repairer of wrongs*, that I discount my plans, that I sacrifice ambition to friendship, to love, to chivalry, that I change the entire plan of my career.

Having set my course, I returned to Mme Doré, and reopening the conversation at the very word at which she had interrupted it, I said to her: *"Is it so very difficult to make a girl's fortune? If that is all that is at issue, I will do it."*

"How and with what, my friend?"

"In thirty ways, but I shall take the shortest. Give me two years, you will have no regrets."

Whether Mme *Doré* allowed herself to be impressed by my affirmative tone and by her inclination for me, or whether she judged that there was no drawback to holding a *fall-back position* in reserve, which, moreover, she never imagined could raise any obstacles to such an advantageous proposition as the marriage with M. *des Naudières* seemed to her, she did not deprive me of hope. The habit of irony that she had, and that I had never understood, gave her every facility to encourage me without risk, and left her free to say later that she had been mocking me.

I was not mocking: I am very serious in business. It did not take more than a half an hour to join Mlle *Le Dée,* to give her an account of the important conversation that had taken place—in which I spoke to her neither of my walk nor of my deliberations—to rejoice in a tear that hung on the edge of her eye, to clasp hands, and to agree that she would be your mother.

Although she was not passionate and although her imperturbable reason frequently provoked and tormented me, she honored me with an attachment, a goodness, a confidence that made the charm of my life. Never did she permit herself to doubt that I would succeed at whatever I undertook. She found herself with me in the most unfortunate positions and said: *"I do not know what he will do, he will have a terrible time, but he will pull himself out fine!"* And the encouragement that this thought gave me, my pride that wanted to justify it, the efforts of the one and the other rendered me capable and pulled me out in effect.

She was therefore calm, consoled, even gay at my word, as if our fortune and our marriage had been accomplished.

As for me, I began to feel the difference between a positive engagement and an objective determined by all the chimeras that up until that time had flattered my imagination. When I had only had to think of myself and a friend, to whom cold, hunger, bullets, or blows of a sword were nothing at all, it mattered little that events messed up my castles in Spain; the materials were not expensive, and I built another on the spot. They all seemed good to me, provided that they required intelligence, promised glory, and gave me the pleasure of saying to the honest and courageous *de Pradt: So are you pleased with me? If you require something better we will look in my bag.* Here, it was another matter: a worthy woman who was full of the most interesting candor had just placed on my head her happiness and her existence. It was essential not to disappoint her hopes. I was unpardonable if I had been presumptuous, if I had boasted inopportunely. It was no longer a question of losing oneself on the seas; it was on the earth that I had to walk, in the midst of

the thickets and brambles. And twenty-four hours of reflection sufficed to show me that there would be greater difficulty in obtaining
an income of only a thousand livres than in trying to become King
of Corsica. Nonetheless, it was no longer time to withdraw. I could
not even allow my own anxieties to be suspected; the ship was
launched, already the wind distanced it from the shore. It was
necessary to steer. *"Fidens animi, Diis faventibus."*[8]

I returned to Paris. I informed *Pradt,* not without excuses, not
without regret, not without pressing him to my heart, that the
voyage to Corsica was over. On an occasion that offered itself and
that I encouraged him to seize, I built another castle for him in
Russia, on which he himself placed many turrets and battlements
and many snares; and which he then traded against a vessel that
was sailing to Santo Domingo, then to Philadelphia, from whence,
passing over the lakes with snowshoes into Canada, and having
united with the furs of the Hurons a share of the treasures of
Candide,[9] he returned without them to France, by the convenience
of a shipwreck—in the same way that, thanks to another, I acquired
the leisure to write all this chatter to you.

With my friend gone but this time not left alone—for I had
my love—I completed that beautiful watch to which was attached
the talisman of my liberty. I had engraved on its plate *Du Pont filius
composuit, fecit, dedicavit Patri suo.*[10] On the first of January 1763, I
gave it to my Father, who did not very much regret having a
plausible motive to leave his shop to his nephew *Vaudry,* rather than
to me; we remained friends; and I walked off with my twenty-five
louis, my opinionatedness, my happiness, my genius to fortune, to
power, to glory, to marriage, to *you* who could well be in the end
the unique *net product* of so many beautiful things and of so many
great works.

Notes

[1]Vincent the son was François-André Vincent (1746–1814), whose
best-known paintings included *L'Enlèvement d'Orythie* (painted for his reception into the Académie), *Arria et Paetus, Guillaume Tell précipitant Gessler
dans le lac,* and *Germanicus faisant une harangue à ses troupes* which earned him
the Prix de Rome. He married Adelaide Labille-Guyard, herself a distinguished and successful painter. Vincent the father was François-Élie Vincent, an adroit miniaturist and the painter of Mesdames, who was a

Genevan refugee in France; he died at Paris in 1790. Jacques-Louis David (1748–1825) was the great and influential neo-Classical painter of the period of the French Revolution. His numerous important paintings included *Le Serment des Horaces* (1785), *Paris et Hélène* and *Brutus* (1789), and the great paintings of the Revolution, *Le Serment du jeu de paume* (never finished), *Le Pélétier est mort* (now known only by an engraving), and *La Mort de Marat*.

[2]Madame Boucher was presumably the wife of François Boucher (1703–1770), a designer and decorator as well as a painter and a protégé of Madame de Pompadour. He became first painter to King Louis XV in 1765. There was a Mademoiselle Boucher who exhibited around 1802 and who may be a daughter; for a passing mention of her, see Germaine Greer, *The Obstacle Race* (New York: Farrar, Straus, Giroux, 1979). I have found no mention of Madame Boucher, but it was still very common in the eighteenth century for women painters to work with, or to get their starts in the ateliers of, male relatives; for the general contours of the experience of women artists, see Danielle Rice, "Women in the Visual Arts," in Samia Spencer, ed., *French Women and the Age of Enlightenment* (Bloomington: Indiana University Press, 1984). A specific illustration is offered by the life of the woman artist whom Du Pont calls Madame Guyard, the Adelaide Labille-Guyard (1749–1803) mentioned in the previous note. Her first husband was the painter Guyard, a student of François-Élie Vincent; her second husband was François-André Vincent. An accomplished painter, she was admitted to the Académie de Peinture in 1783 for her *Portrait de Pajou*. She was also the first painter of Mesdames and of Monsieur. Her style reflected vigor of drawing, composition, and color. Du Pont is in error in calling the future Madame du Barry the little Lançon: born Jeanne Bécu to the unmarried Anne Bécu, she took the name Jeanne Rançon, after the name of the man her mother had married, during her late girlhood and early teens. She was still using it when she came to Paris during her sixteenth year in 1759, which is probably close to the period Du Pont is referring to. See Stanley Loomis, *Du Barry: A Biography* (Philadelphia and New York: J. B. Lippincott, 1959).

[3]On Barbeu du Bourg, see Chapter 9, note 6, *supra*. Théophile de Bordeu (1722–1776) was a renowned eighteenth-century doctor who completed his medical studies at Montpellier, taught there for a while, and in 1752 established himself in Paris. His originality lay in his grasp of the complexity of vital phenomena, their independence and irreducibility, and his refusal of all the simple theories that presented the organs as passively submitted to some external motor. Among his many influential writings, his *Recherches sur les maladies chroniques*, republished in B. A. Richerand, ed., *Oeuvres complètes de Bordeu*, 2 vols. (Paris, 1818), best captures the sophistication of his thought. In the late 1750s and early 1760s, after he had been named doctor to the Hôpital de la Charité with the title of inspector,

his successes indeed earned him the implacable hostility of Michel-Philippe Bouvart (1717–1787), who had entered the Académie des Sciences in 1743, been named professor at the Faculty of Medicine in 1747, and then to the Collège de France. Bouvart resolutely opposed many of the modern currents of medical thought in his day, including inoculation. He published on a variety of topics in both French and Latin; see for example *Examen d'un livre qui a pour titre: T. Tronchin de colica pictorum* (1753); *Consultations contre la légitimité des naissances prétendues tardives* (1765); *De dignitate medicinae* (1747). On the general context of medical thought in the eighteenth century, especially the second half, see Martin S. Staum, *Cabanis: Enlightenment and Medical Philosophy in the French Revolution* (Princeton: Princeton University Press, 1980).

[4]Theodore de Neuhoff was a German adventurer and baron who enjoyed a brief tenure from May to October 1736 as king of Corsica.

[5]Antonio-Filippo-Pasquale di Paoli (1725–1807) had been born into a leading Corsican military and political family. After studying in Naples, notably political economy with Antonio Genovesi, he became a second lieutenant in the Neapolitan Royal Regiment of Farnese, with which he served in Sicily and Elba. A professional soldier by choice and inclination, he nonetheless was restive under a narrowly military existence. In 1755, he enthusiastically responded to the suggestion of his brother Clemente and the Corsican chiefs that he return. In July 1755, he was chosen general-in-chief of the Corsican nation, a position he held until his defeat by the French at the battle of Ponte Nuovo on 8 May 1769. Shortly thereafter, he was forced to flee and the French conquered the island. His exploits attracted the attention of the French, and the Corsican cause the interest and sympathies of many of the *philosophes*; it is easy to understand why Du Pont might have found him such a dashing model. On Neuhoff, Paoli, and Corsica, see Thadd E. Hall, *France and the Eighteenth-Century Corsican Question* (New York: New York University Press, 1971).

[6]The *économistes* was the name by which the physiocrats most frequently were known in their own time.

[7]M. des Naudières was a *receveur des tailles*; literally, a receiver of direct taxes. In general, during the eighteenth century, there were one or two such receivers for each election. From the amount they collected, they took 6,5,4, or 3 *deniers* (cents) per *livre* (pound) as their own remuneration and then passed the remainder on to the *receveurs généraux* (receivers-general). See M. Marion, *Dictionnaire des institutions*, pp. 471–73.

[8]The phrase can be translated as: "With fidelity of the soul [or confidence], the Gods protecting."

[9]The mention of Candide is another of Du Pont's references to Voltaire's hero of the tale of the same name.

[10]The Latin phrase can be translated as: "Du Pont the son designed it, made it, and dedicated it to his father."

11

My First Steps in my New Career and their Little Success. M. de Choiseul. Services that the Abbé de Voisenon and M. Poissonnier Rendered Me.

In truth, I had advanced with confidence and boldness, following the vague and very inconclusive reasoning that a man who had conceived the means to attain a crown certainly would know how to provide bread for himself and his companion. The deduction was unsound, for the project of founding a Kingdom could be worth nothing and would in all probability only have led, had it been executed, to getting its inventor stabbed. As to my new career, everything was for nought, the slate was blank; I had not formed the least sketch of a Plan.

The first side to which my thoughts turned was the science in which I was the most learned and in which success could, it seemed to me, be the most rapid—that of Warfare. I needed a difficult and noteworthy exploit in which routine and even simple valor went for nothing, in which imagination and genius could open new paths and immediately bring distinction to their man. I thought of taking Gibraltar.

I procured all the plans imaginable of this fortress and especially the accounts of the sieges it had already undergone, and I conceived of two ways of overcoming it: one of which I shall not say a word about, for it could be realized one day and could not be used if I had described it; the other coincided in many respects with the Project that has since been formed by the *Duc de Crillon,* and not yet been attempted, although it could be, for this general was only charged with executing that of *M. d'Arson,* which he disapproved of.[1]

I drew and polished my two projects with great care and wrote a very detailed Memoir on each of them. The Memoirs had the fault of being too burdened with phrases and pretensions of great writing, when it was only a question of being an inventive engineer and general.

The union of France and Spain, and the extreme interest that the pride of this first power led it to attach to the possession of Gibraltar, led me to base the greatest hopes for fortune on the taking of this place—just at the moment a peace was concluded that rendered my two projects useless, as it did all those which might have been suggested to me by the only science in which I believed myself truly talented and likely to stand out from the common run.

I burned my Memoirs and my designs, preferring to keep them in my head, from which no one could take them, than in my Satchel in which any experienced man could have found them and claimed the honor for himself. If it had been a question of a Project useful to the human race, I should not have acted thus, but Gibraltar only concerned my self-love, was burdensome to those who possessed it, useless to those who wanted to seize it. The means for taking it were not worth the effort of being left to posterity.

With all military outlets closed, I said to myself: *Thus are the cherished labors of my youth lost, but I must not assume that I am lost myself. They have made peace; let us learn the sciences of Peace.*

My manner of learning, adopted in the time in which I lived alone and without a library, consisted neither in questioning nor in reading but in seeking in Nature and in myself, shutting myself up, and, sometimes while walking, sometimes leaning on a Table, my two eyes covered by my two hands, plunging myself into a deep and sustained reflection on the thing I wanted to know. This form of internal and solitary study is worthless for the physical sciences; for the Metaphysical and moral sciences it succeeds perfectly, and it is even thus that one best accomplishes mechanical inventions. You have already seen that, following the excellent advice of *Fol,*

I even learned the practice of watchmaking thus. When I abandon myself to reading, I read too much; I do not know how to stop. When I receive lessons, the ideas of others do not enter my head in an ordered thread; they create mutual obstacles for each other. My own, to the contrary, are mine and from the very fact that I have conceived them, I understand them clearly: I arrange them in the order that suits the working of my intelligence; I take the shortest path from the point that I know to be closest to that which I do not know on the road to the object at which I propose to arrive. The instruction that I have created for myself goes quickly and profits me: it does not burden my memory; it exercises my judgment and renders me more capable of subsequently giving myself another. I have taken pains to invent several things already commonly known by everyone; it almost always happens that I expressed them more briefly, more clearly, more simply than those who knew them before me.

Through this method and on my own, I found *that the earth and the waters are the unique source of riches, all included in the harvests and subsequently divided, distributed among all men by the different labors of society, exchanges, and wages; that whatever constitutions may be, there are never complete citizens but those people whose interest is absolutely inseparable from that of the public good and whose income actually contributes to its maintenance, but those who harvest the riches and who own the stock that produces them—the proprietors of the land; that the interest of these landowners demands liberty, happiness, and immunity for all the other inhabitants of the Country and for all labor.*

These bases established in my head appeared to me so important for the human Race that the obligation to disseminate the knowledge of them and to apply them as much as I could to the government of Nations and particularly to the well-being of my Country seemed to me a veritable mission, for which I was accountable to God, to humanity, and to my fellow citizens. My character then assumed a grandeur above the vanities that had swelled it in my youth and above all personal interest. I thought less of Fortune and of Glory—the hope for which had first determined me to work—than of the felicity, the prosperity to which I could raise my Country. I no longer saw Ministers as Protectors who were necessary to me, but as Instruments I needed to establish the reign of the useful truths whose beauty and simplicity equally touched my head and my heart.

Such is the sentiment that since that time has directed my

entire life. It was believed that I had served many Ministers, but that is not true. *M. Turgot* alone excepted—for he was worthy of commanding me and the world—*I made use of many Ministers.*[2] And I made them serve—in spite of their prejudices, in spite of their errors, in spite of their faults, in spite of their vices, and, what is stronger, in spite of their prejudices against me and my doctrine— a multitude of paternal operations and promulgate wise and salutary laws that had been dictated by this doctrine of the conservation of property, the foundation of Liberty.

I sought power in the hands that held it, and I directed it to do good. What I may have found in personal advantage was only on a back burner in my thinking.

M. de Choiseul then reigned in France and I heard him spoken of as a brilliant genius, an elevated and generous soul, an easy character; I found him painted in these terms, which had a certain accuracy, in the pamphlets of *Voltaire*; I determined that it was only to him that I should address myself and, if possible, without intermediary, since my intention was to give him ideas, and his pride might not be pleased that one appear to believe in front of others that he needed them.[3]

I wrote a fairly short memoir, although it did contain some excess in a vain display of eloquence. It was divided into several chapters on the encouragement of agriculture; on freedom of trade; on the salt tax; on customs duties and the necessity of suppressing them and the way in which to replace the income they generated; on the militias, what they cost, the best enlistments that could be attained with the same expenditure; on the *corvées* and the civil, economic, and military advantages that would result from replacing them with the employment of troops in the construction of roads. The memoir compelled reading once one had begun it. It is nonetheless more than probable that it was never read, at least not by the Minister to whom I addressed it.[4]

The manuscript was clean; I had hired a writing Master for six weeks and had developed for myself a style of writing that was not precisely beautiful, but very neat, and that I have not neglected since except when I heard the Bureau clerks take pride in writing badly: *because,* they said, *men who have a beautiful hand are taken to be stupid and do not advance,* and I wanted to have the reputation of being an intelligent man and to advance.

According to my idea that the more directly I approached *M. de Choiseul,* the better I would do, I carried my memorandum to him at his audience at Versailles, without being in the least known to him. I did not *Monseigneurify* him at all; the designation of *Monsieur le Duc* seemed to me less servile and more likely to get myself treated with consideration; it is perhaps something to have sensed that at the time, coming from the bosom of the bourgeoisie, and at my age. The Minister looked at the titles of my chapters, told me that their subject matter concerned the Controller General, and advised me to take my work to him. I begged him to keep it; he kept it; my business was in no way advanced.

A week later, I returned with a simple note cast in these terms: "Duke, I knew that the memoir that I turned over to you concerned several operations to be undertaken by the Controller General, but men are free in their initiatives and their choices, and such is mine that I prefer your approbation to the rewards of that Minister."

This somewhat extraordinary gambit struck him; he dropped the distracted and expeditious air that he, more than any other Minister, wore in his audiences, raised his head, fixed me with his eyes, found me very young, and said to me, *Who are you?* I replied, *Duke, you know that there are many people awaiting you; I shall write you in a week.—Come back.*

I believed that my fortune was made, and if I had had the good sense to write him in a week—in four words, with a thunder bolt—perhaps I should have been more successful, for I had grasped the key to his mind well enough. I, like an idiot, let it drop. When I returned, he very graciously received a memoir that was too long, rather gauche, better suited to diminish the first germ of goodwill that he had shown me than to increase it. I had drawn up a little synopsis of my history, which could not interest him, and I concluded flatly by asking him to take my projects under advisement and to employ me under his orders. I do not know how I could have been so stupid. He surely had the wit not to read my memoir, and that was all I could have hoped for; but, what I did not desire, he saw in the flick of an eye that the memoir was not worth reading. I returned a week later without a memoir. I perceived that he had become colder, and I obtained only these words spoken without humor: *I have nothing new to tell you.* The adventure seemed finished to me; it was, and it contained nothing for me to flatter myself about or to boast of.

A few days later he suspended the drawing for the militias, for which he substituted new provincial Regiments based on paid voluntary engagements. This operation, so completely in conformity with my principles, reawakened my verve. I wrote an ode in irregular stanzas that I remember and that you will willingly read here, since I do not think that I have it anywhere except in my memory.

In this day of the God of the Permesse
I shall not address my wishes
I shall sing of Choiseul and his happy works
It is to Patriotism to guide my rapture.
Thee, by whom the Romans mastered the Universe,
Divine love of the Fatherland,
Come, bear all thy fires in my compassionate soul,
Show me the art of verses.

In the shaking countryside
A son, the support and hope of his parents,
From his father torn by the law of duty,
Leaving in sobs his mother and his lover.
The abandoned soil lacked agriculturalists.
The timid shepherdess, prey to her sadness,
Wept for the strength and youth of her lover
As so many misfortunes.

Be reassured, desolate Family!
By Choiseul, informed of your cruel sorrows,
Louis fixes his paternal gaze on you
Your felicity no longer will be troubled.
Like Phoebus disclosing the rays,
The beneficent Zephyr dissipates the storms
And forming the rainbow from the remains of the clouds
Restores warmth to our furrows.

What! the valiant militia of the French people
Walked only enslaved. They doubted its heart!
Choiseul finally did us justice
Cherishing our Prince and burning for honor.
The State will see us all fly to his service.
But our zeal is free and wishes to be so in broad daylight;
Secret constraint offends a proud soul,
It removes merit from its bellicose ardor
And ours is animated by the fire of our love;
Run Citizens, that our arm that is being untied
Raise an altar to the most beloved of Kings.
The liberty which he restores to the sons of the Fatherland
Deserves a saintly, pure, august, immortal Cult.

There at the feet of that altar lies a rustic tier
There let us place the revered bust of Choiseul,
    Fixing his eyes on his adored Master
    And on public utility.
It is thus, that in the past near the Great Henry,
One saw for the happiness and the honor of France,
Humanity, virtue, prudence shine
    In the features of Sully.

The laborers guided by thankfulness
Will come from all parts to assemble at the environs.
    O my King, the splendor of your court
Is not worth their hommage in which innocence shines!
They bring thee the price of thy beneficent attentions;
See these young Beauties in their simple attire
Weave flowers into the yellowing stalks;
See these happy Shepherds on the thick greensward
    Guide their bounding lambs.
    All these mortals are thy children;
All, invoking for thee the God of nature,
At the expense of their days will extend your years.

    Thee, Minister born for glory,
If my verses are not harmonious enough,
If these too hasty fruits of a virtuous impulse
Cannot attain the Temple of Memory,
Believe that thy generous Edict will be engraved there,
    And that the Graver of history
Will know how to make it dear to our last nephews.[5]

These verses, which are not without negligence but also not without poetry or effect, had a very good one. *M. de Choiseul* first read them glancingly and then reread them straight through and said to me: *It is not an edict; it is only an attempt, an order to suspend, with a supplementary institution that I think will lead to the Edict. But why do you never appear except at the audience? Come to see me.*

When, Monsieur le Duc?

Wednesday at eleven o'clock in Paris.

From Sunday to Wednesday I once again believed my fortune was made, that my Projects were on a good course, and I boasted of my success as much to Madame Doré as to my young friend.

At ten-thirty I was at the hôtel. I insisted that I had an appointment; with this assurance I had much trouble in reaching the antechamber. I spoke my name, which no one knew and said that I had been *invited*. I waited for four hours. Finally I entered. The Minister was not alone, but he led me to an alcove: *I have thought of you; I singled you out from the very first day. Have you studied German public law?*

Had I been a less honest man I could have answered *yes*; taken the *Abbé de Mably* and the *Treaty of Westphalia* and in a week have known enough to show that I was not an ignoramus to a Minister who himself was not especially strong on this point.[6] But I had not wanted to approach the Government to dupe anyone, and I replied the truth that: *No, but that I should undertake it with ardor if he ordered me to.*

It is necessary to be ready. You cannot serve for what I had in mind. I shall recommend you to the Controller General. Make me an expanded version of your memoir on the gabelles [salt tax] *and another on the Corvées; and when you have ideas come back to see me here or at Versailles.*

That did not destroy all hope. Nonetheless I understood full well that I had missed my shot; that the recommendation would perhaps never be made; that if it was from one Minister to another it might lead to nothing, for each one wants to have his own creatures. But in the end I flattered myself that since he had once had some design of employing me or having me employed by M. *de Praslin*, who in truth was nothing but his adjunct, the occasion could be recovered.[7] I still did not know how generally frivolous these Ministers are, and how much, with *M. de Choiseul* in particular, the eve had little to do with the next day.

I composed the two Memoirs for which he had asked me only to dismiss me politely, and turned them over to him.

I studied public Law and told him so; he replied that *It was very well done.*

But although he retained for me what is called *entrances* without an appointment, and although he never refused me a word after having made me wait all morning, I saw too clearly that he had only paid attention to me for an instant and that the instant had passed. My hopes and, what I felt more bitterly, those of my friend, of which I was the repository, and my beautiful plans for regeneration of the Kingdom were quietly drowning.

About the same time I came within a hairsbreadth of drowning them very fast and without a trace, in beautiful clear water, in the flesh, in the Seine River across from la Rapée. I had learned to swim when I was preparing for the expedition to Corsica. I crossed and recrossed the river well enough; nonetheless, one day, either because the water had risen or because I was poorly disposed, my strength failed me on the return, toward the middle of the current. I made the greatest efforts, but they could no longer sustain me. I regained a few moments of vigor by diving, but they only sufficed for a small number of strokes. I saw myself perishing and wanted to struggle to the last moment; finally, exhaustion and fatigue rose to such a pitch that life became too costly to preserve for one minute more, and I crossed my arms. My comrades, who had seen me and who fished me out, found me with them locked around my body. They called me back to life. I had lost consciousness for an instant, and for a second time I felt that the moral pain which precedes death and the fight against it are one thing, but that death itself is nothing at all, the simplest and most rapid of accidents. Having returned to myself, I again pitied Mlle *Le Dée* for the danger she had run. To attach one's happiness to another is precisely to place one's treasure in lost funds; there is only the force of the daily interest that can compensate the capital. I have always tried to pay well those whose funds I held in this fashion, and I rejoice with delight in those that are given to me by those to whom I have entrusted my own.

I was not long inconvenienced, and I hastened to resume my projects, but I had learned from experience that in spite of my theory on direct steps it would be very useful to me to have some friends around M. *de Choiseul.* So I went to see Madame *Poly,* who knew many people of all stations, she mentioned the *Abbé de Voisenon* to me and took me to see him.[8]

He was the best man in the world; already old, he retained from the insanities of his youth only one—salty conversation. He spoke in star-studded exclamations. He had the patience to read and correct everything I had done in the way of scarcely readable verses. As to my prose, since it had dealt only with politics and finance, he said to me: *I don't understand any of it,* and sent me off to Dr. *Poissonnier,* whom I had met at his house, and who had something of *Voltaire's* look and a great deal of his ability to tell good tales.

M. *Poissonnier* was very useful in showing me the absurdity of misplaced eloquence. He took one of my memoirs and said to me: *This piece of writing is very good with respect to its substance and ideas but very bad with respect to its form. I will remove the Pathos and you will see how much it will gain.* Effectively, crossing out a quarter of the work with bold strokes and substituting a couple of happy transitions for what he had deleted, he transformed a verbose and overblown memoir into a clear, methodical, interesting dissertation. I shall never forget this service.

The Abbé *de Voisenon* spoke of it to M. *de Choiseul* with considerable warmth on the occasion of *Jean-Jacques Rousseau's* letter to *Christophe de Beaumont.*[9] He ingeniously and adroitly highlighted the small number of ways in which I resembled the great man—being the son of a clockmaker, having spent a great part of my youth at the work bench, having a warm soul, the extraordinary change of direction, and my romantic character. M. *de Choiseul* replied *But he should be happy with me; I like him very much. He comes when he wishes; I accept all his rubbish. There are some good bits. He is a child. One day or another I shall do something for him.*

He did nothing. Six months had passed; my time was running out; my money was being eaten up even though I was very economical. Mlle *Le Dée* had proudly and decidedly refused M. *des Naudières*; she alone remained serene. Madame *Doré* was in a tiff. As for me, I maintained a calm exterior. I offered hopes that my impatient character decreased each day in my heart; in thinking of my friend, I feared, and with remorse, to have had illusions not about my merit (for I was much inclined to judge it favorably, and the ease with which I had just learned a new profession consoled my pride) but about the possibility of making it serve my fortune, or any public utility.

What course to take in these anxieties of the soul? To turn in on oneself and add to one's capacities by study, to one's chances by activity, to one's power by an opinionated and tenacious resolution. It was at this time that I began to use in soliloquy the formula you have sometimes noticed: *We shall see,* by which I say to misfortune, to reverses, to difficulties, to obstacles, to impossibility itself: *I am not overcome and we shall struggle together.*

Notes

[1]The Duc de Crillon, a French general, had served the Spanish crown and would lead 15,000 French and 25,000 Spanish troops in a siege of Gibraltar from 1779 to 1782. They were decisively beaten by the English

in 1782. See Philippe Sagnac, *La Fin de l'Ancien Régime et la Révolution Américaine* (1763–89) (Paris: Presses Universitaires de France, 1952), p. 370.

[2]Anne-Robert-Jacques Turgot (1727–1781) ranks among the great reforming ministers of the *ancien régime*. During his tenure as controller-general (1774–76), he presided over the most thorough attempt to implement liberal economic policies prior to the Revolution. He had had a distinguished career as the intendant of Limoges and was an important economic theorist who had correspondence and personal contact with various leaders of European intellectual life. He never was willing to identify himself as a physiocrat, although his views were close to theirs on many matters, especially the need for freedom in the grain trade. He and Du Pont became extremely close, as the vast collection of letters at the Eleutherian Mills Historical Library, mentioned by Du Pont in Chapter 15, *infra*, attest. In fact, it was Turgot, as godfather, who suggested that Du Pont's younger son be named Eleuthère Irénée for liberty and peace.

Du Pont himself wrote the first biography of Turgot, *Mémoires sur la vie et les ouvrages de M. Turgot* (1781–82). The outstanding modern edition of his writings, including his administrative acts, memoirs, and correspondence remains Gustave Schelle, ed., *Oeuvres de Turgot et documents le concernant* (1913, repr. Glashüten in Taunus: Verlag Detlev Auvermann KG, 1972); for his work as intendant of Limoges, see Douglas Dakin, *Turgot and the Ancien Regime in France* (1939, repr. New York: Octagon Books, 1965); for his tenure as controller-general, see Edgar Faure, *La Disgrâce de Turgot* (Paris: Gallimard, 1961).

[3]Étienne-François, Comte de Stainville, then Duc de Choiseul (1719–1785), was the chief minister of France late in the reign of Louis XV, from December 1758 to December 1770. Rohan Butler recently has published the first volume in what is likely to be the definitive study and what is already an invaluable compendium of information on the reign of Louis XV; see his *Choiseul*, vol. I, *Father and Son 1719–1754* (Oxford: Clarendon Press, 1980).

[4]Du Pont here is attributing to himself plans for the reform of the realm much like those that Turgot would attempt in the Limousin and that the physiocrats and other reformers would advocate with mounting insistency from the 1760s onward. We have no way of ascertaining when or how he actually began to develop his views on these matters, nor precisely which influences shaped his thought.

[5]There is something extraordinary in Du Pont's having cherished these verses in his memory for some thirty-odd years. The original French reads as follows:

En ce jour au Dieu du Permesse
Je n'addresserai point mes voeux
Je vais chanter Choiseul et ses travaux heureux

C'est au Patriotisme à guider mon ivresse.
Toi par qui les Romains domptèrent l'Univers
Divin Amour de la Patrie,
Viens, porte tous tes feux dans mon âme attendrie,
Montre moi l'art de vers.

Dans la campagne gémissante
Un fils, de ses parens le soutien et l'espoir,
A son Père arraché par la loi du devoir,
Quittait en sanglotant sa mère et son amante.
Le sol abandonné manquait d'agriculteurs.
La timide Bergère en proie à sa tristesse
Pleurait de son amant la force et la jeunesse
Comme autant de malheurs.

Rassurez vous, Famille désolée!
Par Choiseul, informé de vos chagrins cruels,
Louis fixe sur vous ses regards paternelles
Votre félicité ne sera plus troublée.
Tel de Phébus découvrant les rayons
Le Zephyr bienfaisant dissipe les orages
Et formant l'Arc en ciel du débris des nuages
Rend la chaleur à nos sillons.

Quoi! du peuple Français la vaillante milice
Ne marchait qu'en esclave. On doutait de son coeur!
Choiseul enfin nous fait justice
Chérissant notre prince et brûlant pour l'honneur.
L'état nous verra tous voler à son service.
Mais notre zèle est libre et veut l'être au grand jour;
La contrainte en secret offense une âme altière,
Elle ôte le mérite à son ardeur guerrière
Et la notre s'anime au feu de notre amour.
Accourez Citoyens, que notre bras qu'on délie
Au plus aimé des Rois élevant un autel.
La liberté qu'il rend aux fils de la Patrie
Mérite un culte saint, pûr, auguste, immortel.

Qu'au pied de cet autel soit un gradin rustique
Plaçons y de Choiseul le buste révéré,
Fixant les yeux sur son Maitre adoré
Et sur l'utilité publique.
C'est ainsi qu'autrefois auprès du grand Henri
On vit pour le bonheur et l'honneur de la France,
Briller l'humanité, les vertus, la prudence
Sous les traits de Sulli.

Les Laboureurs guidés par le reconnaissance
Viendront de toutes parts s'assembler à l'entour.
O mon Roi, l'éclat de ta cour
Ne vaut pas leur hommage où brille l'innocence!
Ils t'apportent le prix de tes soins bienfaisans;
Vois ces jeunes beautés dans leurs simples parrures
Entremêler des fleurs aux épis jaunissans;
Vois ces Bergers heureux sur l'épaisse verdure
Guider leurs agneaux bondissans;
Tous ces mortels sont tes enfans;
Tous, invoquant pour toi le Dieu de la nature,
Aux dépens de leurs jours allongeraient tes ans.

Toi, Ministre né pour la gloire,
Si mes vers ne sont point assez harmonieux,
Si ces fruits trop hâtifs d'un élan vertueux
Ne peuvent pas atteindre au temple de Mémoire,
Crois qu'on y graveras ton édit généreux,
Et que le burin de l'histoire
Saura le rendre cher à nos derniers neveux.

[6]Gabriel Bonnot de Mably (1709–1785), like so many of his distinguished peers, notably Morellet and Turgot, had been educated in a Jesuit college before attending the seminary of Saint-Sulpice in Paris. The brother of the Abbé Condillac, he began his career as the secretary of another relative, the Cardinal de Tencin, but soon broke with him over an issue of religious toleration and thereafter eschewed all worldly success in favor of devoting himself to his increasingly radical writings in social theory. He had prepared the secret treaty that Voltaire had been entrusted with taking to Frederick II of Prussia in 1743, and had participated in preparing the negotiations for the Peace of Breda in 1746. He drew upon this experience as well as his extensive reading for his work, *Le Droit public de l'Europe . . . depuis la paix de Westphalie* (1748)—surely the work Du Pont is evoking here.

[7]Caesar-Gabriel de Praslin, Comte de Choiseul and then Duc de Praslin (1712–1785), cousin of the great Choiseul, began with the obligatory military career before becoming ambassador extraordinary to Vienna (1758) and then serving in various ministries, notably as foreign minister in the period of which Du Pont is writing. His political and administrative career collapsed with the disgrace of his more famous cousin. See Butler, *Choiseul*, vol. I, esp. pp. 474, 498, 511, 553, 917–18, on his early military career.

[8]Claude-Henri de Fuzée, Abbé de Voisenon (1708–1775), had earned celebrity as a poet and playwright. His success in his lifetime has not been sustained by the judgment of modern critics, but then Voltaire, among

many, praised him enthusiastically. As Du Pont suggests, he had a reputation as a sparkling conversationalist. In addition to plays and poems, he wrote a certain number of *contes* (tales), notably *Le Sultan Misapouf* (1746), *Histoire de la félicité* (1751), and *Tant mieux!* (1760). He passed as a quintessential exemplar of the boredom and triviality of worldly life. See Robert Mauzi, *L'Idée du bonheur au XVIIIe siècle* (Paris: Armand Colin, 1969), p. 39; Mauzi also discusses *Histoire de la félicité*.

⁹Rousseau's letter, "Jean Jacques Rousseau, Citoyen de Genève à Christophe de Beaumont, Archevêque de Paris, Duc de St. Cloud, Pair de France, Commandeur de l'Ordre du St. Esprit, Proviseur de Sorbonne, &c.," first published in 1763, is reprinted in J.-J. Rousseau, *Oeuvres complètes*, vol. IV, *Émile, Éducation, Morale, Botanique,* ed. Bernard Gagnebin and Marcel Raymond (Paris: Gallimard, 1969), pp. 925–1007. Christophe de Beaumont had condemned *Émile,* which had appeared in France at the end of May 1762, in "Mandement de Mgr. l'archevêque de Paris portant condamnation d'un livre qui a pour titre: Émile, ou de l'éducation, par J.-J., citoyen de Genève," rendered at Paris 20 August 1762. Christophe de Beaumont, born in 1703, had been archbishop of Paris since 1746 and was known for the independence he attempted to exercise vis-à-vis the political authorities for his struggles against the writings of the *philosophes*—expressed in innumerable *mandements*—and against the influence of the Jansenists. See Marie-Hélène Cotoni, *La Lettre de Jean-Jacques Rousseau à Christophe de Beaumont: étude stylistique* (Paris: Belles Lettres, 1977).

12

My first rural studies. I have two brochures printed which lead me to find a few protectors and some instructors. M. Méliand. M. de Mirabeau, the friend of mankind, Voltaire. M. Quesnay is gracious enough to seek me out and I give myself to him.

With the war over, the dilapidation of the finances was the real malady of the Kingdom. To cure it, few Doctors and many charlatans presented themselves.

Among the latter was M. Roussel de la Tour, whom I believe to be the same one who has since engaged in a disagreeable suit with M. *Watelet* and who still presents himself to imbeciles as a great Financier.[1] Under the title *Wealth of the State*, he had printed a plan of taxation reinvigorated by a hundredfold, in which, beginning with Population, assuming that it is composed of many more taxpayers than there are, lowering the highest rates, arbitrarily multiplying the middling and lowest ones, he presented the apparent possibility of a yield far superior to public needs.[2] The author proposed an income of *seven hundred and forty millions,* which would relieve, he said, *everyone*; he dazzled almost *everyone*, for almost everyone in France was very ignorant.

Although I was not clever, my solitary reveries had endowed me with a small number of principles that I laid out for you in the last chapter and that sufficed to show me that the author was seriously mistaken and that the general enthusiasm he inspired had no common sense.

I had guessed several fundamental truths concerning agriculture, but, being an unabashed city dweller, I knew only that little of its practice which it had been possible for me to learn in my trips on foot from Paris to Nemours while chatting along the way with a few carters who worked beside the road.

To control my theory, while verifying its consequences and applying them to the facts, I was obliged to consult the only person whom I knew who had any rural notions, *my Father's Cook!* She came from Brie and had been a hired girl in a chicken yard there. By dint of questioning her, I obtained some very imperfect information on the number of persons and animals and the amount of advances necessary for the exploitation of a farm the size of which I postulated.

As defective as my materials were—which no Parisian was in any state to recognize—they proved, on the basis of evidence, that the author of the *Wealth of the State* did not have the first idea of the bases of the operation he proposed; that the true number of taxpayers was infinitely less than he suggested; and that it amounted to barely one out of thirty individuals.

From the observations I constructed a brochure the manuscript of which I sold for *two louis* to the bookseller *Grangé*, who still owes them to me, and I do not think that you had better count this credit for much in the positive balance of my succession.[3]

A young man who gets published for the first time believes that he will not have the full honors of the press if he does not write a dedication: I dedicated my brochure to the *Abbé de Voisenon*. *Voltaire* wrote me that it was to pull a *good joke* on the author whom I refuted; and those who knew the *Abbé de Voisenon* better than I did may have believed that such was my intention, which only would have required that the *joke be good*—but I never suspected that one could be found in it.[4] I had the simplest character. I only knew the Abbé for his plays and his society verses; I had not read his tales. I saw in him only a man of letters who was going to enter the Académie Française, and who, with a gay and, even more, an obliging natural manner was gracious enough to correct my feeble writings, even though their subject matter was serious, and to teach me what I lacked in taste or in style. It was with the sentiment of sincere gratitude and with the greatest good faith that I thanked him for such goodness.

I had published my brochure hastily so as not to miss the timely moment and so that my Protector, who seemed very well disposed, would not confuse my ideas on Finance with the dreams of the author of the *Wealth of the State,* and would not drown them together in the oblivion that his deserved. But I knew that my rural calculations would inevitably lack precision, and so as not to fall into such an error, I attempted to voyage to *Nemours,* going around by *Meaux, Château-Thierry, Coulommiers,* and *Provins,* in order to study the agriculture of Brie en route. I stopped at several farms and acquired a fairly clear idea of the principal labors, the expenditures, and the products of the cultivation of grain; I learned to be no longer a *Parisian ninny.*

In the course of my travels, I found a poor bean-grower from the election of *Château-Thierry,* named *Charles Bocquillon,* who complained bitterly of the subdelegate in the matter of the Corvée.[5] I wrote a very stiff memoir for him, harder perhaps than the case required, which would surely have harmed rather than helped him if his good fortune and mine had not willed that I meet the Intendant of the Province at almost the same moment.

I remained only a short time at *Nemours,* only the time necessary to reap my first laurels as an Author and rejoice in the hopes that they rekindled in me. Having returned to Paris, I went to recount my trip to the *Abbé de Voisenon,* as the man most interested in me; I have always been very much the *son* of my Protectors. I spoke to him of the Peasant *Bocquillon* and of the vigorous memoir I had written for him. Just as I had finished, the Intendant of Soissons entered, M. *Méliand,* a rather close relative of the Abbé, who said to him: *You have arrived very propitiously; here is a young man who is vigorously scolding your subdelegates.*[6]

M. *Méliand* had no reputation because he had a rather nasty wife with a very sharp wit who amused herself by demeaning him; and in addition he was deaf and he had once said *something stupid* to the Queen, which can very easily happen to an intelligent man.*

---

*I had better cite it rather than let it appear more serious than it was. Queen *Leczinska,* having crossed the generality of Soissons and having spoken of it only with praise at a party that M. *Méliand* gave for her, he had the misfortune to say to her: *I very much wanted your majesty to be content with my Province.* The saying could have dropped, but the Queen picked

And he really was an intelligent man; I have hundreds of his letters full of grace and salt, mingled with happy and graceful verses. He was in addition a very honest man, sweet, moderate, wise, conscientious, having no faults other than an extreme weakness of character. He was poor and had a reputation for being stingy because he was orderly. I have seen him do several deeds of great humanity, charity, generosity, and I have personally had reason to praise him on this account. Renown is a very mendacious Goddess; an infinite amount of good fortune and bad fortune enter into the account that she verifies.

The administrative Magistrate assumed a *dignified* air to inquire what the subdelegate and the young man had done. To explain matters the latter evoked as much moderation, even timidity and blushing, as there had been vehemence in his Memoir. M. *Méliand* told me to bring him the memoir, so that he would write a letter to his subdelegate; that he would communicate the response to me; that once the facts had been clarified, I could rest assured that my protégé would have full satisfaction.

I brought him the Memoir the next day and spoke to him in detail of what I had seen in the part of his generality I had crossed. He told me to write it down. I did so with great care and saw on that occasion how much the science of political economy, when studied beginning with agriculture, is more illuminating than when one tries to reach it by any other path. I was certainly very little educated, but for having known from the start that agriculture is the source of wealth and that property is the only social basis, and for having looked attentively at a few farms, I appeared cleverer than a Magistrate who had been administering a province for twenty years.

M. *Méliand* said to me: *You are a real student of Mirabeau.*[8] To my shame and to that of my manner of studying like a hermit, or like a surly dog, I did not know that there was any Mirabeau other than the translator of Aristotle. The good Intendant, who took kindly to me immediately, gave me *The Friend of Mankind* and the *Theory of Taxation*. I devoured them, not being able to contain the pleasure I felt at finding myself on the right road. I jumped up, I

---

up the impropriety of the expression by this little phrase, which she would have done better to forego: *I did not know that the King had ceded the Soissonais to you.* Since it was obviously necessary that the Queen have said something charming, it was agreed at Court that M. *Méliand* was a Fool.[7]

clapped my hands, I cried out with joy; anyone watching me read would have taken me for crazy.

I wrote to the author, still in exile *at Bignon* after having been imprisoned at *Vincennes* for this same book with which I found myself so happy to share some common ideals.[9] I asked him to be gracious enough to continue to help my education. He had taught me that *subsistence is the measure of population*: that was the only economic truth that was entirely his own.

He replied obligingly and with encouragement, suggesting to me in his somewhat enigmatic style *another Master greater than he, whose shoes*, he said, *he was not worthy to untie*. The other Master was M. *Quesnay*, whom he did not name to me, and whom he designated only by the words of St. John the Baptist.[10] I have always been impatient with the prophetic elocution of my Master *Mirabeau* when I think that, had he written me as any other would have, I should have been *Quesnay's* son three months earlier. But I was at that time more than happy enough to know *The Friend of Mankind*, who rendered me the greatest service by his lessons, by his goodness, by his defects, and even by his rigidities.

I promptly sent him a second brochure, which reflected the new enlightenment I had drawn from his writings. It was a *Reply* to the so-called *Marquis de M.*, who had done me the honor of criticizing my first production by trying to establish that merchants and artisans are taxpayers, and that the taxes imposed on commerce are the best—the system of the Colbertists, which cannot sustain examination and which I fought with a decided superiority although still very much of a novice in the career.[11]

I had also sent my two brochures and my Ode to M. *de Voltaire*, which began my correspondence with that great man who never ceased to encourage me. I have always used his spelling. M. *de Mirabeau* could not stand it, brought all his authority to bear on me, from the first moment and at three different intervals, to get me to relinquish it. In spite of my respect for *The Friend of Mankind*, I resisted, not so much because this spelling seemed better to me as because I had adopted it, and I find it antipathetic to retreat in anything, and because I could not have done so without giving offense to M. *de Voltaire*, which would have been to acknowledge his kindness very poorly.

M. *Méliand* grew fonder of me with each passing day. His protection better suited my kind of work than that of the *Abbé de Voisenon*; it was more sustained, as if descending from less lofty places, and with fewer distractions than the intermittent fancies and agreeable smiles of M. de Choiseul.

M. Bertin, then the Controller General, handled agriculture according to good principles.[12] He had just decreed the *freedom of the circulation of grain from one Province to another in the Kingdom*, and established the *Agricultural Societies*.[13] M. *Méliand* presented me to him as a man who could be useful to his views, and who could be advantageously dispatched on voyages, or used in the Bureau of the administration of agriculture, which had just been confided to M. *Parent*.[14] He also presented me to this head Clerk, who received me much less well than the Minister and who has always blocked the good intentions that M. Bertin had for me on various occasions. M. *Parent* led the Government to prefer our neighbor, M. des *Pommiers*, who was at that time a spice merchant whose business was going poorly in *Cheroy*, and who has since become the financial *Governor* of that town.

I consoled myself very well by reading, following the advice offered me by M. *de Mirabeau's* letters, the articles *Fermiers* and *Grains* of the *Encyclopedia*, into which M. *Quesnay* had introduced the first principles of his doctrine, and in which can be found the ingenious and accurate observation of the difference that exists between the position of the first sellers of grain, who have only a little to sell in the years of shortage and of high prices and who dispose of a great deal at low prices in the years of abundance, and the lot of consumers, who buy an equal quantity every year and who experience no variation except in price.[15] In this way, the more the prices vary the more the sellers lose, with no profit for the consumers; from which M. *Quesnay* concluded that it was impossible to pay too much attention to forestalling great variations in prices, and that this necessary effect of free trade assured agriculture a considerable profit without harming the inhabitants of cities, and even worked to their advantage since the profits of agriculture prompted the success of their labors and the abundance that ensued. I learned to follow the profound thoughts of this great man whom I did not yet know and who was to provide me with a Father.

Meanwhile I registered with very tender gratitude that the good *Méliand* always was thinking, with the zeal of a true friend, of ways he could be useful or agreeable to me. He submitted to the *Agricultural Society of Soissons*, as if from me, my two brochures and the memoir that he had had me write on the cultivation of a few cantons in his generality, and he proposed me as an *Associate*. I was admitted on the basis of these three memoirs and his word; and he sent me the diploma, of which I had never dreamed, without having forewarned me that he was taking care of it for me.

I was at my Father's when the letters from M. *Méliand* and from the secretary of the Society arrived. I fell into a stupor of happiness to see myself a member of any *Academy* at all at the age of twenty-three years, having only begun my new political and literary career *eight months* before. I embraced my Father, my Sister, even my cousin; I bounced around the room; I was delirious. My Father said to me gravely: *What is that worth to you?* Never had a question seemed so ignominious to me; my poor Mother would not have asked it! I replied: *It is worth to me . . . It is worth to me . . . and, by Jove, it is worth to me that I belong to an Academy that would not have come looking for me at my work bench!*

I took double pleasure in these little steps forward, for they sustained, together with the hope for the success of my great political views, the confidence of my friend, and they reanimated that of Mme *Doré*.

Soon I attained a more practical success the fruits of which were even more precious to me, and decided the place that I would occupy in the world. I was adopted by the venerable *Quesnay*. It is worth telling you how and with what sentiment on his part.

My two brochures were really superior to the three or four hundred rhapsodies that appeared on the question of Finance at that time. *Quesnay*, who every morning leafed through those which had been published the day before, and who dispatched them immediately to the closet, except mine, wrote *good* on the first page, kept them on his desk, and asked everyone who was their author. Since it had to do with Finances, he especially asked the Controller General; at the time all the Ministers assiduously cultivated M. *Quesnay*, who was more than a Minister since he had the intimate confidence of Madame *de Pompadour*. M. *Bertin* remembered that I had been introduced to him by the Intendant of Soissons, who had spoken to him of the profession of my Father, and somewhat confusing his ideas, he replied: *I know that author; he is a young man, son of a goldsmith or a watchmaker of Soissons.* My two brochures were signed with the initials D.P.

M. *Quesnay* wrote to the Mayor of Soissons to beg him to send him the list of the goldsmiths and watchmakers of Soissons, hoping with this list and the two initials to unearth his man. By chance there was in Soissons a M. *Du Ponchel*, goldsmith, who was very much surprised to receive a letter that informed him that, *If M. his son wished to take the time to come to Paris to the hôtel de Pompadour or to the Château at Versailles, to ask for M.* Quesnay, *he would find people delighted to make his acquaintance and to render him all the favors that were in their power.*

M. *Du Ponchel* had precisely a son *seventeen* to *eighteen* years of age, and without understanding anything of the motives of the goodwill that was extended to him, but on the brilliant hopes attached to the words *hôtel de Pompadour* or *Château de Versailles,* he packed his son into the coach and sent him off. The young man arrived at M. *Quesnay's,* the letter that bade him come in his hand. M. *Quesnay,* nonetheless suspecting a *qui pro quo,* asked him if, *he were not the Author of two little brochures on the Wealth of the State?* The good child replied that *he had never produced any brochures; that he was beginning to make buckles for shoes and garters pretty well.* M. *Quesnay* fell all over himself with excuses, invited him to dinner, sent him back to his region, and gave up his fruitless research.

Sometime thereafter, he obtained a revocation of the exile of *The Friend of Mankind,* who ran to Versailles less to thank him than to rejoice in his conversation, which was always salty and brimming with insights and good sense. One of the first things that M. *Quesnay* told him was: *but tell me, then, who wrote these two little brochures? It must have been you or I who showed him how.*

It is neither you nor I, replied Mirabeau, *it is nature and reason, which are well worth us. The author wrote to me twice; twice I replied to him. Here is his address.*

Then *Quesnay* invited me. Then I gladly glued myself to him as to my Master, to my Instructor, to my Father. He received me, treated me for *eleven* years like his son, the *Disciple he loved.* His strong soul and his profound genius did not easily succumb to tender feelings, and nonetheless I had the happiness to see many in him for me.

I was only a child when he opened his arms to me; it is he who made me a man.

Notes

1. Roussel de la Tour was a councillor of the Parlement of Paris in the 1760s. Claude-Henri Watelet (1718–1785) followed his father as receiver-general of taxes in Orléans beginning in March 1741. Watelet, a

writer and artist who had been in debt for years, had accumulated a deficit of over a million *livres,* partially through the misuse of royal funds. He avoided bankruptcy by shifting his debt to the account of his clerk, Charles-Nicolas Roland. Roland published a *Mémoire au Roi Louis XVI en dénonciation d'abus d'autorité . . .* (London, 1784), in which he accused Watelet of having had him arbitrarily imprisoned. For this affair, to which Du Pont seems to be referring, see John Bosher, *French Finances 1770–1795; From Business to Bureaucracy* (Cambridge: Cambridge University Press, 1970), pp. 106, 288, and 342.

²Roussel de la Tour published *Richesse de l'état* in May 1763 on the eve of a *lit de justice* at which Louis XV intended to impose the registration of new taxes. Roussel de la Tour proposed substituting a single, personal *capitation* (income tax) for the vast panoply of taxes that were crushing the people. Du Pont's disdain to the contrary, *Richesse de l'état* enjoyed a tremendous instantaneous success, according both to Bachaumont, *Mémoires secrets; à partir de 1763,* 36 vols. (1777–89), I, p. 248, and to E. J. F. Barbier, *Chronique de la régence et du règne de Louis XV,* 8 vols. (Paris, 1857), IV, p. 455. See Georges Weulersse, *Le Mouvement physiocratique en France (de 1756 à 1770),* 2 vols. (Paris: Felix Alcan, 1910, repr. 1968), I, p. 83, and II, pp. 349–51. For a partial list of the many brochures written in response to it, see Institut National d'Études Démographiques, *Économie et population: les doctrines françaises avant 1800. Bibliographie générale commentée* (Paris: Presses Universitaires de France, 1956), p. 548.

³Du Pont's brochure was entitled, *Réflexions sur l'écrit intitulé: "Richesse de l'état" (de Roussel de la Tour),* and was also published in 1763. The work is briefly discussed in the standard works on Du Pont and physiocracy. See among many Gustave Schelle, *Du Pont de Nemours et l'école physiocratique* (Paris: Guillaumin, 1888), pp. 9–11; James J. McLain, *The Economic Writings of Du Pont de Nemours* (Newark: University of Delaware Press, 1977), pp. 39–40; and Weulersse, *Mouvement physiocratique,* I, pp. 86–88.

⁴Schelle, *Du Pont de Nemours,* p. 11, quotes a passage from Voltaire's letter. For titles of Voisenon's *contes,* see Chapter 11, note 8, *supra.*

⁵An election was a tribunal that heard cases pertaining to the distribution of the *tailles* (land tax), *aides* (sales tax), and other related taxes; it was also the district that was subject to the jurisdiction of an election. These tribunals, which had been established by the Estates General of 1355, had fallen into decay and corruption by the eighteenth century but persisted as juridical and administrative units. Subdelegates had appeared not long after the office of intendant had been firmly established in the mid-seventeenth century, to help with the tremendous burden of work that exceeded the capacities of any single man. The office of subdelegate was not specialized with respect to geographic area or task: in principle, the subdelegate performed many of the functions of the intendant and

exercised the same power, but in the name of the intendant, not in his own. In principle, also, subdelegates received no salary and to receive some income would combine the office with some other function such as treasurer of France or officer of the presidial court. More often, however, the intendant would recompense his subdelegates out of his own pocket. Certainly that seems to be the case with M. Méliand's subdelegates, although the intendant did not always think to pay them. See Chapter 15 *infra*.

Corvée, in the most general sense, simply referred to the obligation of the people to perform a certain amount of labor for their lord. The royal *corvée* to which Du Pont is referring entailed the obligation to work on constructing and repairing roads for a certain number of days per year. The institution existed under Louis XIV, but only became generalized under Louis XV, presumably in conjunction with the improvement of the kingdom-wide system of roads at that time. During the same period, it also came under the attack of physiocrats and others as counterproductive and a gross interference in the lives and agricultural work of the peasantry. As the equivalent of a tax in kind on the labor of those who were subject to it—or *corvéables*—it was unevenly distributed throughout the kingdom and bitterly resented. During his intendancy in the Limousin, Turgot converted the *corvée* in that province into a monetary tax, perceived to be more just and economically beneficial. See Dakin, *Turgot and the Ancien Regime*; Schelle, *Turgot*, II, esp. pp. 183–244: Marion, *Dictionnaire des institutions*.

[6]The Chevalier Charles-Blaise Méliand de Thoisy, intendant of Soissons, had begun as a *maître des requêtes*, a magistrate in the Chambre des Requêtes of the Parlement of Paris and the first stage in a career in the royal administration. He apparently came from a provincial family of robe nobility. Vivian Gruder, *The Royal Provincial Intendants: A Governing Elite in Eighteenth-Century France* (Ithaca & London: Cornell University Press, 1968), p. 64, gives the dates of his tenure as intendant from 1743 to about 1751. These dates clearly do not correspond to the tenure of the Chevalier Méliand for whom Du Pont worked off and on throughout the mid-1760s, beginning in 1763, but he may have been a son or nephew of the other. Mentions of Méliand's role as intendant of Soissons throughout the 1760s can be found in Weulersse, *Mouvement physiocratique*, and Saricks, *Pierre Samuel Du Pont de Nemours*.

[7]Marie Lesczinska (1703–1768), queen of France, wife of Louis XV, was the daughter of the Polish king Stanislas Lesczinski, who lost the throne of Poland while she was still a girl and emigrated to France (1719). The royal match was an extraordinary coup for the displaced princess, but her married life was marred by the king's unending parade of mistresses.

[8]By the time Du Pont began to correspond with him, Victor de Riqueti, Marquis de Mirabeau (1715–1789), "the oldest son of the doctrine,"

already had spent some time in the prison of Vincennes as punishment for his indiscretion in discussing the financial condition of the realm in his *Théorie de l'impôt* (1760). On *L'Ami des hommes*, see Chapter 3, note 1, *supra*. The best account of Mirabeau's life remains Louis de Loménie, *Les Mirabeau: nouvelles études sur la société française au XVIIIe siècle*, 5 vols. (Paris: E. Dentu, 1889), esp. vol. II; on his economic doctrines, see Henri Ripert, *Le Marquis de Mirabeau, ses théories politiques et économiques* (Paris, 1902), and my *Origins of Physiocracy*.

[9]Mirabeau's correspondence for the period of his imprisonment at Vincennes is at the Bibliothèque de l'Arsenal, Paris. On Bignon and the Mirabeaus' relations with their peasants, which departed somewhat from Mirabeau's idyllic picture of rural life, see *Les Mirabeau et leur temps, actes du Colloque d'Aix-en-Provence, 17 et 18 décembre 1966* (Paris: Clavreuil, 1968).

[10]François Quesnay (1694–1774), "the Confucius of Europe" to his most devoted disciples, developed the economic analysis and, with Mirabeau, the political economy that came to be known as physiocracy. Quesnay's thought—especially his celebrated and puzzling "zig-zag," the *Tableau économique*—has challenged all the great historians of economic thought, including Karl Marx and Joseph Schumpeter, although his dictum that land constituted the source of all wealth did not withstand the rise of industrial capitalism and classical economics. The literature on Quesnay is voluminous. For an introduction, see the account of his life by Jacqueline Hecht and essays by other scholars in Institut National d'Études Démographiques, *François Quesnay et la physiocratie*, 2 vols. (Paris: INED, 1958), vol. 1; this volume also includes a complete bibliography of Quesnay's work and a comprehensive bibliography of works about him; volume 2 consists in the most convenient French edition of his writings. The best edition in any language has been prepared by Marguerite Kuczinski in German; see her François Quesnay, *Okonomische Schriften 1756–59*, 2 vols. (Berlin: Akademie-Verlag, 1971) and *Okonomische Schriften 1763–67*, 2 vols. (Berlin: Akademie-Verlag, 1976). See also my *Origins of Physiocracy*.

[11]Du Pont's second brochure was *Réponse demandée par le M. le Marquis de*** à celle qu'il a faite aux Réflexions sur l'écrit intitulé: "Richesse de l'état"* (Paris, 1763). The term Colbertists frequently was used to refer to the mercantilists who, although far from a unified school, were taken to follow the prescriptions of Jean-Baptiste Colbert, the great financial minister of Louis XIV. In a general way, those lumped together as Colbertists tended to favor restrictions on trade, state intervention in economic life, and state assistance for industry, among other policies. In short, they were taken as systematically opposed to the systematic espousal of economic freedom advocated by the physiocrats. Du Pont doubtless would have included among the Colbertists such figures as François Véron de Forbonnais and Jean-Joseph-Louis Graslin, eighteenth-century economic theorists who, whatever their differences, favored the encouragement of industry and

commerce, as well as Roussel de la Tour whom he was attacking. See Weulersse, *Mouvement physiocratique, passim,* for some of the debates.

[12]Henri-Léonard-Jean-Baptiste Bertin (1719–1792) served as controller-general from 1759 to 1763 and was responsible for encouraging the establishment of the Societies of Agriculture and for the first draft of the declaration for the reform of the laws governing the grain trade. A protégé of Madame de Pompadour, he resigned his office in the face of opposition from the Parlements to the new taxes he felt obliged to impose to remedy the disastrous financial situation occasioned by the Seven Years War. His policies are discussed in Steven L. Kaplan, *Bread, Politics and Political Economy in the Reign of Louis XV,* 2 vols. (The Hague: Martinus Nijhoff, 1976).

[13]A declaration of 25 May 1763 proclaimed free circulation of grain within the kingdom and permitted some exportation. This bold attempt, which was to meet with considerable opposition from the people and urban magistrates, undid centuries of royal and urban legislation designed to control the marketing of grain and to ensure subsistence to the king's subjects. See Georges Afanassief, *Le Commerce des céréales en France* (Paris, 1894), and Weulersse, *Mouvement physiocratique.* On the early history of the development of the Paris market and regulation, see Abbot P. Usher, *The History of the Grain Trade in France* (Cambridge, MA: Harvard University Press, 1913); on the development of the agricultural societies, see André J. Bourde, *Agronomie et agronomes en France au XVIIIe siècle,* 3 vols. (Paris: SEVPEN, 1967), III, pp. 1109–20. Bourde also provides a fine discussion of Bertin's career as controller-general.

[14]In 1763, Bertin separated the administration of agriculture from the general business of the controller-general, creating a separate department that would last until 1780. Bertin entrusted Parent, his first clerk, with direction of this department. See Weulersse, *Mouvement physiocratique,* II, p. 159; Henri Pigeonneau and B. de Foville, *L'Administration de l'agriculture au contrôle général des finances* (Paris, 1882); and André Bourde, *Agronomes,* III, pp. 1131–39.

[15]For the text of Quesnay's articles, see INED, *François Quesnay et la physiocratie,* II; for a discussion of their place in the development of his thought, see my *Origins of Physiocracy.*

13

M. Quesnay. His doctrine: the point to which he had brought it before I attached myself to him.

M. *Quesnay,* a famous Doctor, after having been a Surgeon of the first rank and Secretary of the Academy of Surgery, which he had helped to found, left in medicine the *Traité de la Saignée,* which launched his reputation, the *Préface des Mémoires de l'Académie de Chirurgie* and several precious *articles* in these *Mémoires,* the *Traité des Fièvres,* the *Traité de la Gangrene,* the *Traité de la Suppuration,* and the *Traité de l'Économie animale,* in which, not limiting himself to the merit of a physiological scholar, he took his place among the leading Metaphysicians, which was his most particular vocation.[1]

Called to the Court as a Doctor, he restored life and beauty to Madame de *Pompadour,* and, with two such important services, had acquired her entire confidence, which he used with circumspection, with ability, sometimes with courage, never for himself, always for the public good.

He had refused to have his Son made a Farmer-General.[2] *I do not want,* he said, *there to exist in myself or in my family the slightest motive for desiring or tolerating the perpetuation of abuses.*

He had even twice refused the office of *First Doctor of the King,* because an income of about *fifty thousand livres* from the sale of mineral waters and the permissions to sell remedies was attached to it, and because he disapproved of this kind of revenue. He preferred to remain the *First Ordinary Doctor.*

In this second office he was admitted to the intimate society of the King and the Favorite.

Louis XV had a just spirit, did not lack taste, took pleasure in *Quesnay's* original thoughts, and even more in the familiar and stinging expressions in which the old doctor knew how to package them in conversation. He gave him letters of nobility, composed the arms himself, and designed them as three pansies in the state of nature with this motto: *propter cogitationem mentis.*[3]

M. *Quesnay*, who every day saw enormous and deadly faults committed because the government sometimes followed beaten paths out of irrational habit, sometimes the vagaries of passions, asked himself if, when each of the other human labors is enlightened by a positive and specific science, it was not an absurdity to believe that the Government of Nations should be abandoned to fortuitous combinations or to blind routine. He soon convinced himself that a very solid and profound *Science* should determine it, and the *Science of Political Economy* seemed to him to be a kind of *Public Medicine,* as far above the *individual Medicine* that he had practiced up till then as the entire Nation is above each of the citizens that compose it.[4]

He sought this *Science,* which was not to be found in books, in Nature, considering it a duty to seize the occasion to make some of its principles or some of its results penetrate to the mind of the Persons whose will disposed of the fate of the Empire.

His work did not address the greater or lesser perfection of Constitutions, but those economic Laws which would be applicable to all Constitutions and which would make the happiness of men anywhere they were followed no matter what the Constitution might be.

Effectively, whatever may be the distribution of the legislative Power, the executive Power, and the Judicial Power—which are the object of constitutions—and in whatever manner Peoples are represented, they will be rich, numerous, happy, powerful, and morally sound if agriculture is flourishing, if labor is honored, if commerce prospers, if there is *freedom* of thought and action, *security* of persons and of the *property* of goods. And, to the contrary, if Liberty, Security, Property are not sufficiently guaranteed, if labor, agriculture, and commerce decay, the Country will become uninhabitable, whatever the extent of political rights and the established forms of their exercise may be.

It is not, therefore, by the *Science of the Social Contract*, the bases of which are established in *Jean Jacques Rousseau*; it is that of *Political Economy*, which M. *Quesnay* has cultivated, or rather created.[5] And at an advanced age, in haste to be useful to France, not being able to serve his fellow citizens except by his influence on the will of the King, to whom the greatest share of the legislative Power and public authority were confided, he had chosen his study well.

He observed that men would propagate so long as they had the means to live and to raise their children; that in vain would they bear more children than could be nourished, since then they would be condemned to misery and to death—truth that the *Friend of Mankind*, like him, had recognized on his own. But the discovery of the following truths belonged exclusively to M. *Quesnay*, who first saw that it is impossible to furnish perpetual consumption except by new and renewed productions; and that only the earth, the waters, the mines, and the quarries provide renascent productions or raw materials.

That labor applied to existing productions or primary materials merely transforms them, adding to the value of those primary materials only that of greater or lesser wages and salaries—in other words, consumptions for which competition establishes the level for the same kind of laborers.

That Commerce is reduced to exchanges of value for equal value, with preference only in the choice on the part of the contracting parties.

That the wages or salaries of the labors of transformation, of storage, and of carting included under the generic names of *Manufacture* and *Commerce* are always paid, like those of domestic servants and boarders, by the wealth of which someone was already the Proprietor.

That, in contrast, the labor of cultivation, of fishing, and of the exploitation of mines or quarries pays for itself, by drawing from the bosom of nature the new objects of consumption or exchange that it offers for enjoyment, or that it places in Commerce.

That there are, accordingly, *productive Labors* and *sterile Labors* and that the fruit of the first pays the wages of both.

M. *Quesnay* invented, under the name of *Tableau économique*, a formula to depict and calculate the effects of expenditures, exchange, and circulation, which distributes, which shares throughout society, which leads to the consumption of commodities and raw materials that which the *productive Labors* generate.[6]

He distinguished two portions in the value of the harvests that result from these labors.

First that which is necessary to pay back the costs of cultivation, maintain the capital, and continue the work of cultivation—a portion that cannot be deflected from this destination without weakening cultivation, diminishing population, and ruining society. He called this regenerative portion of the harvest *Returns of Cultivation.* Then, the portion that remains after the costs of exploitation have been deducted, and that can be used for one thing or another according to the will of the Proprietor. He called this second portion of the value of the harvest, the *Net Product.*

He demonstrated that if one did not wish to induce famines, impoverish citizens, deprive them of the means to support their families, dry up all sources of national prosperity, one could take from the *Net Product* only those funds necessary for public expenditures.

Applying the formula of his *Tableau économique* to the different hypotheses, he calculated the frightening and progressive degradations that result from even the lightest blows directed against the advances, the costs, the Capitals of Cultivation.

He showed that it was not possible to attempt to subject manufacturers and merchants to taxation without having the manufacturers and merchants, who always need the salary of their labor and the interest of their capital, include this contribution in their bills; without their adding, as with all other employment of their capital, the interest of the advance that would have been required of them.

And that the wages, the salaries, the interest on capital of these agents of circulation, being necessarily paid either by the Proprietor's expenditure of the *Net Product* or by that of the cost of exploitation administered by the Cultivators, it was truly on the Proprietors and on the Cultivators that would fall the taxes that were intended to be established on manufacturers and merchants.

That there was, with respect to the portion returned to them by the expenditure of the *Net Product,* no benefit for the Proprietors in having other citizens forced to support the tax; that there was, on the contrary, a surcharge of all the artificial costs of the interest on the money advanced by the Merchants and the Manufacturers.

But that the loss for the Proprietors was altogether more considerable with respect to the portion of the taxes on the shops and the Commerce subsidized by the expenditure of the costs of exploitation, for then the cultivators' advances being diverted from their productive employment, the harvest weakened, in such a way that the Proprietors, in settling their accounts with the Cultivators, were forced to underwrite the tax and the diminution of the harvest caused by the tax.

That finally the harm for Society is even infinitely larger when the cultivator tied up by a lease cannot immediately throw back on the Proprietor both the repayment of the tax and the diminution of the harvest; for in this case the advances of the exploitation are absorbed and the harvests degraded following a growing progression from year to year, so much so that it is necessary, if the lease is long, that the rural enterprise be ruined, that the livestock disappear, that the lands become thinner and denuded, that the manure be destroyed, that cultivation end, or that it at least experience a horrible deterioration.

If the Proprietors of the land, said M. *Quesnay*, were instructed in these truths, which are so important to them, they would demand in all countries the suppression of all taxes on agriculture, on manufacturers, on crafts, on consumption, on commerce; they would insist on paying directly all contributions out of their *Net Product*, for this is the only way of discharging them that does not add a surcharge and that can ensure the duration and the success of the cultivation that is the foundation of all their wealth.

M. *Quesnay* perceived in addition that an evil entirely similar to this deadly effect of all the indirect taxes would result from all the hindrances, all the obstacles that encumbered labor in agriculture, arts, crafts, manufactures, and commerce, since it amounts to the same thing for the industrious citizen if one burdens the wage of his labor with a tax, or if one squelches his industriousness and deprives this labor of a part of its efficacy.

All regulations, all inquisitions, all prohibitions on labor or commerce are thus a truly aggravated tax on the *Net Product*, a true cause of degradation in the advances of cultivation; and to the contrary all increases in liberty for industry, all facilities given to commerce, all constructions of roads or canals, all perfections added to navigation, all ingenious inventions that save labor and expenditure in the arts induce progress in cultivation, the extension of its advances, the increase of the harvest, the growth of the *Net Product*. It is thus that the *Net Product*—the interest of the Proprietors of the land—is the thermometer of all good and bad in society.

Since the *Net Product* alone underwrites public expenditures, it seemed just and useful to M. Quesnay that it do so by having a proportional share of this product, which increased and decreased with the product attributed to the political Body; since when a State is rich, it can permit itself expenditures of public utility that could not be dreamed of when the State is poor, and above all since once taxation that is invariably proportional to the net product is established, it no longer costs anyone anything. Lands are sold, bought, inherited, divided with the obligation of meeting the Tax. The Capital of the revenue destined for the political Body no longer participates in commerce; it remains stable with respect to society. Individuals only possess and only transmit with their various contracts that portion of the *Net Product* which is not mortgaged to the expenditures of the State, and the Capital of individual revenue that underwrites their needs. Thus one could say that to institute *public co-property* in the *Net Product* of the landed Proprietors in this manner is not to impose a Tax but to abolish taxes forever.

M. *Quesnay* has since written an excellent work that contains very new principles on the *natural law of men united in society*. He has perfectly discussed the moral part of the Science that he had invented; but his first care was to base it on interest and to fortify it by calculations. He wanted to teach it to Kings and to ensure its influence over a corrupt court: *If I speak to them of morality,* he said, *they will only listen to me as to a philosophical dreamer; or they will believe that I wish to lord it over them and they will dispatch me to manna and rhubarb. If, on the contrary, I limit myself to telling them—Here is your interest, here is your pecuniary interest, the interest of your power, of your possessions and of your wealth—they will pay attention as to the discourse of a friend.*

When he had thus linked all his ideas in such a way as to form a true science of public interest, of that of each Citizen, and of the interlocking of these two interests, it was a question of accustoming the Favorite and the King to the fundamental maxims of this science, without one or the other's perceiving that the Doctor presumed to give them lessons, which would immediately have removed any inclination to listen to him and would have had him harshly *put back in his place*, as was said at the time, in such a way that his zeal and his understanding not only would have become useless but would have discredited the salutary truths that he would have prematurely divulged.

Here is the prudent course that M. Quesnay followed.

He insinuated to Mme *de Pompadour* that to amuse the King and give him some new recreations, to tear him away from the boredom of the court and the dangers that ensued therefrom, it would be good if she provided him with the tools of different crafts, even appeared to take pleasure in them herself, worked with them, and made him work with them.

He did not initially propose the one he had in mind; instead he gave priority to the lathe.

They were provided with superb tools; they succeeded splendidly. The king tried his hand and made wooden stools for his entire court.

But one should not always stick to the same craft, and the next one suggested was Printing.

A *Founder* was ordered to make the most beautiful *type* that existed at the time; he was even told to add a silver alloy, which he had the good sense not to do; perfectly cast *forms* were produced in well-polished iron; there were gold *composing sticks,* a Mahogany press, the most beautiful *marbles* for the press as well as for imposing; *cases* of rosewood and Brazilwood, which give off an agreeable odor. A printshop suitable to make decorations was set up in the small apartments, and *Quesnay* was entrusted with directing it.

The King applied himself even more than he had to the lathe. He learned to recognize the *cases* and to set the type. Mme *de Pompadour* did as much. The Doctor was admired for having such a beautiful press built and he arranged to have a friend suggest that a delicate way of thanking him would be to have an edition of one of his works set by the royal hands and those that governed them. But it had to be a work that no one knew, that, like the setting of it, would be a mystery for all who were not initiated into the secret pleasures of the court.

It also had to be a work that was not long and that offered the opportunity to show off all the riches of the press, that had notes, that required *italics, small* and *large capitals,* and characters of several different sizes.

Quesnay gave a brief *Explanation* of his *Tableau* économique saying to the King: *During your hunts, you have seen many estates, many farms, and many laborers; you have seen everything that concerns your Kingdom and your Majesty. You will print how those people generated all your riches and how they are shared in society.* He put at the end of this *Explication du Tableau,* as an *Extract of the Royal Economics of Sully,* thirty *Maximes du Gouvernement d'un Royaume agricole,* with *notes* on several of these maxims.[7]

In this work he had surpassed himself. All his other writings have precision and depth; this one had in addition warmth and abundance. In it he energetically described the Kingdom and the causes of its impoverishment, and revealed, with elevation and sensibility, the means to make it flourish. It was there that he had the Monarch set and print the following phrases, while teaching him to distinguish them by striking characters.

That the property of land and liquid assets is guaranteed to those who are their legitimate Owners. The security of Property is the essential foundation of society.

The land is the unique source of wealth, and it is agriculture that multiplies it.

That the advances of the Cultivators be adequate. The advances of agriculture must be preciously conserved for the production of the tax, the revenue, and the subsistence of all classes of citizens.

Above all, the Kingdom must be populated with rich cultivators. Poor Peasants, poor Kingdom.

The urbanite is nothing but a mercenary paid by the wealth of the countryside.

That the multiplication of livestock be favored.

That each be free to cultivate in his field the Productions that his interest, his abilities, the nature of the land suggest to him.

That the Tax not be destructive or disproportionate to the bulk of the revenue of the Nation; that it be established directly on the net product of landed property, and not on the wages of men or on commodities, where it would multiply the costs of perception, prejudice commerce, and annually destroy a part of the wealth of the Nation; that it also not be collected from the wealth of the Farmers of landed property, otherwise the tax would degenerate into spoliation and cause a decay that would probably ruin a State.

That the nation be educated.

That outlets for and transport of productions and fabricated goods be facilitated. As is the market, so is Reproduction.

That the price of commodities and merchandise in the Kingdom not be lowered. As is the market value, so is the revenue. Abundance without value is not wealth. Shortage and costliness is misery. Abundance and good price is opulence.

That the entire freedom of trade be maintained. The surest, most exact, most preferable Administration of internal and external Trade for the Nation and the State consists in complete freedom of competition.

That the administration of finance either in the collection of taxes or in the expenditures of government never give rise to pecuniary *fortunes* that remove a part of the revenues from circulation, distribution, and reproduction.

That the state avoid borrowing.

That one count on no resources for the extraordinary needs of the State but the prosperity of the nation, and not the credit of the financiers; for pecuniary Fortunes are clandestine riches that know neither King nor Fatherland.

The King set about half of the copy and looked over the proofs on several occasions until the edition was correct; the pains were not entirely lost. The work seemed interesting to him: *It is a pity* he said, *that the Doctor is not of the trade; he knows more than all the rest of them.* But *Louis XV*, who was altogether unable to understand the Science of government, was the last man in the world to be concerned about it; he did not consider it his affair and lampooned his Ministers before the Public.

The Favorite was more interested.[8] *Quesnay's* discourses began to direct her ambition toward the glory and utility of a good government. She had been hated by the French, like all the favorites whose morals scandalized and whose fortunes revolted them, and in addition for having very poorly conducted the war. She wished to deserve and to win their esteem by real services. She loved agriculture, or convinced herself that she loved it. She said to M. *Bertin* that *it was necessary to encourage agriculture.* She understood the advantages of free trade and emboldened the same Minister to permit that of the circulation of grain. Finally we owe to the influence that *Quesnay* assumed over her, and to the stimulation that he was able to give to the Courtiers, to the Philosophers, to men of letters, and that the changes of Ministry and of Principles could not stop thereafter, the generous movement that turned the entire Nation toward agriculture and free trade—a movement whose immense advantages are registered by a very impressive fact. In 1763, at the time of the Peace, there were no more than 22,500,000 inhabitants in France, according to the calculations of MM *Moheau, Expilly,* and *de la Michodière,* who were themselves accused of exaggeration; and in 1790, according to a still incomplete count, there were found to be 27,250,000.[9]

Such is the service that *Quesnay,* his doctrines and his students—mocked, persecuted and, what is worse, contravened by an expensive war, by deadly and burdensome loans and enormous depravations of the Court, but determining, enlightening, directing several great operations of the Government—rendered to this Country. It is a beautiful philosophy that, in spite of a bad constitution and a corrupt Administration, increases the population of a Kingdom by a fifth in twenty-seven years.

I could not progress in my Memoirs without giving you an

idea of the Science that would occupy my life from the point at which I had arrived when I began to cultivate it, of the great man who invented it, who taught it to me, who was to serve as my Father, who enabled me to contribute to the success of the profound views to which he had devoted himself for the happiness of the human race.

Notes

[1]On Quesnay's medical works, see Jean Sutter, "Quesnay et la Médecine," in INED, *François Quesnay et la physiocratie*, I, pp. 197–210, and my *Origins of Physiocracy*. The "Preface" to the *Mémoires de l'Académie Royale de Chirurgie* and excerpts from *Essai physique sur l'économie animale* were reprinted in Auguste Onken, ed., *Oeuvres économiques et philosophiques de F. Quesnay fondateur du système physiocratique* (Frankfurt and Paris, 1888).

[2]A farmer-general was a member of the United General Farms, which had played a central role in the collection of taxes since its founding at the time of Colbert in the 1670s, during the reign of Louis XIV. As a method of fiscal administration, revenue farming rested on the practice of granting the right to collect taxes as a property or legal right to an income or source of revenue, for a limited period of time and in return for payment of a lump sum. The practice of revenue farming had a long history in France and permitted the monarchy to count on a regular income without worrying about the difficulties and delays of tax collection. The farmers-general were the proprietors of the right to collect specific taxes including the royal salt monopolies (*gabelles*), the tobacco monopoly (*tabacs*), customs duties (*traites*), sales taxes (*aides*), and various town and registry duties. They and their activities attracted resentment, hostility, and charges of corruption. This reputation, as well as Quesnay's hostility to the kinds of taxes and methods of collection they represented, accounts for his unwillingness to allow his son to become a farmer-general. See George T. Matthews, *The Royal General Farms in Eighteenth-Century France* (New York: Columbia University Press, 1958); and Yves Durand, *Les Fermiers généraux au XVIIIe siècle* (Paris: Presses Universitaires de France, 1971).

[3]In French, pansies (*pensées*) are a pun on thoughts (*pensées*). The flower, of a deep violet hue, was considered an emblem for memory or recollection (*souvenir*). As Ophelia said in *Hamlet,* "Pansies are for thoughts." *Propter cogitationem mentis* can be roughly translated as: "On account of the cogitation of the mind."

[4]The relation between Enlightenment thought and medicine has been receiving growing attention; see Peter Gay, "The Enlightenment as

Medicine and as Cure," *The Age of the Enlightenment: Studies Presented to Theodore Besterman* (Edinburgh and London, 1967). Other scholars have sought the origins of Quesnay's notions of free trade and economic circulation in William Harvey's theories of the circulation of the blood. For a discussion of the specific relations between Quesnay's medical and economic work, see my *Origins of Physiocracy*, "Quesnay as Physician and Metaphysician." To the best of my knowledge, no one has ever developed Du Pont's idea that Quesnay viewed the economy as needing a kind of public health. But it is difficult to determine if Quesnay really thought in this fashion or if, as is more likely, Du Pont himself began to think that way with the growing attention to public health from the 1760s and 1770s onward. Cf. the discussion of Samuel-Auguste Tissot's growing interest in public health in Antoinette S. Emch-Deriaz, *Towards a Social Conception of Health*, part III.

[5]For Du Pont's criticisms of Rousseau, see Jean Perkins, "Rousseau jugé par Du Pont de Nemours."

[6]There have been innumerable studies of Quesnay's *Tableau* and heated debates concerning its meaning and, especially, whether or not it "works." For the history of the early versions of the *Tableau*, see Marguerite Kuczynski and Ronald L. Meek, eds., *Quesnay's Tableau économique* (London and New York, 1972); for the various interpretations of it, see my *Origins of Physiocracy*, "The Tableau."

[7]Du Pont himself is the source for this story which Gustave Schelle picked up when he read the manuscript of the memoirs. See his "Quesnay et le Tableau économique," *Revue d'économie politique* 19 (December 1905): 490–521, and published separately (Paris, 1905); and especially his *Le Docteur Quesnay, chirurgien, médecin de Madame de Pompadour et de Louis XV, physiocrate* (Paris: Alcan, 1907). The full text of the thirty maxims which Du Pont summarizes hereafter can be found in Kuczynski and Meek, eds., *Quesnay's Tableau.*

[8]Jeanne-Antoinette Poisson (1721–1764) became Mme Le Normant d'Étioles before her rise to Marquise and then Duchesse de Pompadour. As Louis XV's official mistress, the Favorite, from 1745 to her death in 1764, she displayed a deep—and frequently criticized—interest in the affairs of government about which she managed to learn a great deal. Working in close association and friendship with Choiseul, she was credited with a decisive role in such affairs of state as the diplomatic alliance and the expulsion of the Jesuits. Her warm relations with Quesnay are well-documented by her lady-in-waiting, Mme du Hausset, in her *Mémoires de Madame du Hausset, femme de chambre de Madame de Pompadour* (Paris, 1824). For the beginnings of her political career and her relations with Choiseul, see Butler, *Choiseul*, vol. 1, *passim.*

[9]Moheau (for whom we do not have a first name) was probably the author of *Recherches et considérations sur la population de la France* (Paris, 1778);

the work also has been attributed to Antoine-Jean-Baptiste-Robert Auget, Baron de Montyon, whose other works appeared in 1796 and thereafter. Abbé Jean-Joseph d'Expilly, the author of a *Dictionnaire géographique, historique et politique des Gaules et de la France*, 6 vols. (Paris, 1762–70), and *La Cosmographie, divisée en cinq parties, qui comprennent l'astronomie, la géographie, l'hydrographie, l'histoire ecclésiastique et la chronologie* (Avignon, 1748), published *De la Population de la France* in 1765. La Michaudière, identified as intendant of Lyon in INED, *Économie et population*, actually wrote *Recherches sur la population des généralités d'Auvergne, de Lyon, de Rouen et de quelques provinces et villes du royaume, avec des réflexions sur la valeur du bled tant en France qu'en Angleterre, depuis 1674 jusqu'en 1764* (Paris, 1766), which is usually attributed to the better-known populationist Messance, a *receveur des tailles* in the election of St.-Etienne. Maurice Garden, *Lyon et les Lyonnais au XVIIIe siècle* (Paris: Belles Lettres, 1970), pp. 492 and 540, confirms the existence of an intendant of Lyon named La Michodière between 1757 and 1762; John Bosher, *French Finances 1770–1795: From Business to Bureaucracy* (Cambridge: Cambridge University Press, 1970), pp. 51 and 56, identifies a Jean-Baptiste-François de la Michodière (1720–?), who was a councillor of state in charge of the Bureau of Population tables in the 1780s and a master of requests under Calonne later in the same decade. Variations in spelling notwithstanding, this is the same man, and one whom Du Pont almost certainly would have known and certainly would have known of, since they worked for the same ministers and frequented the same circles. La Michodière's predecessors in the intendancy of Lyon had included Trudaine (see Chapter 15 *infra*) and Méliand. Du Pont's reference thus provides excellent confirmation that La Michodière did write a treatise on population, although he is not mentioned in the fine standard work on French population thought in English by J. J. Spengler, *French Predecessors of Malthus: A Study of Eighteenth-Century Wage and Population Theory* (Durham: Duke University Press, 1942).

14

*The intimacy with which M. Quesnay honored me.
Small annoyances that M. Abeille caused me. My part
in the general administration of the intendancy of
Soissons. My book on the export and import of grain.
My stay at Bignon. Mirabeau the Son. Mme de
Pompadour's projects and what she intended to do for
me. Illness and death of this lady. Abandon into
which this death threw M. Quesnay and his student.*

You have seen, dear friends, in the preceding chapter, that
M. *Quesnay* had a genuine and deep passion for public usefulness.
He treated the different people who came to see him in accordance
with what he took to be their capacity to be *useful* to Society. And
judging it possible to expect much of a young man who had found,
all on his own, three or four sound principles of political economy,
he granted me from the very first day the same freedom and showed
me the same familiarity as if I had known him for ten years, and
it was ten years later. Taking me with one hand and my two
brochures with the other, he said to the others of his students who
were present: *Gentlemen, here is M.* Du Pont, *and here is his work* ex

ungue leonem.[1] *He has been our friend for twenty years; he was before he was born.*

M. *Abeille*, who held one of the first places among his most favored disciples, was shocked by the distinguished kindnesses he so rapidly showered on an urchin.[2] He developed a feeling of antipathy and ill humor toward me that still persists, although it is almost thirty years old, and he displayed it from the very first weeks.

M. *Quesnay* gave me different economic questions to discuss. I cannot, I have never been able to, contemplate with dispassion these materials so important to the happiness or the misery of the human race; but at that time especially I almost always infused what I wrote on the subject with too much abundance and too poetic or too oratorical turns of phrase. M. *Abeille* bitterly picked up these defects, observed that what I had just done was in poor taste, that one did not express oneself in this fashion on serious questions, that my style would make me seem like a man poorly suited to this type of study; he repeated to me like a Pedagogue: *ornari Res ipsa negat, contenta doceri.*[3] M. *Abeille* had merits and reputation; his age and his name impressed them on me; I would have disputed principles with him, for exact truths belong to everyone; but when it was a question of style and taste, short of demonstrating a ridiculous pride, I could only keep still; nonetheless the frequency and the severity of his criticisms made the blood rush to my face, and sometimes brought tears to my eyes. *Leave this young man in peace,* Quesnay said to him, *if he did not have too much of something at his age, he would be caught very short at ours.* I felt a great tenderness for the old man of seventy years, the instructor of us all, who thus protected me against a scholar of forty.

I considered one of the first duties of my gratitude for the *graciousness* of M. *de Choiseul* to tell him of my liaison with M. *Quesnay*, of the friendship that he had demonstrated for me, and of the lessons that he was gracious enough to give me. I did not know that M. *de Choiseul* had broken shortly before with Madame *de Pompadour*, that he feared the advice *Quesnay* could give her, and that he deeply hated the Doctor. I did not even have the wit to recognize this in the reply he made to my tale: *So much the better, Du Pont, you have nothing more to do with me.* But returning and struck by the coldness that succeeded his caressing manners, I asked him the cause of this change, and in what I had had the misfortune to displease him. He led me into a back room and said to me: *I have not changed; you do not displease me. You must have noticed that I have wished you well since the first day that I saw you. I have showed you as much on a thousand occasions. But it is you who are changing your career . . . I am going to speak to you as to a man whom I respect and whom I believe incapable of abusing what I say to him . . . The friends of M.* Quesnay *are not mine. Choose.* I had a liking and even some gratitude for M. *de Choiseul,* even though he had never done anything for me but open his door and speak obligingly to me. But between a sage, a great man, an enlightened philosopher, who honored me with a sincere affection and deigned to teach me each day as his child, and an amiable and powerful Minister who could not know me well nor grant me more than a superficial interest, the difference, the distance seemed so enormous to me that I did not hesitate an instant. I replied without weighing: *I am deeply sorry, Monsieur le Duc; I will not choose. I shall never forget the signs of goodwill that you have given me; and I shall profit from the instruction of each of my benefactors to make me more capable of deserving and justifying the bounties of the other.* This conversation terminated, I only returned to see M. *de Choiseul* one time; sure of being poorly received that time, but also sure of not being so twice. I never spoke of the matter to M. *Quesnay,* and only very vaguely of the relations that I had had with M. *de Choiseul;* I should have considered it base to seek to make use of this with my old Master; and with him there was enough to keep busy with philosophic truths so that tales could have only a small place in the time that one spent at his side.

I went to dine with him every day he was in Paris. He never served at the table and offered nothing: *You have every bit as much intelligence as mutton,* he said, *here is the meadow, seek your grass.* He was impatient for the company to withdraw; as soon as it had left we set ourselves to work, and he kept me until eleven at night. He had me come to Versailles, where Mme de *Montmort,* at his request, provided me with a lodging.[4] I went to him at the crack of dawn; we worked with extreme ardor. His lodgings were very cramped; his bedroom served as his study; he left me there when he went to see Madame *de Pompadour* and the King. The rest of the time and especially after dinner he was overwhelmed with visits, as are all people in favor; he then set me at his desk and frequently said to me: *do not disturb yourself*—so that the others would not disturb me. The comings and goings of the court annoyed him with a multitude of stupidities, most of which were said with the intention of pleasing him. He replied with lively epigrams. And when, in the middle of the noise, I had written something reasonable, or made a sound observation, or an exact calculation, he said to me as soon as we were alone: *Here is something that is going well; it is thus that Archimedes worked at Syracuse.*

He said on another occasion to M. *de Mirabeau: We must cherish this young man for he will speak after we are dead.* M. *de Mirabeau* reported this to me; you can imagine how much I wanted to retain my instructors and to deserve their *cherishing* me. That time was extremely happy for me.

I had to interrupt the pleasure to go to Soissons with M. *Méliand,* who had proposed that I make a tour of his generality with him. M. *Quesnay,* having judged that the instruction I might draw from this trip would be worthwhile, and having charged me with a multitude of questions, himself encouraged me to go and to take with me, in addition, the draft of my treatise on *the export and the import of grain* in order to occupy me, he said, *in the breaks.* There were few, and I took very little advantage of those there were.

With M. *Méliand,* I visited the election of *Crespy,* where we did what was called *the department,* which is to say the distribution of the Taille among the Parishes and the judgment of the protests. Then we crossed a part of the Election of Soissons and stayed in the city. M. *Méliand* reserved many more affairs than he ordinarily did for his own examination. We undertook this examination together, or I did it in his absence and reported to him. My reports were precise, and the letters I suggested to him as a result had a novel character. Never had M. the Intendant been so decisive with his subdelegates, so firm nor so ready to argue cases with the Ministers; and you can well understand that since still today I am deemed to have a bold and somewhat singular stance in affairs, at twenty-three, at a time in which everything was swaddled in pedantic forms, I must have appeared a very extraordinary *Intendant.* M. *Méliand* contained my ardor a little bit by his prudence and his experience; but he frequently ceded by his gentleness. I did indeed earn him some quarrels which at first frightened him considerably, and which we then conducted honorably; and since the result was happy, he believed himself courageous so long as I was beside him.

But any rapid rise to favor has its dangers. I became odious to the first secretary, whose name I have forgotten, and to almost all the subdelegates. I had done nothing intentionally to deserve it; to the contrary, I had done everything I could to be extremely polite and to manifest every deference to those senior to me; but I had doubtless fallen into more than one impropriety, for that was almost inevitable on the part of a man who had always lived alone and who had no knowledge of the world.

Meanwhile, my book did not progress. I was to bring it back done to M. *Quesnay,* and I could barely manage the flood with which M. *Méliand* deluged me. I begged him to go without me to do the department of the Elections of Laon, Noyon, Clermont and Guise, leaving me alone at the Intendance with a junior secretary whom he had given me. He had a bed put in the library for me; dinner was brought in to me, and I only went out twice in three weeks. But after having put the work on the Intendance, which M. *Méliand* had given me, in order, I did not advance my own as I should have.

For a poor boy who passionately loved to read and who had been for so long deprived of books, a large and beautiful library was a dangerous snare. I found myself there like a young hermit suddenly transported to the middle of a seraglio. I read all day long; I read while I dined; I read at night; I read ceaselessly; I read in this fashion for two weeks straight. Finally, knowing that M. *Méliand* was due to return, I drafted in four days, and as it came, a Memoir on *the freedom of the grain trade* that I was to read, on his return, at the reopening of the Agricultural Society—a memoir that I should have been very much embarrassed to submit to print in that state.

The Court had already moved to Fontainebleau. There M. *Quesnay* awaited my book, of which the memoir that I read at the Agricultural Society was barely a sketch. I asked M. Méliand's permission to go shut myself up in some corner, where there was no library, to work. He gave me my freedom, and for my retreat I chose Madame Doré's house at Nemours, not so much because it was very calm, very convenient, very agreeable, very close to Fontainebleau, but because Mlle *Le Dée* lived there. From Soissons, I had informed these two ladies of this resolution; and I know not which one of the two had told Mlle *Le Dée's* father, nor who awoke his prudence above and beyond need, but on the eve of my arrival, he had come to Nemours and had taken away his daughter. Madame *Doré* seemed to me to be offended by his act as if it were inconsiderate to her. I was very much affected by it. I lost in talent in the first days, but gained in leisure in the others, and when the terminal date presses with honor at its side, talent pretty well has to return.

I wrote a manuscript that was more worthy than its predecessor of being submitted to my Master, and I took it to him at

Fontainebleau. He suggested many corrections and additions, but he found the core of the work good enough to decide that it should be dedicated to Madame *de Pompadour*. He had several reasons for wanting this dedication. The first was to engage the Lady to be and to appear to be the Protectress of the Principles set forth in the book, and thus to remove most of the difficulties that the absolute freedom of the grain trade would have encountered in a Council that was timid and routine-ridden and, even more important, fawning and servile. The second was to secure for myself a useful and powerful Protectress.

He spoke to her of the need to favor the sale of the principal productions of the territory, as the most efficacious way of elevating Agriculture and with it Population and Finances; of my work as a way to attain this goal by preparing the way for the law through education, which would do her honor when it would be seen that it was under her auspices that this salutary education was disseminated; of me finally as a young man whose precocious intelligence and activity could make him useful for everything and worthy of every support. He asked her permission to present me to her. With equal, and even inferior merit, it is a great advantage with women to be young. Madame *de Pompadour* took an interest in me and showed a kind of infatuation for me. She told the Doctor to bring me sometime when she was alone. She referred to me by the expression of goodwill, *our young Agriculturalist*. She spoke good naturedly of her good intentions, with interest in the public good, with gratitude to the people who were showing her the means, and she did it all gracefully, for she was still very beautiful and did not lack wit.

M. *Bertin*, and even some of his projects whose substance was very reasonable, had been half-sacrificed to the Parlement by giving the position of Controller General to M. *de Laverdy*.[5] It was M. *de Choiseul* who had named him. Madame de Pompadour, a friend of M. *Bertin* and his views, in order to satisfy this company even more and to counterbalance the credit that M. *de Choiseul* had acquired with the Parlementaires, was to have selected from the Parlement a *Commission* charged with examining and drafting the memoirs of each of their parties.[6] M. *Quesnay*, who had probably influenced this resolution and who never lost an occasion to propagate his useful principles, had had me appointed secretary of this Commission, expecting much from the inevitable influence that any instructed and hardworking secretary has on any company to be instructed, and of which each member, preoccupied with his pleasures and his affairs, wants glory at a discount. I was at the height of my desire to acquire the freedom to write without constraint on all the abuses of disastrous taxes and on the operations necessary to their reform, supporting my projects and those of my wise Instructor with all the weight of an accredited body such as the Commissioners of the Parlement would have been. I believed myself already to be triumphing over the arbitrary Taille, the Corvées, the Gabelle, the Aides, the Droits de Traite, and, as a consequence, the other indirect and vexatious taxes. I saw the realization of all the desires of my heart: public utility, glory, rapid advancement, a happy marriage.

Full of these sweet hopes, I returned to my solitude at Nemours to intoxicate Madame *Doré* with them; she then set herself to protect my love for her cousin with the greatest warmth. I stayed to complete in peace the corrections to my book that my Master desired, and to read *Rural Philosophy*, a first copy of which he had given me in proofs.[7] Reading this book, which had been written by M. *de Mirabeau* under the direction of M. *Quesnay*, to whom the seventh chapter belonged entirely, led me to spend a few days with the author on his estate at *Bignon*, which is only five leagues from Nemours.

There I saw and admired the *Friend of Mankind* engaged in fertilizing the land as a veritable Benefactor of the human Race, enriching and populating his village by the advances he showered with genius as well as with profit for the improvement of his property.[8] He was surrounded by the better part of his family. His Mother, a respectable woman of an imposing character; his Sister-in-Law, a little German countess, who was amiable on account of her goodness; his Daughter *Caroline*, today Madame *du Saillant*, beautiful, sweet, tender, witty, the only one of his children of whom he had never had reason to complain and who always gave the others advice. At the time she was about fifteen with the air of an ingenue that would not have permitted the presumption that she would one day be the mother of sixteen girls and one boy.

Madame de *Pailly* of whom I shall speak later was among the company.[9]

Finally at Bignon I found the *Mirabeau* who has since become so famous, for whom France perhaps owes me since I formed him over a long period of time and several times saved him; to whom she gave the finest honors of the Pantheon; whom I tenderly loved, who did me many wrongs but far fewer than to any of the others who loved and served him in his youth; incomprehensible man, gifted with a very rare talent, with a sparkling character, the most brilliant and even the most amiable qualities intermingling with the most shameful and even the lowest vices.[10] The quarrels between his Father and him had already multiplied; already I was charged to study him and to attain as much influence as I could over his mind and his heart; and, under the pretext of hunting together, I spent two days in tête-à-tête with him. He devoted his art and attention to pleasing me and succeeded perfectly. I judged that in showing him esteem, deserving his, and giving him an affection mixed with firmness, one could draw out of him what one wanted. Effectively, I retained over him the greatest ascendancy that he ever accorded any man, up until the National Assembly when, without actually breaking, we became distanced from one another; he, because he knew that my severe morality could not approve part of the means he employed; I, because having guessed these measures did not want any part of them. Liberty has always seemed such a noble thing to me, and seemed attainable by such a noble road, that whenever it has been used as a pretext for indulging in imposture, intrigue, calumny, active or passive venality, I have considered the pretense as maladroit as it is vile, entirely beneath Liberty and myself. Forgive me, my friends, if my heart, still bleeding from all the crimes that I have seen committed, leads me here to anticipate the order of time. I come back to say that I attached myself tightly to *Mirabeau the son* and that he attached himself to me in the same way from my first trip to *Bignon*.

I returned, my book corrected, expecting soon to take possession of the fine place as agent of a Commission on Finances that seemed to have been created specially for me. I found Mme *de Pompadour* dangerously ill, and her projects suspended until the restoration of her health. *Quesnay* cured her without contravening nature, which was itself curing her. She had a brief convalescence during which she remembered me, asked him for news of me, permitted me to see her, read my dedicatory epistle, and treated me even more affectionately than she had done at Fontainebleau. *The Doctor would not have failed to tell you,* she said to me, *how much, in spite of my poor health, we have thought of you. We have prepared a great career for your talents.* I was deeply touched; a beautiful, powerful woman who had barely escaped death, a kind of Queen who promised and gave her support to my patriotic and romantic Projects could not fail to impress my heart vividly.

My dream and joy were of short duration. The invalid who was thought to be cured had a relapse that appeared so dangerous and decisive that M. *de Choiseul*, whose falling out with her was not generally known, whose affection had perhaps revived—although the public had attributed his action to hatred and fear more than to friendship—and who in all likelihood had retained some hold on the Favorite that did not allow her to resist, took over the household in spite of her; decried *Quesnay's* opinions, saying that he had become crazy, that his long nights of watching and his great attachment for the invalid had deranged his mind; obtained the King's agreement that *Richard*, whom he had brought, would have the preponderant voice and would alone decide on the treatment.[11] The most serious symptom consisted in violent palpitations of the heart; *Richard* redoubled them by the most active tonics and cordials. A few days of this insane regimen, which was continued up until the last moment, made the illness incurable and carried off Madame *de Pompadour*, who saw herself dying and said on several occasions to Quesnay: *Do what you want, my poor friend; we are not the masters.*

It was claimed that she had been poisoned. It was not *Quesnay's* opinion that she had taken any of the substances ordinarily called *poisons*, but that the use of incendiary remedies in an illness that required relaxation and calm had killed her—which would not be a *poisoning*, but an *assassination*. M. Quesnay did not doubt that it had been *intentional*; I was never able to believe it; and it was enough to have read what M. *Richard* had written in medicine to judge that by the weakness of the logic, the imperfection of his observations, the absence or contradictions of medical philosophy, which glare from each page, the Doctor could have in very good faith, with a zeal as real as misplaced, thrown oil and spirits on the fire that water would have put out.

Whether M. *Quesnay* expressed his thoughts on this treatment too freely, or whether M. *de Choiseul*, offended by the gossip that was spreading them around and taking them personally, gave in to the impetuosity of his character, or whether he only wanted to intimidate him, there was talk of shutting up my old Master in a Citadel and his young student in the Bastille. We were warned by the Marquis *de Scépeaux*, by M. *d'Angiviller*, and by Mme de *Montmort*, who was willing to take charge of my papers, and we waited patiently for what the Despots would order.[12] M. *de Choiseul* did not have a lasting temper; his friends made him understand that to persecute the Ordinary Doctor of the deceased, whom he had shoved aside during her illness, would redouble the insinuations and the suspicions. He left us alone. I almost laughed in thinking of the trust one should place in the friendship of Ministers, and in seeing that after so frequently having promised me *a place,* the only one that he was ready to give me was in the Bastille.

My book had been printed but not yet published; it had been held up by the need to make pasteboards for it, as a result of a declaration that M. *de Laverdy* had been stupid enough to send to the Parlement on 28 March 1764, and the Parlement had been base enough to register, *to prohibit writing on the past, present, and future administration of finances under pain of being extraordinarily pursued.* If Mme *de Pompadour* had not been considered dead, and *Quesnay* lost, never would the Controller General have dared to propose this Law. In the fear that had gripped all my friends, I was urged to suppress my dedicatory Epistle. I insisted that it was the one moment at which the publication of this epistle would become noble and interesting for me. I only prefaced it by this little announcement: *The author believes that the dreadful event that has occurred since the printing of this writing should not cause him to suppress an homage that is dictated to him by gratitude and truth. Woe to the man who would fear to throw a few flowers on the tomb of those to whom he offered his incense.*

The death of Madame *de Pompadour* taught me a very good lesson in showing me, through two examples, the influence that real or apparent credit has on the affections of the majority of men.

M. *Quesnay,* while in her service, was overwhelmed with the importuning friendship of a mob of people who through an excess of tenderness did not leave him a free moment. M. *Quesnay,* deprived of his Protectress and threatened by the principal Minister, was abandoned by everyone except M. *de Mirabeau,* M. *du Val,* the surgeon at the Château, Mme *de Montmort,* and me; and I was the only one who could continue to see him every day. We spent them in a profound peace; no one came to disturb our work. *These events,* he said to me, *afford a fine sorting out of friends, but in addition those who remain become even more dear; they inherit from all the others.*

The second example bears on myself and caused me great sorrow. With Mme *de Pompadour* alive and protecting me, Mme *Doré*'s enthusiasm for me was continuously growing. M. *Le Dée,* the father, appeared to share it; he invited me to dinner and received me with great consideration; he was approved in all this by his Relatives. Mme *de Pompadour* buried, I was taken to be eliminated. Mme *Doré* became much chillier. The Chevalier *de la Corderie,* brother-in-law of M. *Le Dée*, advised him to close his door to me. The advice was followed. My leave was indicated to me. Mlle *Le Dée* was severely forbidden to see me or to have any correspondence with me. *Nitimur in vetitum.*[13]

As for me, I in no way believed myself lost; I saw in our science of political economy an admirable use of my time, a beautiful Treasure for my country and for myself.

Notes

[1]The Latin phrase can be translated: "from the claw of the lion."

[2]Louis-Paul Abeille (1719–1807) served as secretary of the Agricultural Society of Brittany, the deliberations and papers of which he had published as *Corps d'observations de la Société d'Agriculture, de Commerce et des Arts établie par les états de Bretagne* [par Abeille et Montaudoin] (Rennes, 1760), for the years 1757–58. In 1763, with the publication of *Lettre d'un négociant sur la nature du commerce des grains*, he publicly espoused physiocratic principles and remained associated with the school until 1769. His principal economic writings appeared during this period, although he continued to publish the writings and memoirs of the Agricultural Society of Brittany, at least in 1789, 1790, and 1791. He made important contributions to the dissemination of physiocratic ideas, but his break in 1769 was complete and would be definitive, according to Weulersse, *Mouvement physiocratique*, I, pp. 188–89, who also points out that Abeille, who held the positions of inspector general of manufactures and secretary of the Bureau of Commerce, was a serious defection.

[3]The phrase can be roughly translated from the Latin as: "This thing itself refuses to be embellished, it is sufficient to be taught."

[4]The Duc de Luynes, in his *Mémoires du duc de Luynes sur la cour de Louis XV*, ed. L. Dussieux and E. Soulié, 17 vols. (Paris, 1860–65), vol. 16 (1757–58), pp. 376–77, for March 1757, describes Mme de Montmort's presentation at court with Mme de Prie on Wednesday, 1 March 1757. "Madame de Montmort was presented by Mme the Princess of Beauvau. Mme de Beauvau was charged with this commission as the wife of a captain of the guards. Those who know Mme de Montmort saw that she is a woman of much wit and great amiability; she is the daughter of M. Dudoignon, a lieutenant general who distinguished himself at the siege of Lille of 1708 . . . ; M. and Mme de Montmort have two sons who are here."

[5]Clément-Charles-François de Laverdy replaced Bertin as controller-general in November 1763 when the Parlements proved intractable in their opposition to Bertin's proposals for increased taxes. Laverdy, a member of the Parlement of Paris and the son of a well-known lawyer, had no

previous political career worthy of attention and was suspected of extreme Jansenist sympathies, but he also enjoyed a solid enough judicial reputation to raise hopes for his ability to handle the difficult job, especially to make peace with the Parlements. Laverdy's tenure as controller-general, which ended in his disgrace for no clearly identified reason in 1768, witnessed the most extensive attempt to date to liberalize the internal and external grain trade. He did not repeal Bertin's declaration of May 1763 and, in 1764, promulgated the edict of July, of which Du Pont writes below and which he helped to draft. This July edict permitted exportation of grain from the kingdom, although with more restrictions than the physiocrats would have liked. These measures aroused considerable opposition, especially on the part of the municipal officers and populace. In fact, Laverdy himself frequently permitted interventions in the market and other ad hoc restrictions on free trade. Steven Kaplan, *Bread, Politics and Political Economy*, esp. pp. 241–45, defends Laverdy's commitment to liberalism and ascribes his departures from it in practice to the difficulties of implementing a liberal grain policy under the *ancien régime*. The physiocrats seem never to have considered Laverdy fully their man, and they always ascribed the difficulties that free trade in grain encountered under his administration to his unwillingness to adopt total free trade and to defend it rigorously. See Weulersse, *Mouvement physiocratique, passim*.

[6]Apparently the commission was never appointed, or at least never met.

[7]*Philosophie rurale ou économie générale et politique de l'agriculture* appeared in 1763. It reflected the fruits of Quesnay's and Mirabeau's collaboration, and Quesnay drafted the chapter on the *Tableau économique*.

[8]On Mirabeau at Bignon, see Loménie, *Les Mirabeau*, II, and *Les Mirabeau et leur temps*.

[9]Mme de Pailly, born about 1730, was a Swiss Protestant, possibly from Berne, who had married a Swiss army officer of probable French origin like her own family. She lived separated from her husband, who had retired to Lausanne, and had spent several years in the company of her sister in the Luxembourg Palace. A friend of the Countess of Rochefort, she was acquainted with polite society. Mirabeau apparently met her about 1755, at a time when his own disastrous marital relations were worsening. In 1762, Mirabeau's wife definitively left the conjugal roof; sometime thereafter, Mme de Pailly moved in and remained Mirabeau's devoted companion for the rest of his life. See Loménie, *Les Mirabeau*, II, pp. 503–58, and his *La Comtesse de Rochefort et ses amis: études sur les moeurs en France au XVIIIe siècle* (Paris: Michel Levy Frères, 1870), esp. pp. 155–215.

[10]Honoré-Gabriel, Comte de Mirabeau (1749–1791), the great tribune of the Revolution and eldest son of the Marquis de Mirabeau, was a decade younger than Du Pont. At the time of which Du Pont is writing,

the young count already was distinguishing himself as an unusually bright and difficult child, whom tutors would find unmanageable and whose own father would have confined by *lettre de cachet* first in house arrest and then in the dungeon of Vincennes. The war between the Mirabeaus father and son made that between Du Pont and his father look pale. During the 1770s and 1780s, Du Pont was in correspondence with Mirabeau the son and kept trying to effect a reconciliation between him and his father. On the Comte de Mirabeau, see Loménie, *Les Mirabeau*, and *Les Mirabeau et leurs temps*; the Duc de Castries, *Mirabeau* (Paris, 1960); F. M. Fling, *Mirabeau and the French Revolution* (New York and London, 1908); and Sheila Catherine Kamerick, "The Political Thought of Mirabeau" (Ph.D. diss., University of Rochester, 1982). Some of Du Pont's correspondence with both Mirabeaus during the 1770s and 1780s can be consulted at the Eleutherian Mills Historical Library.

[11]Richard was another doctor. He relied on a more vigorous or "heroic" treatment than Quesnay, who much preferred to let nature work with only the modest assistance of appropriate rest and diet. On conflicting views of medical treatment in the eighteenth century, see Antoinette Suzanne Emch-Dériaz, "Towards a Social Conception of Health in the Second Half of the Eighteenth Century: Tissot (1728–1797) and the New Preoccupation with Health and Well-Being" (Ph.D. diss., University of Rochester, 1983); Georges Gusdorf, *Dieu, la nature, l'homme au siècle des lumières* (Paris, 1972), pp. 424–525, "Le Progrès de la conscience médicale," *passim*. For testimony on Quesnay's attitude toward treatment, see Madame du Hausset, *Mémoires de Madame du Hausset, femme de chambre de Madame de Pompadour* (Paris, 1824), *passim*.

[12]Charles-Claude de Labillarderie, Comte d'Angiviller (?-1810), member of the Academies of Science and of Painting and Sculpture, served as director-general of buildings and gardens for Louis XVI. Marie-Paul-Alexandre-César Boisguignon, Vicomte de Scépeaux (1769–1821), became the leader of the Vendéen forces and fought the republicans during the Revolution. The d'Angiviller and the de Scépeaux to whom Du Pont is referring were probably their fathers and were certainly members of the court of Louis XV, as was Mme de Montfort.

[13]The rough Latin translation would read: "We are exalted by things forbidden."

15

*M. Turgot becomes friendly toward me. MM de
Trudaine give me work on his recommendation and
treat me kindly. M. de Fourgueux. I enter the world.
I lose time there. How I withdraw. Advice that M.
Quesnay gives me. I am employed to undertake the
description of the Generality of Soissons.*

My book on the *Export and Import of grain* is one of my works
that attained the greatest success. The Edition sold out in two
months and the printer *Simon*, who had given me *twenty-five louis*
and one hundred and fifty copies, told me that he had made a very
reasonable profit.[1] The same occurred for so many bad works that
it proves nothing in favor of mine. But what was much more flattering to me, much more useful, what contributed infinitely to the
happiness and honor of my life, I owe to this book the beginning
of the friendship that M. *Turgot* deigned to show me. Barely had
he read it, but he came to seek me at my Father's and showed me
an esteem, a confidence, a tender interest that, coming from him,
were more touching than can be said.

The ideas of M. *Turgot* were perhaps not as profound as those
of M. *Quesnay*, but their compass was much broader; he dug them

less deeply and linked them up with each other more. The Doctor sought his principles in nature and in Metaphysics. He said: *This is what should reign in the world,* and he could be understood only by a small number of vigorous thinkers. The Magistrate included in his the entire mass of human knowledge and the general history of the universe. He showed that men had only reasoned well and had only been happy to the extent that they had approached the truths that he was exposing. One could follow him provided that one had some logic and sense, but what especially made M. *Turgot* more amiable was that he was more loving. To please M. *Quesnay* it was necessary to have intelligence and talent *good for something.* To be cherished by M. *Turgot,* it was enough to have a *good, honest, and sensible heart.* Yet one did not recognize immediately the full charm of his company. At first, he only appeared wise, learned, and sweet. One had to have lived with him to know how affectionate and demonstrative he was.

He took me to see MM *Trudaine,* father and son, who were then occupied in writing the Edict issued in July 1764 to establish the freedom of the external grain trade, and consolidate that of the internal trade. All four of us worked on it separately and together. M. *de Laverdy* did not want to adopt it precisely as we proposed it to him.[2] He added some restrictions, and while we were putting the last touches to the salutary law of which we were the moving spirits and the authors, I prepared ahead of time, in a memoir entitled *The antirestrictor,* a criticism of the defects that were being introduced into the Edict and an exposition of the dangers that would result from them. You will find this memoir in my boxes, and you will see that it had predicted all the events that led minds astray and caused the destruction of the freedom the advantages of which had been recognized. It is because it was incompletely established that it was not possible to sustain even the amount that was introduced. Nonetheless, although spoiled, restrained, and regulated, it increased the net Product of the territory by about *three hundred millions*; it caused the reclamation of an immense quantity of lands that up until then had lain uncultivated; it forestalled the famines that would have occurred if free trade had not animated cultivation, increased the harvests, and distributed their products more equally. It multiplied subsistence goods of all kinds; it gave the means to live, and consequently life itself, to *two million French people.* I am far from having the sole honor of having rendered this service to the Fatherland, but it is something to have walked, by their admission, with those to whom it is indebted for this service.

In this important branch of administration it is impossible to have too much courage and to place oneself too far above the glory that is one's due and that one does not obtain, of the gratitude of which one is worthy, and of the ingratitude of which one can be certain. The Prejudices that plague this matter date from the furthest antiquity. They come to us from the very *aristocratic* Greek and Roman *cities,* where those who were called *Citizens* lived from the labor of their slaves and the tribute paid by conquered Peoples subjugated under the name of allies. Transmitted from age to age, these tyrannical Prejudices still reign over the majority of the nation. Despite thirty years of the efforts of reason, of arithmetic, and of Philosophy, despite the principles of liberty and of equality, the citizens of the urban municipalities are more disposed than ever to treat their fellow citizens of the rural municipalities as *serfs of the soil* and to dispose arbitrarily of their labor, their time, their harvests, and their carts. The tendency toward this unjust and dire abuse of power even seems increased in the cities by the opinion of the *Sovereignty* that the citizens of each populous municipality wish to exercise, as if they represented the totality of the Republic of which they are only articulating parts, and to whom alone belongs the deployment of sovereign authority. In 1764, I begged my readers' pardon for insisting on truths that then seemed trivial to all good minds, and that today are almost entirely ignored even by most of the administrative bodies. Nonetheless, for having stated them, I experienced some small aversion from my own family, which had not raised itself to the highest degree of enlightenment. My Uncle *Nicolas* wanted to disinherit me because I had proved that the only good policing of the grain trade lay in the competition between cultivators and merchants; and my Uncle was an independent farmer.[3] In 1789, I saw in the Constituent Assembly, my respectable colleague, M. *Hanoteau,* also such a farmer, a good man, a man of heart, a man of spirit, a man of mind, who was no more enlightened.

I was afflicted by the anger of my Uncle, but primarily for him; and I consoled myself by much weightier supporters. M. *de Montclar* wrote to me and had me contacted by M. *Tamisiey,* clerk of the court of the Parlement of Provence, in the name of the Commissioners charged to examine the Project for the Law on the grain trade.[4] He also sent me, on their behalf, questions pertaining to the best system of taxation. I replied to them with a very carefully worded letter in which I included the better part of my Memoir against restrictions. They never received that letter, which was intercepted in the Mail following a usage common at the time, now proscribed on pain of death, and always followed by the government, of opening letters suspected of discussing public affairs and of suppressing them when they were not found satisfactory; or to use them as evidence for committees of Inquisition. I very much regret having lost the rough draft of that one.

I was luckier with the Parlement of Dijon. M. *de Malteste,* who was its under-Dean, asked for my ideas on the subject of the ridiculous declaration of March 28, 1764, which prohibited writing on the administration of finances.[5] He included my reply almost in its entirety in the Remonstrances that this Parlement appended to its refusal to register—remonstrances that were published. This Law, worthy of Constantinople, was in like manner repudiated by all the Provincial Parlements; and I found no member of the Parlement of Paris who did not deny his own role in its registration. Such is the danger that arises from the ease of disavowing one's own role in errors committed as a Company, and it is what has guaranteed that the greatest injustices, the greatest cruelties, the most unworthy acts, the greatest stupidities, have always been the work of Companies, especially those that deliberate in secret.

The MM *Trudaine* passed on to me all the work that had already been done toward the suppression of the customs duties in the interior of the Kingdom and the preparation of the uniform Tariff that was to be established for its external borders. For the continuation of this work they had a fairly large number of Memoirs prepared for me, offered me much praise, to which they appended some gratuities from the Commerce funds that I had not taken the trouble to request, and which they thought of my needing, or of which M. *Turgot* reminded them. MM *Trudaine* were two men of very great merit. No one ever had a spirit more just, wiser, more manly, more nervous than the Father; no one ever had greater enlightenment, more perfect honesty, more rapid or more facile work than the son.

Through them and through M. *Quesnay* I made the acquaintance of M. *de Fourqueux,* who subsequently honored me with great friendship; a man who had only one defect, the excess of modesty in which he enveloped and hid from his own eyes an immense learning, a profound manner of considering all the questions of political economy and of reducing them to calculations, the talent of writing well in verse and in prose, and a gaity to which only his most special friends were privy.[6] M. *de Fourqueux's* modesty was one of the rarest qualities I have ever seen. M. *Turgot,* who did not understand it any better than I, imitating a common saying, said: *Can you imagine that M.* de Fourqueux *is stupid enough to believe that M.* Abeille *is more intelligent than he?*

Among so many men of the first rank, my education could only have made rapid progress, and I should have had neither wrongs nor sorrows if I had not also found myself tied to the women of their society.

The first who brought troubles upon me was Madame *de Pailly.* It was difficult to see her without being dazzled. It is impossible to be more beautiful or to have a more imperial air. Add to that the intelligence, the talents, and the character of Madame *de Maintenon,* and you will have her portrait in three words.[7] I do not know on what occasion I wrote some verses for her. I had no intention of their being taken as consequential, for I was far from wanting to make myself guilty of the least infidelity to Mlle *Le Dée*; but I introduced a little gallantry, without which women attach no importance to poetry. I had not yet noticed the extent to which M. *de Mirabeau* was intimate with her. As soon as I noticed, I withdrew from her with the respect that I should have for him. It is still one of the traits of her sex not to be able to bear movements of withdrawal. Women are happy to send you away if you displease them, or when you have ceased to please them, but they cannot suffer that you spare them that pain. Be on guard when you say an obliging word to them; if they have attached more significance to it than you intended, they will not be undeceived without becoming your implacable enemies. Madame *de Pailly* never forgave me for the verses that led to no prose. She constantly spoke of me to M. *de Mirabeau* in the most unfavorable light possible; she arranged to have showered on the Abbé *Baudeau,* who behaved in a very different manner than I, all the kindnesses of which the *Friend of Mankind* was capable, and on me all the rigors that derived from his somewhat haughty temperament.[8] I had to triple my efforts to retain that part of my Master which was dear to me, a fund of friendship that was my due; and for twenty years I was punished by him for a conduct for which he should have been grateful to me.

I had a more substantial failing, if only that of being frivolous and wasting my time in the society of Madame *de Fourqueux* and Madame *de Trudaine.*

It was not through a spirit of dissipation that I had introduced myself into their society. It was on account of vanity, for it did not please me to have only male Protectors, since I did not want to grant them the honor of that title if they refused to be also my friends; and I had, in addition, calculated, with sufficient good sense, that in limiting myself to seeing only in the mornings the well-placed men from whom I hoped to promote my advancement, and in speaking only to them of business, I would class myself in a much inferior rank from which I should not be allowed to escape; and that with respect to advancement itself I ran the risk of being bettered by those to whom would be granted the honors and the freedom of familiar society in which the ladies could be interested.

Madame *de Fourqueux* had invented a very pleasant way of offering supper; this kind of supper was called *a Café*. The dining room and the drawing room were filled with a multitude of little tables. The Mistress of the House and her two daughters did the honors in large white aprons. The Company was chosen, yet not invited. They had drawn up a list of thirty-six people who did not all always come, but when it pleased them, and at the hour that suited them, after eight o'clock at night. Those who came walked about or sat at a table with the companion that pleased them the most. They changed companions according to whim. They were served, on request, primarily liquid refreshments, compotes, fruits, and also more solid food if they desired it. Supper in this guise was at once brilliant, gay, free, and not costly. The Café frequently ended with little games and sometimes some dancing.

I wanted to be admitted to it; I was; and I even moved from this general company to a more intimate society. Madame *de Fourqueux* and Madame *Trudaine* were both infinitely amiable, although they did not resemble each other in any way. Madame *d'Invau*, whom I never pleased, was in the first flower of her youth.[9] One would have taken them for three sisters. (The oldest and especially the Mother excused my idiosyncracies.) But their evenings lasted very late; the need for sleep subsequently held me in bed; the morning became short. A part of the day was lost in the society of others. (Once known in the world, I wished to enjoy through the eyes of my relatives my small emerging glory by seeing the people that they were accustomed to respect the most, the *de Jaucourt* family.) I had sent my various works to Mademoiselle *de Jaucourt* and to Madame *de Jaucourt-Epénilles* née *Vivens*, both women of intelligence. They had welcomed my homage as much on account of the interest that a young man who is doing well can inspire as to oblige, through me, MM and Mlle *de Monchanin*, whom they liked. I visited them frequently; I often ate at the home of the one or the other, which took up a part of the afternoon.

Thus my time slipped away, and while M. *Quesnay* was good enough to leave me in Paris to pursue the work that the MM *Trudaine* and M. *Turgot* could give me, I dined, I supped in town, I consumed my days and my nights in vain conversations, in amusements that in truth did not amuse me and satisfied only my vanity; I did not save enough free time to do enough things, or to do them well enough.

Close to six months passed in this fashion and finally shamed me. *How then,* I said to myself, *you took three weeks to write a Book; the Book and a few distinguished men that granted it their approbation allowed you to be received in polite society, and here is half a year during which you would be hard-pressed to say what you have done that is really useful, or in what direction you have progressed. This must stop.* I took my scissors and cut the entire front of my hair on the left side.

Having thus torn myself away from the society of the ladies, I wrote a brochure on *large-scale and small-scale cultivation,*[10] under this epigraph taken from the eleventh song of the Iliad: *The rows traced by the mules, for they are preferable to oxen for working the fields with a heavy plough.*

M. *Quesnay* found my work very good since it supported a doctrine that he had set forth in the article *Fermiers* for the *Encyclopedia,* and in *La Philosophie rurale.* Nonetheless, neither he nor I had grasped the real point of the question. We attached too much importance to the work of horses or to that of oxen, whereas the true character of the two forms of cultivation consists in the abundance of capital and the advances multiplied by entrepreneurs who are disposed to lease lands and bring them to a condition that permits remunerative exploitation; or in the absence of this capital, which makes it impossible to find farmers, reduces the Proprietors to having to provide themselves and to provide poorly the advances for exploitation, the work of which they confide to miserable sharecroppers denuded of everything, whom they force to furnish everything, and whose inadequate and not very productive labor is paid by a share of a meager harvest. Rich Farmers almost always prefer horses that cost more, work more rapidly, and are better suited to a large operation. Poor Proprietors can only raise themselves to the level of advances for cultivating with oxen, which is less expensive, and ordinarily less profitable, both in relation to the extent of the land and in proportion to the capital invested.

Labor with oxen or with horses thus generally offers a rather faithful indication of large-scale and small-scale cultivation, but is not what constitutes it. One can find, especially in mountainous country, some large-scale cultivations executed by oxen, and in the plains of very poor countrysides there are miserable cultivations in which horses are used. Here is the true story to which I did not return until after a long controversy, and which was never well explained except subsequently by M. Turgot.[11]

As for me, it practically sufficed for my happiness, and I convinced myself too easily that it sufficed for my glory, that I set myself to work with ardor. The work that I have just finished always seems excellent to me—only after a few months do I discover its defects. As soon as I see them, I correct them and, the correction finished, the book is again perfect until a third edition or until, having forgotten it and seeing it again cold, my laggardly, but by then severe, judgment accords it its just value.

My happiness was not reduced to the illusions of vanity. The prohibitions thrown down by M. *Le Dée* had in no way detached me from his amiable daughter. I had touched the heart of the old governess, who, a little exhorted by my friend, encouraged by all the good she had for so long heard spoken of me in the house, and perhaps also by the great hopes that we founded on my proximate fortune, believed herself to be doing, and in the event did, a good action in serving us.

I had won over her Gardener, the most honest drunkard in the world, who delivered my letters and brought back the replies.

I had found an old *Mother Saulnier*, a keeper of women in labor, a good teller of adventures, good for all trades, who saw the Gardener, the Governess, and sometimes the beautiful Young Lady.

I had even succeeded in interesting a great-aunt of M. *le Dée*, called Madame *Bénévault*, deaf, but good, witty, a little romantic, who sympathized with the sorrows of honest love and who had come to love me enough to lend me the money with which I paid the three others.

I exchanged bouquets. I received sword's knots and ruffles embroidered by the hand of the Fairies, or by those of love. From time to time, I even obtained meetings at the good Aunt's, at the Gardener's, at Mother *Saulnier's*, even at M. *le Dée's*, in the dining room or in his garden, an hour after he had gone to bed. The light set at a certain angle announced that there was an opportunity to receive me; a few dried peas tossed against the panes from the other side of the street announced that I had arrived, and the door was opened for me. I had been fully pardoned for having hair over only one of my ears when it was learned that it was in the interests of working better and not seeing other ladies.

This kind of life, which was very sweet gave me great facility for all kinds of work, for the influence of my heart on my mind has always been a function of the extent to which those whom I love have praised me, caressed me, made me happy. Oh! if women only knew what they can do with us when we have some substance.

Most of those whom I have known and who have influenced me, since they were singularly good, true, and naive, have decisively confirmed in me, and even in the use of what mind I had, a childlike simplicity of which I cannot think today without laughing at my own expense—even though it has not yet disappeared entirely. I shall give you an example, and I have yet others of the same kind.

Du Belloy put on a play, the *Siege of Calais,* during the winter of 1764 to 1765, and I saw it several times with the enthusiasm that ideas of honor and of Fatherland could not fail to excite in the heart that you know.[12]

The Play was printed; I read it and found it, as it was, pitiably written in half-barbaric verses. I imagined that I would give the author great pleasure by correcting his verses; during the period in which the theater was closed, I redid *five hundred and eighty* and sent them to him with a beautiful letter, so that he could benefit at the reopening from making his versification worthy of the sentiments that it expressed. With the best faith in the world, I awaited enthusiastic expressions of gratitude! *Du Belloy* did not reply; and I subsequently learned to my great surprise, that I had mortally offended him and that he would never pardon me!

I recounted the occurrence to M. *Quesnay,* and it is not for not having known either the human heart in general, or the *genus irritabile vatum* in particular that he reproached me—it was for having myself expended a time and a talent in making verses that I owed to the public good. I had not yet ever told him that I was a Poet. He learned the fact with great anger. My Father had no greater antipathy for Poetry than did M. *Quesnay.* He only admired a few lines of *Corneille* and even these only on account of the thought. *All the beauty of a writing,* he said, *is in the thought, as that of a woman is in her charms. Fools that you are who think to embellish her with pompoms. She cannot be too naked.* The same principle led him to disdain the eloquence of *Cicero,* which he found too dependent on words. To show that true eloquence was in things, he cited this passage of *Demosthenes: You fear, Athenians, the expenditure of war. Very well! Philip will come: he will burn your houses; he will massacre your young people; he will carry off your women, your children, and yourselves into slavery; and you will see the fruits of your economy.* Express, he added, this thought as you will, try to weaken it by a poor style; the stupidest of translators, the flattest of writers will not be able to prevent its being a model of eloquence.

My old Master scolded me so sharply, so frequently, for having written these verses that he almost stifled my disposition to let it run freely. I spent four years without daring to read Poets, far indeed from walking in their steps, and it was only after having lived with M. *Turgot* at Limoges and having applauded his energetic verses, so abundant and sweet, that I allowed myself to return occasionally to my natural inclination.

In truth, M. *Quesnay's* severity was exaggerated. Thoughts are certainly the foundation of any good writing, as invention and drawing are those of any good painting; but thoughts gain tremendously from being expressed with force, with elegance, with harmony; just as the painting draws a large part of its merit from the degree of expressiveness and of richness, from the truth of the colors. Imagine a simple stroke from the very hand of *Raphael*: you will have thought, invention, fundamental drawing, and you will have no painting. Beautiful verses and excellent prose, no less difficult, have therefore the advantage of better expressing beautiful thoughts, of fixing them more forcefully in the memory, of transmitting them more surely to posterity, thus to render them more useful by rendering them better known and more lasting.

M. *Quesnay* more efficaciously disgusted me with another occupation that was absorbing a large part of my time. I liked to write letters, and in writing them I abandoned myself to all the philosophical views that crossed my mind. My letters became long, sometimes rich. They contained perceptions, dissertations, developments, some of which seemed to me to deserve being submitted to my master, if only to ascertain that my verve was not leading me astray. He much reproached this prodigality of work. *I do not know what you are thinking of*, he said, *thus to spend your mind and your enlightenment in private letters. If you knew what those who receive them do with them you would never want to address them any more. You should write nothing except for the Public, and nothing that is not to last for two thousand years.*

The better to accommodate the maxims of my Master with the pleasure that the chattiness of letters gave me, I have, since that time, only selected one or two persons, other than your Mother, to whom I have written regularly, freely, expansively. As long as M. *Turgot* was alive it was to him, and he received at least eighteen hundred letters from me, of which he replied to about one thousand. He saved most of mine, which have been returned to me. I have all of his; they are very curious. When I lost him, M. and Mme *de Lavoisier* inherited that abandon of my heart, and, if they did not burn them, they too should have a couple of thousand letters from me.[13] If I am unable to finish these memoirs, you will find, especially since the year 1768, material for completing them, more or less, in my correspondence with M. *Turgot* or with M. *de Lavoisier*. Madame *Poivre* also had a great many letters from me.[14] I think that she did not keep them. I have written to no one else except in indispensable necessity.

I thus worked as a philosopher, as a citizen, as a free man, an amateur of moral and political sciences; I had even received some gratuities from the fund designed to encourage commerce, for which I had worked; but I had no clear function, I was not among the number of government employees. I became one.

M. *Méliand* had a great desire to become *Councillor of State* and to retain simultaneously the administration of the Generality of Soissons. He decided the best means to attain both goals promptly and surely would be a remarkable work, such as an economic description of that Province, that would set forth the advances of cultivation in each Election, each Subdelegation, each community, their total product and their net product, and would furnish the means to place the assessment of the tax on solid and luminous foundations. This enterprise correctly seemed to him the most in conformity with his duty, the most useful in any case, the most appropriate justification for the favor he wished to obtain.

He asked me for an outline of the work and charged me with executing it. I neither refused nor bargained with him. He gave me eighteen hundred francs remuneration. There was no proportion between the magnitude of the operation, the costs that it required, and the mediocrity of this salary. The stupidity and niggardliness of the Controller General *Laverdy* had refused to authorize him to make a larger outlay for such important research, which the stupid minister only supported on account of complacency and what he considered simple curiosity. M. *Méliand* gave me the money from his own pocket, to be collected from his business agent, and I economized stringently to pay for the trips that the nature of the project made indispensable.

In the jobs that have been confided to me I have never considered more than two things: their present usefulness for the state and my fellow citizens, their future utility for my reputation and my fortune. If I have executed them rapidly, in a brilliant and distinguished manner, the honoraria of the year, such as they have been offered to me, never appeared to me to merit a moment's thought. It was the great offices to come that I perceived and that I wanted to deserve and to assure myself of by care, effort, and a perfection of work above all competition.

Believing myself certain that my stubborn and indomitable will would furnish me the continuously renewed means of a perpetually sustained application, and counting on my laborious activity, my hopes were apparent in my face and perhaps too much in my words. My vain and ambitious joy at receiving an appointment that was by its nature of short duration and so badly paid earned me from Mlle *de Jaucourt* a fairly good pleasantry in which the slightly caustic salt of her wit appeared clearly, as did the inclination of people of quality to rebuff, without forsaking the politeness of an obliging familiarity, the vanity of those they believe inferior to them. *Finally, Gil Blas,* she said to me, *here you have reached the King.*[15] Effectively, I joined to the brilliant hopes of *Gil Blas* when he entered the Duc de Lermes's service the real poverty out of which he never climbed.

With eighteen hundred francs in emoluments I hired five secretaries. It is true that they, like me, were very poor devils, several of whom had intelligence. I gave the first *five hundred francs*, the second *four*, the third *one hundred écus*, and *nothing* to the two others. They all worked more or less as supernumeraries to get some training and to deserve to follow my destiny. Altogether convinced myself, with my customary modesty, that I should one day be either Controller general or at least Intendant of finances, I convinced them, and I promised the future reward of my clerks out of the net product of my glory. The honest young men believed their fortune made; a few of them succeeded. As for me, with my *six hundred* francs that remained, a few little debts that I had contracted, the great personages who liked me, and my facility to cradle myself in dreams, I was perfectly happy.

Notes

[1] *De l'exportation et de l'importation des grains, mémoire lu à la Société Royale d'Agriculture de Soissons* (Soissons and Paris: Simon, 1764). Close to three hundred of Turgot's letters to Du Pont are preserved at the EMHL, Winterthur MSS, Group 2, Series A. Gustave Schelle published many of these surviving letters in his *Oeuvres de Turgot* and separately as *Lettres de Turgot à Du Pont de Nemours de 1764 à 1781* (Extraits des *Oeuvres de Turgot . . .*, Paris, 1924).

[2] Daniel-Charles Trudaine (1703–1769), the son of a *prévôt des marchands*, became a master of requests, councillor of state, intendant of the generality of Riom, and, under the controller-general Orry, in 1743, director of the service of the Ponts et Chaussées (bridges and roadways). His son, Jean-Charles-Philibert Trudaine de Montigny (1733–1777), became his associate in these various projects beginning in 1757 and succeeded him as intendant of finances and director of the Ponts et Chaussées in 1767. Both became honorary members of the Academy of Science. Although they were more closely associated with the tradition of Vincent de Gournay than with the physiocrats, they were both stalwart defenders of free trade in grain. Trudaine de Montigny in particular believed that Laverdy should take a very hard line against the resistance to free trade in the mid-1760s. The Edict of July 1764, on which Du Pont and Turgot collaborated with the Trudaines, established limited freedom of export for grain: when the price of grain rose above a certain level in the port cities, export was to be suspended. The final form of the edict promulgated by Laverdy thus included restrictions that the authors of the draft had not favored. See Kaplan, *Bread, Politics and Political Economy;* Weulersse, *Mouvement physiocratique*; Saricks, *Pierre Samuel Du Pont de Nemours*; Schelle, *Du Pont de Nemours*; Du Pont, *De l'exportation*; and Louis-Paul Abeille, *Premiers opuscules sur le commerce des grains* (1763–64, repr. Paris, 1911). On the Trudaines' work on the administration of roads, see Jean Pétot, *Histoire de l'administration des Ponts et Chaussées* (Paris: Marcel Rivière, 1958), esp. pp. 139–232, *passim*.

[3] Du Pont's uncle was a *laboureur*. These independent peasants could vary in wealth from comfortable self-sufficiency with a couple of horses, fifty acres, and twenty cows, to affluence based on 250 acres and perhaps even tithe rights. The wealthiest stratum of this independent peasantry offered access to urban wealth and the bourgeoisie. On *laboureurs*, see Goubert, *The Ancien Regime*, pp. 113–15.

[4] Du Pont's M. de Montclar is almost certainly J.-P. François, Marquis de Ripert de Monclar, who wrote a number of works on financial and economic questions beginning in 1749. In 1768, he published a *Lettre sur le commerce des grains* in which he staunchly insisted on the necessity for free trade in grain. His works, for many of which there are no known

extant copies, are listed in INED, *Économie et population*, and identified and discussed in Gilbert-Urbain Guillaumin, *Dictionnaire de l'économie politique, contenant l'exposition des principes de la science . . .* , 2 vols. (Paris: Guillaumin, 1852–53). Ripert de Monclar is not mentioned in Weulersse, *Mouvement physiocratique;* Kaplan, *Bread, Politics and Political Economy;* or identified in Saricks, *Pierre Samuel Du Pont de Nemours.* On the economic views of the Parlement of Provence in this period when it favored freedom of the grain trade, see Paul Beik, *A Judgment of the Old Regime, Being a Survey by the Parlement of Provence of French Economic and Fiscal Policies at the Close of the Seven Years War* (New York: Columbia University Press, 1944). He does not mention Tamisiey, but a *greffier* was a clerk of the court.

[5]The declaration of 28 March 1764 prohibited publishing anything concerning matters of state and finances. Jean-Louis, Marquis de Malteste, came from an old Burgundian robe family. In the seventeenth century, one of his ancestors, Claude Malteste, had written *Anecdotes du Parlement de Bourgogne ou histoire secrète de cette compagnie depuis 1650 par Claude Malteste conseiller au dit Parlement . . .* , ed. Charles Muteau (Dijon, 1864). Du Pont's Malteste published *Esprit de l'Esprit des Lois* (1749) and *Oeuvres diverses d'un ancien magistrat* (London, 1784). He apparently worked closely with the president of the Parlement of Burgundy, M. des Brosses, in defending its views and interests against the crown. He receives passing mention in Marcel Bouchard, *De l'Humanisme à l'Encyclopédie: l'esprit public en Bourgogne sous l'Ancien Régime* (Paris: Hachette, 1930); see also E.-F. de la Cuisine, *Le Parlement de Bourgogne* (Dijon, 1857).

[6]Bouvard de Fourqueux was prosecutor-general at the Chambre des Comptes through the middle decades of the eighteenth century. As early as 1754, he collaborated with Trudaine, Gournay, and others, all of whom had been influenced by the ideas of Claude-Jacques Herbert, author of *Essai sur la police générale de grains* (London, 1753), in preparing the first royal decree favorable to greater freedom in the grain trade and the development of agriculture. He remained a friend and collaborator of the Trudaines; one of his daughters married Trudaine de Montigny, and Fourqueux thus was bound by ties of family and common interest to the partisans of greater freedom of trade and reform throughout the closing decades of the *ancien régime.* He served in the Chambre des Notables in 1787 and very briefly as controller-general, following the forced resignation of Calonne as controller-general in April of that year. On his friendship with Du Pont, see brief mentions in Saricks, *Pierre Samuel Du Pont de Nemours,* and Schelle, *Du Pont de Nemours.*

[7]Françoise d'Aubigné, the granddaughter of Agrippa d'Aubigné, was raised in Martinique. Not long after her return to France, she married the novelist Paul Scarron. Deeply devout throughout her adult life, she is credited with a decisive influence on the religious policies of Louis XIV, whom she came to know when she went to court as governess of the royal

children and, having herself been widowed, whose morganatic wife she became in 1685. As the Marquise de Maintenon, she was renowned for her charm, her piety, her extensive culture, her determination in the service of causes in which she believed, and her role in developing the education of the daughters of the poor nobility through her writings and, especially, the school she founded for them at St. Cyr. See Carolyn Lougee, *Le Paradis des Femmes: Women, Salons, and Social Stratification in Seventeenth-Century France* (Princeton: Princeton University Press, 1976), esp. pp. 188–208, and Madeleine Danielou, *Madame de Maintenon éducatrice* (Paris: Bloud & Gay, 1946).

[8]Abbé Nicolas Baudeau had begun writing on economic questions in 1763 with the timely *Idées d'un citoyen sur l'administration des finances du roi* (Amsterdam, 1763). In 1765, he founded a journal, *Les Éphémérides du citoyen*, on the model of Addison and Steele's *Spectator*. By 1766, both Baudeau and his journal had been converted to physiocratic principles. For the next decade and more, he remained one of the most prolific and successful popularizers of the school. His relations with Du Pont, who took over the direction of *Les Éphémérides* in the late 1760s when Baudeau went to Poland, were strained by differences over the finances of the journal and probably personality as well. See Weulersse, *Mouvement physiocratique*; Schelle, *Du Pont de Nemours*; Saricks, *Pierre Samuel Du Pont de Nemours*; Earle E. Coleman, "Éphémérides du Citoyen, 1767–1772," *Papers of the Bibliographical Society of America*, 56 (1962): 17–45; and Du Pont's correspondence with Baudeau in the EMHL, Winterthur MSS, Group 2, Series A.

[9]Madame Mayon d'Invau was the daughter of Bouvard de Fourqueux, by birth and by marriage a member of this close circle of the financial and administrative elite. Her husband, Étienne Mayon d'Invau (b. 1721), served as controller-general from October 1768 to December 1769. Her older sister had married Trudaine de Montigny.

[10]Du Pont's "Lettre sur la différence qui se trouve entre la grande et la petite culture" appeared in the *Gazette du commerce* (January 1765). The author rather blindly followed the distinction that Quesnay had drawn between large-scale and small-scale cultivation in *Fermiers* and *Grains* for the *Encyclopédie*: large-scale cultivation was performed with horses, small-scale with oxen.

[11]Turgot always reminded Du Pont of his disagreements with him with respect to the nature and respective merits of large-scale and small-scale culture. See his letters to Du Pont in Schelle, *Oeuvres de Turgot*, II, esp. those of 10 May 1765, pp. 438–39, and 9 December 1766, pp. 517–19. For the full elaboration of Turgot's own views, see his "Les Réflexions sur la formation et la distribution des richesses," ibid., pp. 534–601.

[12]Pierre Laurent De Belloy's *Siège de Calais* proved a tremendous success from the beginning of its first run at the Comédie Française in 1765, and probably would have broken all records for attendance had the

run not been cut short by a quarrel among the actors. Du Pont's rather proprietary admiration for the play may be due in part to its plot, which properly belonged to the new genre of the *drame* rather than to that of heroic tragedy; it depicted as heroes the burghers, the mayor of the besieged Calais and his sons, instead of their aristocratic opponents. These attitudes closely resemble those of Du Pont himself, not merely in his physiocratic insistence on the need to alleviate the burdens on the rural population, but also in his behavior during the Revolution, during which he cast his lot with the Third Estate but remained deeply loyal to the crown. On the reception of the *Siège de Calais*, see John Lough, *Paris Theatre Audiences in the Seventeenth and Eighteenth Centuries* (London: Oxford University Press, 1957), pp. 188, 216–17, and 238–39; Lough cites the passage from the play, p. 239, but the translation here is mine.

> Harcourt trahit son prince, et d'Artois l'abandonne;
> Un maire de Calais raffermit sa couronne! . . .
> Quelle leçon pour vous, superbes potentats!
> Veillez sur vos sujets dans le rang le plus bas:
> Tel qui sous l'oppresseur loin de vos yeux expire,
> Peut-être quelque jour eût sauvé votre empire.

> "Harcourt betrays his prince and d'Artois abandons him;
> A mayor of Calais secures his crown! . . .
> What a lesson for you, superb potentates!
> Watch over your subjects of the lowest ranks:
> Those who expire under the oppressor far from your view,
> Might, one day, have saved your empire."

[13]Antoine-Laurent Lavoisier (1743–1794), celebrated as the founder of modern chemistry, was also a farmer-general of taxes under the *ancien régime*. Influenced by the ideas of the physiocrats, he devoted considerable attention to agricultural and statistical problems, conducted an experimental farm, and played a leading role in the committee on agriculture organized by Calonne in 1783, of which Du Pont also became a member. From this time on, the two men became close friends and collaborators. Lavoisier drew up the instructions for the deputies from Blois to the Estates General, as Du Pont did for the deputies from Chevannes. They worked together on various financial committees during the early years of the Revolution. In 1784, Lavoisier published *De la richesse territoriale du royaume de France*; this, together with his and others' writings on political arithmetic, was published by P.-L. Roederer shortly after his death as a guide to the economic policies of the Directory: *Collection de divers ouvrages d'arithmétique politique* [par Lavoisier, Lagrange, etc.], ed. P.-L. Roederer (Paris, An IV). See also G. Schelle and E. Grimaux, *Lavoisier, Statistique agricole et projets de réforme* (Paris: Guillaumin, 1895). On the friendship between

Lavoisier and his wife and Du Pont, see Saricks, *Pierre Samuel Du Pont de Nemours.*

Madame Lavoisier, whom Du Pont would like to have married after her husband's death during the Terror, had translated scientific works and subsequently married Count Rumford. The Lavoisiers held the mortgage on Du Pont's property at Bois-des-Fossés and had loaned him money to open a printshop during the Revolution. Furthermore, Du Pont's younger son Irénée began to study the manufacture of gunpowder in 1787 at the Régie des Poudres, where Lavoisier was a director. Du Pont's letters to the Lavoisiers have not survived, nor have his to Turgot. The EMHL, Winterthur MSS, Group 2, Series A, contains close to three hundred letters from Turgot to Du Pont, most of which were published by Schelle in *Oeuvres de Turgot.*

[14]Françoise Robin (1748–1841) was the widow of Pierre Poivre, a well-known traveler and former intendant of the islands of France and of Bourbon (Réunion). Du Pont had met Poivre, who was also known for his writings on agriculture, in the late 1750s. In 1786, Du Pont published a eulogy of him. On at least two occasions, he pressed Madame Poivre's case for a pension with the royal government. In the fall of 1794, after his release from hiding, he started to court the widow Poivre who agreed to marry him in December of that year. The marriage banns were published in July 1795, and the marriage celebrated on 26 September. This marriage proved as happy as Du Pont's first. For a light but charming portrait of Françoise Poivre, see Edmond Pilon, "Le roman de Madame Poivre," *Revue des deux mondes,* 8th series, 18 (15 November 1933). 368–83, which depicts her relations with the writer Bernardin de St. Pierre in 1769–70; for her relations with Du Pont, see Saricks, *Pierre Samuel Du Pont de Nemours.*

[15]Du Pont is referring to the novel by Alain René Le Sage (1668–1747), *Histoire de Gil Blas de Santillane,* published in three parts between 1715 and 1735. Book VIII, in which Gil Blas enters the service of the Duc de Lermes, appeared with Books VII and IX in 1724.

MEMOIRS

of
Pierre Samuel Du Pont (de Nemours)
addressed to His Children

Rectitudine Sto

September 1792

To my Sons Victor and Irénée Du Pont

from the . . .   4 September 1792

Uncertain, my dear Children, if I shall ever have the happiness of seeing you again, and in what fashion I shall leave my present retreat, I think I should profit from it by giving you some necessary information concerning your Family, and some Memoirs of my life that will at least be pleasurable for you.

I myself shall find consolation and sweetness in writing you a very long letter. It will be divided into chapters, which I shall have delivered to you successively.

If the outcome were to occur before the end of the story, you will fill in the gaps as you can.

First Chapter
What I know of my Paternal Family
Extract

The copyist of these Memoirs believes that he should [   ] give an extract of this chapter [torn page; missing lines] established; but for which it suffices that the other Readers have a very succinct notice, if only so that the Characters that they will see on the stage in the course of the work not be entirely unknown to them.

The author observes that his name is extremely common in all Countries and in all languages. *Pontius* among the Romans and the Samnites; *Pontanus* in modern Latin; *Pontio,* which we translate as *Ponce,* among the Spaniards and the Portuguese; *del Ponte* or *da Ponte* among the Italians; *von Brück* among the Germans; *Van Brugh* or *Van Breughen* among the Dutch and the Flemish; *Bridge* among the English; *Mostowski* among the Poles; *Du Pont* in France are all the same name that applies equally to Families that are descendants of *a Warrior,* distinguished for the defense of a Bridge; of *a Chatelain,* responsible for guarding a Bridge; of *an Architect,* renowned for having built a Bridge; of a Toll-collector, who collected the dues for crossing a Bridge; and of a *Child found* on a Bridge. Everywhere, there is a great number of men who fall into one of these five cases, and especially in the last two: from which it follows that there have always been many *Du Ponts* of every profession and of every rank, but most in the least elevated classes.

As to the Family of which these memoirs speak, it is Protestant, norman, and believes itself to have been originally from Brittany.

The Author's Ancestors were in trade at Rouen for more than two centuries. One of them had [torn page; missing lines] . . . [left?] their descendants a natural fund of virtue and of uplifted character.

But in protecting the youth of such a famous Poet and in devoting himself to literature, the new Magistrate diminished his fortune, that had not been large to begin with. His children were not able to sustain the noble status that he had acquired for them: the office was sold off. They returned to commerce. The great-grandfather and the grandfather of our Writer took up the commerce of iron, copper, and all the kitchen utensils that are made with these two metals. With the esteem due to probity, they acquired a mediocre fortune of which the largest part consisted in two houses in town and two farms in the country.

This family is numerous. It has two masculine and four feminine, or feminized, branches in France; two branches in England; three in Holland, including one masculine; one in Switzerland and one in Carolina.

The Father of the Author had five brothers: *Jean,* who followed the trade of their ancestor; *Pierre* and *Abraham,* who were clockmakers in London; *Jacques* and *Nicolas,* who were farmers, one at *Fontaine sous Préaux,* the other at *la Robinette,* near Rouen.

He also had two Sisters: *Anne* who married *Abraham Pouchet-Belmare,* a manufacturer of cotton and linen cloths and a man of great merit; and *Marie* who married *Jacques Oulson,* a captain of a merchant vessel who was subsequently ruined by a shipwreck.

Jean and *Pierre* died without children. All the others left posterity.

Second Chapter
What I know of my maternal Family
Extract

The maternal Family of the author is named *de Montchanin* or *de Monchanin*; for the way of writing this name has varied almost from generation to generation. The family came from the *Charollais*, was heretofore noble and even ancient; divided into three branches of which the eldest, which is extinguished, had incontestably made illustrious alliances, as can be seen in the book of Father *Anselme* on the great officers of the crown.[1]

The second branch was Protestant and, at the beginning of the century, included four Brothers, of which one died in the service of France, one in that of Prussia, another in Switzerland, and the fourth, *Héléodore de Monchanin*, after having himself served the Republic of Holland, returned to France to collect a small inheritance, was welcomed by the Marquis *de Jaucourt-Epénilles* to whom he believed himself to be related, who entrusted him with the stewardship of his estates in Burgundy and in Nivernais, and lodged him in the Château of *Brinon les Allemands* at the center of these properties.

Héléodore left five children, of which the youngest boy, *Etienne Auguste* was a bad egg and the only one who did not derogate—in the language of the time—from nobility. This fact shows how strange an institution legal nobility was. He was a constable in France and died as a Captain in the service of England, leaving a son who has long since disappeared.

All the others took up *trades* to live. *Alexandre*, the oldest boy became an engraver in clockmaking; *Pierre* specialized in watch cases, also in clockmaking.

Françoise, the oldest of all of *Héléodore de Monchanin*'s children was the chambermaid of Mlle *de Jaucourt*, of whom she nonetheless considered herself a relative, although a fairly distant one.

Anne Alexandrine married *Samuel Du Pont*, clockmaker in Paris, Father of the author.

Alexandre and *Françoise* died without children.

From *Pierre's* branch, there remains *Pierre Héléodore de Monchanin* who is employed in the office of the national liquidation.

From *Anne Alexandrine's* branch came the author and his children; and *Anne Du Pont* who is married to *Philippe Jean Gudin de la Ferlière*, with whom she had a boy and a girl who are both living.

Note

[1]The identification of Father Anselme and an explanation of national liquidation, mentioned below, can be found in notes 2 and 8 to Chapter 2 of the text of the autobiography.

Index

Abeille, Louis-Paul, 13, 250, 259n2, 267
Académie de Peinture (Academy of
    Painting), 208n2, 261n12
Académie des Sciences (Academy of
    Sciences), 143, 209n3, 261n12,
    275n2
Académie Française, 152n6, 168n3, 226
Agricultural societies, establishment of,
    230, 236n12
Agricultural Society of Brittany, 259n2
Agricultural Society of Soissons, 230–31,
    253
Aides (taxes), 92n7, 111n7, 233n5, 246n2,
    255
Alembert, Jean le Rond d', 143–44,
    152n6, 172–73
    Letter on the Theaters, 173
Alfred the Great, king of England, 117,
    125n4
Amanzé family, 93, 99n3
Angiviller, M. d', 257, 261n12
Angiviller, Charles-Claude de
    Labillarderie, Comte d', 261n12
Anselme de Sainte-Marie, Father, 93,
    99n2, 285
Argenson, Marc-Pierre de Voyer de
    Paulmy, Comte d', 160, 161,
    168n3

Argenson, René-Louis de Voyer de
    Paulmy, Marquis d', 159–61,
    168n2, 173, 179
Ariosto, Lodovico, 121, 127n10
Armide see Lully, Jean-Baptiste
Arson, M. d', 212
Asselin, the Abbé, 133
Assignats, 11, 149
Aubigné, Agrippa d', 276n7
Augustine, Saint, *Confessions*, 39
Austin, Helen, 29
Autobiography, considered as a genre,
    38–42
Avila, M. d', 163

Baden, Carl Frederick, Margrave of, 19
Barbeu-Dubourg, Jacques, 190–93,
    195n6, 200
Barents, Willem, 116, 124n3
Barre, Mme, 88
Bastille prison (Paris), 122, 257, 258
Baudeau, Abbé Nicolas, 13, 19, 267,
    277n8
Beaufort, Madame, 86
Beaumont, Christophe de, 60, 220, 224n9
Beauvais, the Baron de, 145